ROUTLEDGE LIBRARY EDITIONS: PHONETICS AND PHONOLOGY

Volume 6

THE LEXICAL PHONOLOGY OF SEKANI

THE LEXICAL PHONOLOGY
OF SEKANI

SHARON HARGUS

LONDON AND NEW YORK

First published in 1988 by Garland Publishing, Inc.

This edition first published in 2019
by Routledge
2 Park Square, Milton Park, Abingdon, Oxon OX14 4RN

and by Routledge
711 Third Avenue, New York, NY 10017

Routledge is an imprint of the Taylor & Francis Group, an informa business

© 1988 Sharon Hargus

All rights reserved. No part of this book may be reprinted or reproduced or utilised in any form or by any electronic, mechanical, or other means, now known or hereafter invented, including photocopying and recording, or in any information storage or retrieval system, without permission in writing from the publishers.

Trademark notice: Product or corporate names may be trademarks or registered trademarks, and are used only for identification and explanation without intent to infringe.

British Library Cataloguing in Publication Data
A catalogue record for this book is available from the British Library

ISBN: 978-1-138-60364-6 (Set)
ISBN: 978-0-429-43708-3 (Set) (ebk)
ISBN: 978-1-138-31727-7 (Volume 6) (hbk)
ISBN: 978-1-138-31731-4 (Volume 6) (pbk)
ISBN: 978-0-429-45528-5 (Volume 6) (ebk)

Publisher's Note
The publisher has gone to great lengths to ensure the quality of this reprint but points out that some imperfections in the original copies may be apparent.

Disclaimer
The publisher has made every effort to trace copyright holders and would welcome correspondence from those they have been unable to trace.

The Lexical Phonology of Sekani

Sharon Hargus

Garland Publishing, Inc. ■ New York & London
1988

Copyright © 1988 Sharon Hargus
All Rights Reserved

Library of Congress Cataloging-in-Publication

Hargus, Sharon.
   The lexical phonology of Sekani / Sharon Hargus.
      p. cm.— (Outstanding dissertations in linguistics)
Revision of the author's thesis (Ph. D.—University of California, 1985)
Bibliography: p.
ISBN 0-8240-5187-4
1. Sekani language—Phonology. 2. Sekani language—Grammar, Generate. 3. Lexical phonology. I. Title II. Series.
PM2285.H37   1988
497".2—dc 19

Printed on acid-free,250-year-life paper
Manufectured in the United States of America

In memory of my sister

ROBIN LYNN GOODMAN

1956-1983

Preface to the Garland edition

I have made some revisions to my 1985 dissertation for this edition.

The abstract analysis proposed in the original Chapter 8 (The Strict Cycle Condition) has not stood the test of time. A reanalysis of the data presented in this chapter can be found in Hargus (to appear (a)). In addition, some of the data from Ch. 8 now appears in Chapter 1 (Sekani).

I have reorganized Chapter 2 (Lexical Phonology) in an attempt to present a better overview of the evidence for the theory. I have paid particular attention to the rather abstract theory of morphology which is assumed by most adherents of the theory.

In other chapters, I have kept changes to a minimum, only deleting or altering analyses which I no longer believe to be correct.

I would like to acknowledge here my deep appreciation for the friendship and support of my colleagues at the University of Washington: Mike Brame, Heles Contreras, Joe Emonds, Ellen Kaisse, Fritz Newmeyer, Sol Saporta, and Alice ter Meulen.

TABLE OF CONTENTS

List of maps..x
List of abbreviations..xi
Acknowledgments..xiii

Chapter 1: Sekani...1
   1. Introduction...1
   2. The position of Sekani within Athabaskan.............................1
   3. Previous studies of Sekani...5
   4. The present study..7
   5. Surface and underlying segments......................................7
      5.1 Orthographic conventions...9
      5.2. Labio-velars...11
      5.3 Nasal vowels..13
   6. Distinctive features..14
   Notes..15

Chapter 2: Lexical Phonology...17
   1. The organization of grammar in the Lexical Phonology model..........17
   2. Comparison with the SPE model of grammar............................19
   3. How abstract is morphology?...21
      3.1 The Chomsky/Jackendoff approach to morphology and the
           lexicon...21
      3.2 Level ordering..23
           3.2.1 A level ordered model of the English lexicon.............25
           3.2.2 The negative prefixes in English..........................28
           3.2.3 Zero-derived verbs..29
           3.2.4 Summary...31
           3.2.5 The abstractness of level ordering........................31
      3.3 Advantages of abstract morphology...............................34
           3.3.1 Inadequacy of word-based morphology.......................34
           3.3.2 Consequences of lexically listing unproductive
                 affixes in English...................................36
      3.4 Problems with abstract morphology...............................39
           3.4.1 Overgeneration..40
           3.4.2 Idiosyncracy of outputs...................................45
      3.5 Summary...51
   4. Orderings of phonological and morphological processes...............51
      4.1 Tagalog Nasal Substitution and Syncope in reduplicative
           forms...53
      4.2 Danish Lengthening and imperative formation.....................56
      4.3 Summary...59
   5. The lexical/postlexical rule typology...............................59
      5.1 An example from English...60
      5.2 The derived-only restriction....................................63
           5.2.1 A closer look at 'derived'................................63
           5.2.2 Deriving the derived-only restriction.....................64
   Notes..70

Chapter 3: Level Ordering: The Verbal Prefixes...........................73
1. A level-ordered overview of the verbal prefixes..................75
2. Level 1...76
   2.1 Morphology..76
      2.1.1 Aspectual stem suffixation...........................76
      2.1.2 Classifier prefixes (position 13)....................79
         2.1.2.1 h̲...80
         2.1.2.2 d̲...83
         2.1.2.3 d̲+h̲ (*1̲).....................................87
         2.1.2.4 Phonological effects of the classifiers.....88
   2.2 Level 1 phonology...92
      2.2.1 Voicing Assimilation.................................92
         2.2.1.1 Domain of Voicing Assimilation..............94
         2.2.1.2 The classifier prefixes.....................96
         2.2.1.3 Summary.....................................97
      2.2.2 The D-Effect Rule....................................97
         2.2.2.1 Domain of the D-Effect Rule................100
         2.2.2.2 Order and formulation of the D-Effect Rule..100
      2.2.3 Palatalization......................................102
   2.3 Level 1: Summary...105
3. Level 2..106
   3.1 Morphology...106
      3.1.1 Subject prefixes (position 12)......................106
      3.1.2 Mode prefixes (position 11).........................107
      3.1.3 Conjugation prefixes (position 10)..................109
      3.1.4 Position 9..110
         3.1.4.1 Order of prefixes within position 9........111
         3.1.4.2 Order with respect to position 8 and 12
               prefixes...................................112
         3.1.4.3 Affix order: Summary......................115
   3.2 Level 2 (vs. 3) phonology..................................116
      3.2.1 The s̲-conjugation rules.............................116
         3.2.1.1 Formulation of the s̲-Conjugation rules......117
         3.2.1.2 Domain of the s̲-Conjugation rules..........120
      3.2.2 n̲-conjugation ə̲ Fronting............................123
4. Levels 3 and 4...126
   4.1 Morphology...126
      4.1.1 Subject prefixes (position 8).......................126
      4.1.2 Object prefixes (position 7)........................126
   4.2 Levels 2 and 3 phonology...................................128
      4.2.1 Prefix Vowel Deletion...............................128
         4.2.1.1 Formulation of Prefix Vowel Deletion.......128
         4.2.1.2 Domain of Prefix Vowel Deletion............130
      4.2.2 Conjugation Tone Mapping............................132
         4.2.2.1 Formulation of Conjugation Tone Mapping....132
         4.2.2.2 Domain of Conjugation Tone Mapping.........134
      4.2.3 L Deletion..135
         4.2.3.1 Formulation of L Deletion..................135
         4.2.3.2 Domain of L Deletion.......................136
      4.2.4 Vocalization..138
         4.2.4.1 Formulation of Vocalization................138
         4.2.4.2 Domain of Vocalization.....................141
      4.2.5 Conjugation ə̲ Deletion..............................142
         4.2.5.1 Formulation of Conjugation ə̲ Deletion.......142
         4.2.5.2 Domain of Conjugation ə̲ Deletion...........145

                4.2.5.2.1 /gha/...................................145
                4.2.5.2.2 /`sə/ and /`nə/........................146
                4.2.5.2.3 Domain of Conjugation a Deletion:
                           Summary....................................151
        4.2.6 na Absorption...151
        4.2.7 Levels 2, 3 and 4: Summary.............................155
    4.3 Level 3 vs. 4 phonology..157
        4.3.1 Similarities of ʔa, ts'a and gha to other position
               7-9 prefixes..157
        4.3.2 ʔa, ts'a, gha and the domain of Conjugation Tone
               Mapping...159
5. Level 5..161
    5.1 Morphology...162
        5.1.1 Inceptive prefix (position 6)...........................162
        5.1.2 The na prefixes (position 5)............................163
               5.1.2.1 Reversative na................................164
               5.1.2.2 Customary, habitual na........................164
               5.1.2.3 Positional properties of the na prefixes
                        (I)...165
        5.1.3 Distributive prefixes (position 4)......................166
        5.1.4 Incorporated stems (position 3).........................167
        5.1.5 Adverbial prefixes (position 2).........................169
        5.1.6 Incorporated postpositions (position 1).................170
    5.2 Level 5 phonology: a Raising...171
        5.2.1 Formulation of a Raising................................172
        5.2.2 Domain of a Raising.....................................173
        5.2.3 Positional properties of the na prefixes (II)...........174
6. Postlexical phonology..181
    6.1 Devocalization..182
    6.2 Glottal Stop Insertion..184
        6.2.1 Underlying tone or glottal stop?........................185
        6.2.2 Characteristics of Glottal Stop Insertion...............190
7. Summary..192
Notes..193

Chapter 4: Level Ordering: Nominals and Postpositions........................197
1. Stems..198
2. Level 1 suffixes...200
    2.1 Possessive suffixes...200
    2.2 -e..202
    2.3 -hu human plural..204
    2.4 Instrumental stems..205
    2.5 Nasalization..205
    2.6 Summary...207
3. Level 5 suffixes...207
    3.1 Nominalizing suffixes...207
        3.1.1 Examples..207
        3.1.2 Level Ordering: Nasalization...........................210
        3.1.3 Possessed derived nominals..............................212
        3.1.4 Locative Nominals.......................................215
    3.2 Diminutives and other adjectives......................................217
        3.2.1 Diminutives...217
        3.2.2 -záʔ prototypical.......................................221
    3.3 Human plural -ge/ghe..222
    3.4 Level 5 suffixes: Summary..223

    4. Compounds and prefixes..................................223
        4.1 Possessive prefixes and oblique objects.............224
        4.2 Compounds...226
        4.3 Continuant Voicing..................................228
             4.3.1 Basic data...................................228
             4.3.2 Incorporated stems...........................231
             4.3.3 Continuant Voicing vs. Voicing Assimilation..233
             4.3.4 Possessed continuant-initial compounds.......234
        4.4 Level ordering......................................236
             4.4.1 Nasalization.................................236
             4.4.2 Domain of Continuant Voicing.................237
             4.4.3 The loop.....................................238
        4.5 Summary...239
    5. Conclusion..239
    Notes...239

Chapter 5: The Bracketing Erasure Convention.........................243
    1. Motivation for Bracketing Erasure...........................244
    2. Motivation for non-cyclic, level-final Bracketing Erasure...246
    3. Violations of the Bracket Erasure Convention in Sekani......248
        3.1 Conjugation a̱ Deletion..............................249
             3.1.1 Evidence for Bracketing Erasure..............250
             3.1.2 The problem for Bracketing Erasure...........253
             3.1.3 Possible reanalyses of Conjugation a̱ Deletion......255
                    3.1.3.1 Merging levels 2-4.................256
                    3.1.3.2 A morphological formulation........257
                    3.1.3.3 A syllable-based rule..............258
             3.1.4 Conjugation a̱ Deletion: summary.............259
        3.2 Perambulatives......................................259
        3.3 Continuant Voicing in derived nominals..............263
        3.4 Suffix Vowel Deletion...............................267
             3.4.1 Basic Data...................................267
             3.4.2 Stem vs. suffix vowels.......................269
             3.4.3 Problems for Exceptionless Bracketing Erasure......272
                    3.4.3.1 Possessed derived nominals.........272
                    3.4.3.2 Stem-final vs. suffixal -[e] and -[è?]......273
    4. Conclusion..276
    Notes...277

Chapter 6: Epenthesis..279
    1. Introduction..279
    2. The domain of Epenthesis--a first approximation.............282
    3. Formulation of Epenthesis...................................285
        3.1 The importance of stem bracketing...................285
        3.2 A syllable-based rule of Epenthesis?................286
    4. Rule Ordering...288
        4.1 Conjugation rules...................................288
        4.2 Position 12 subject prefixes........................291
        4.3 Summary...292
    5. Level 5 Epenthesis..292
    6. Epenthesis and Stray ṉ Deletion.............................294
        6.1 Stray ṉ Deletion....................................294
        6.2 Rule ordering.......................................297
    7. Conclusion..299
    Notes...299

```
Chapter 7:  The Cycle.................................................301
     1. Do cyclic rules exist?........................................302
     2. Which rules are cyclic?.......................................304
     3. Cyclic rule application in Sekani.............................306
          3.1  Diphthongization and w Vocalization....................306
               3.1.1  Diphthongization................................307
               3.1.2  w Vocalization..................................307
               3.1.3  Rule ordering:  the gho-gho forms...............309
               3.1.4  Diphthongization and w Vocalization are cyclic..312
          3.2  Possessive suffixation and Nasalization................315
               3.2.1  Nasalization....................................315
               3.2.2  Repossessed nouns...............................316
               3.2.3  An ordering paradox.............................318
               3.2.4  Nasalization is cyclic..........................319
     4.  Non-cyclic rule application in Sekani........................320
          4.1  Schwa Lowering.........................................321
               4.1.1  w Vocalization and second person plural forms...321
               4.1.2  Schwa Lowering is not cyclic....................322
               4.1.3  Is Schwa Lowering a post-lexical rule?..........324
          4.2  a Deletion.............................................324
               4.2.1  a Deletion is not cyclic........................326
               4.2.2  a Deletion is not post-lexical..................327
               3.2.3  a Deletion is a level 5 rule....................327
          4.3  Non-cyclic rules:  summary.............................329
     5.  Conclusion...................................................329
     Notes........................................................... 330

Appendix:  Sekani Rules...............................................333

References............................................................339
```

ix

List of Maps

Finlay-Parsnip Drainage Basin*..2

British Columbia*...3

Northern Athabaskan Languages**...4

* Guy Lanoue generously allowed me to reproduce these two maps from his dissertation (Lanoue 1983).

** This map was provided to me by Jim Kari.

List of Abbreviations

1	first person
2	second person
3	third person
4	fourth person
adv	adverbial prefix
ar	areal prefix
asp	aspectual affix
C	customary/habitual mode
clf	classifier prefix
cnj	conjugation prefix
con	conclusive aspect
cont	continuative aspect
d/du	dual
ddim	double diminutive suffix
dem	demonstrative
der	derivational prefix
dim	diminutive suffix
dstr	distributive
epen	epenthetic segments
excl	exclusive
Fut	future mode
hum	human
Imp	imperfective mode
incp	inceptive prefix
loc	locative
mom	momentaneous aspect
N	noun
neg	negative affix
nom	nominalizing suffix
O	object prefix
Op	optative mode
P	postposition
p/pl	plural
per	perambulative aspect
Pf	perfective mode
Prg	progressive aspect
psd	possessed noun suffix
Psr	possessive prefix
Q	interrogative morpheme

recp	reciprocal prefix
refl	reflexive prefix
rev	reversative prefix
S	subject prefix
s/sg	singular
stm	stem-final suffix
term	terminative aspect prefix
thm	thematic (lexically specified) prefix
typ	prototypical suffix
unsp	unspecified
V	verb
vb	verbalizing suffix
voc	vocative

Acknowledgments

Many people, all indispensible in unique ways, have helped this dissertation come into existence.

The Sekani data contained in this dissertation was collected during fieldwork in McLeod Lake, B.C., from June 1982-May 1983, October 1983, and May 1984. In 1982 the McLeod Lake Indian Band generously granted me permission to study their language. For their continuing friendship, hospitality, and enthusiasm for their language, I thank Patricia and Harry Chingee, Victor and Beverly Chingee, Sam Chingee Sr., Sam Chingee Jr., Alec Chingee Sr., Gilbert Chingee, Margaret Fisher, Peter Solonas, and Josephine and Max Tylee. For their help in the translation of such crucial forms as 'we [du] habitually vomit separately,' I single out Josie Tylee, Sam Chingee Sr., and especially Peter Solonas for help above and beyond the call of duty.

Dave and Kay Wilkinson of Ft. St. James, B.C., helped me get started on my fieldwork when I first arrived in B.C., making available to me copies of their published and unpublished materials on Sekani and Carrier. Their help smoothed the way in many respects. Gerry and Sandy Cross performed the invaluable service of keeping my car running. Greg and Linda Allen and Gerry and Joan Sheanh helped me reorient myself from the land of all-night supermarkets to a rural lifestyle and real winters.

*

It would be easy for me to list the parts of my dissertation that various committee members agree or disagree with. None of my committee members is responsible for failing to bring me to my senses with regard to specific analyses. However, I gratefully acknowledge their efforts to do so: Bill Bright, Bruce Hayes, Paul Kroskrity, Pam Munro, Keren Rice, Alan Timberlake. The name of Donca Steriade would have appeared on my signature page, but for the requirement of the UCLA Linguistics Department that all committee members be present at the defense. The reader will be grateful for Donca's generous help in weeding out preposterous earlier analyses. Other UCLA people who have contributed to this dissertation in one way or another are: Steve Anderson, George Bedell, Scott Busby, Mike Hammond, Dan Kempler, Ian Maddieson, Laurie Tuller.

I thank the Athabaskan linguistic community for their helpful comments on my earlier analyses of Sekani: Jim Collins, Ed Cook, Victor Golla, Jim Kari, Mike Krauss, Jeff Leer, Keren Rice, John Ritter, Leslie Saxon, Gill Story, Chad Thompson.

I thank Leanne Hinton and the members of the UC Berkeley Linguistics Department for welcoming me to the Survey room. (I lived in Berkeley while writing this dissertation.)

I owe a special debt to Keren Rice. A future historian might be able to reconstruct from our several hundred pages of correspondence the development of the more coherent analyses of Sekani reflected in this dissertation. Moreover, Keren's Slave grammar has helped me understand the structure of Athabaskan languages as no other other piece of writing on Athabaskan has. If other linguists find this dissertation useful and interesting, it is largely because of Keren's prior research on Athabaskan.

I am indebted to Bruce Hayes for his constant encouragement and interest, his help in improving specific analyses, and his careful, thorough reading of this dissertation. Many improvements in my presentation of analyses and general exposition have come about largely because of Bruce.

Finally, I thank Scott for being around whenever I needed moral support.

*

I gratefully acknowledge the financial assistance I received in support of this research from the following sources: the British Columbia Provincial

Museum, Victoria; the National Museum of Man, Ottawa; the Arctic Institute of North America; the UCLA Graduate Division; the Jacobs fund of the Whatcom Museum, Bellingham, WA; the Wenner-Gren Foundation for Anthropological Research; and the Department of Indian and Northern Affairs, Prince George, B.C.

Chapter One

Sekani

1. Introduction

Sekani is an Athabaskan language. Together with Eyak, the Athabaskan languages form one branch of the Na-Dene family of languages (Krauss and Golla 1981):

(1)
```
              Na-Dene
             /       \
        Tlingit    Athabaskan-Eyak
                    /         \
                  Eyak      Athabaskan
```

Some linguists include Haida in the Na-Dene family, but this is not generally accepted by Na-Dene scholars. See Levine (1979) and Greenberg (1987) for discussion of this controversy.

Sekani is spoken in the northern central interior of British Columbia, Canada. The territory of the Sekani-speaking peoples includes what were originally the Finlay and Parsnip River drainages of the Rocky Mountain Trench.[1] See Maps 1 and 2.[2]

Sekani is spoken in three communities: Ft. Ware, Ingenika, and McLeod Lake. Some lexical and phonological differences between Sekani dialects are discussed in Hargus (1985, in preparation).

2. The position of Sekani within Athabaskan

Map 3 shows the location of Sekani with respect to neighboring Athabaskan languages.[3]

There is abundant linguistic and historical evidence that Sekani is most closely related to Beaver within the Athabaskan family.

The impression of McLeod Lake Sekani speakers is that Beaver people speak 'our language' or 'the same language', whereas equally nearby Carrier is not

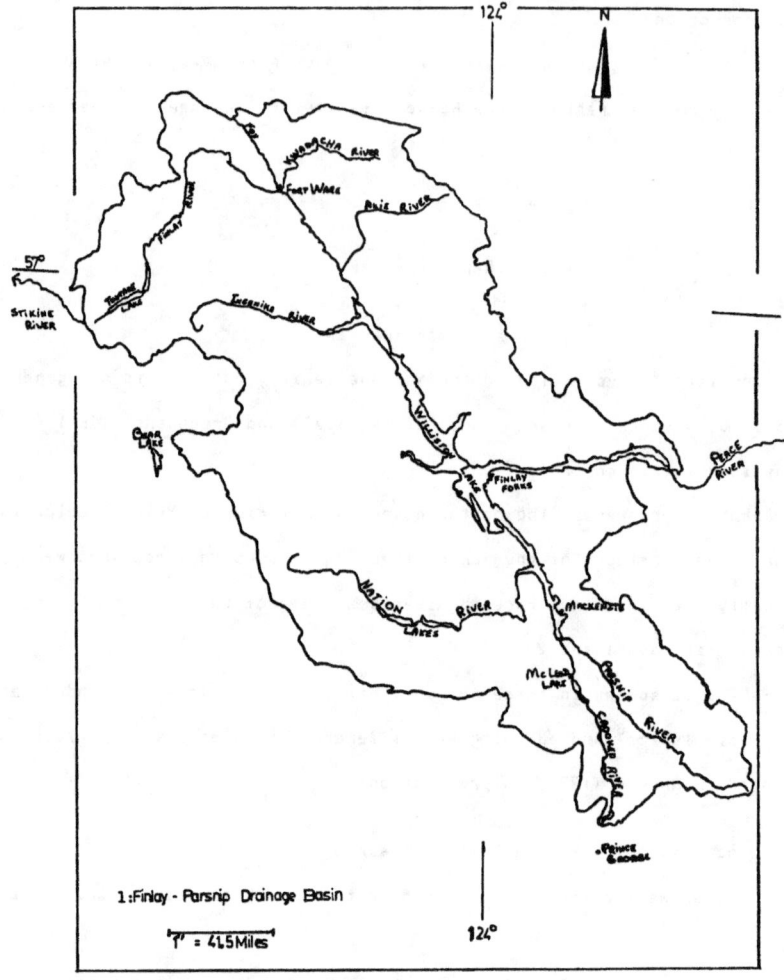

Map 1. (Lanoue 1983)

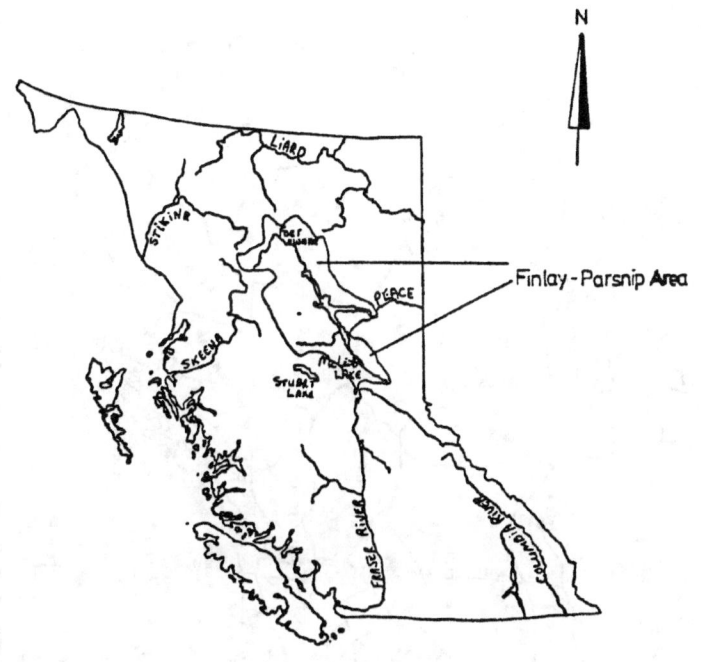

Map 2. (Lanoue 1983)

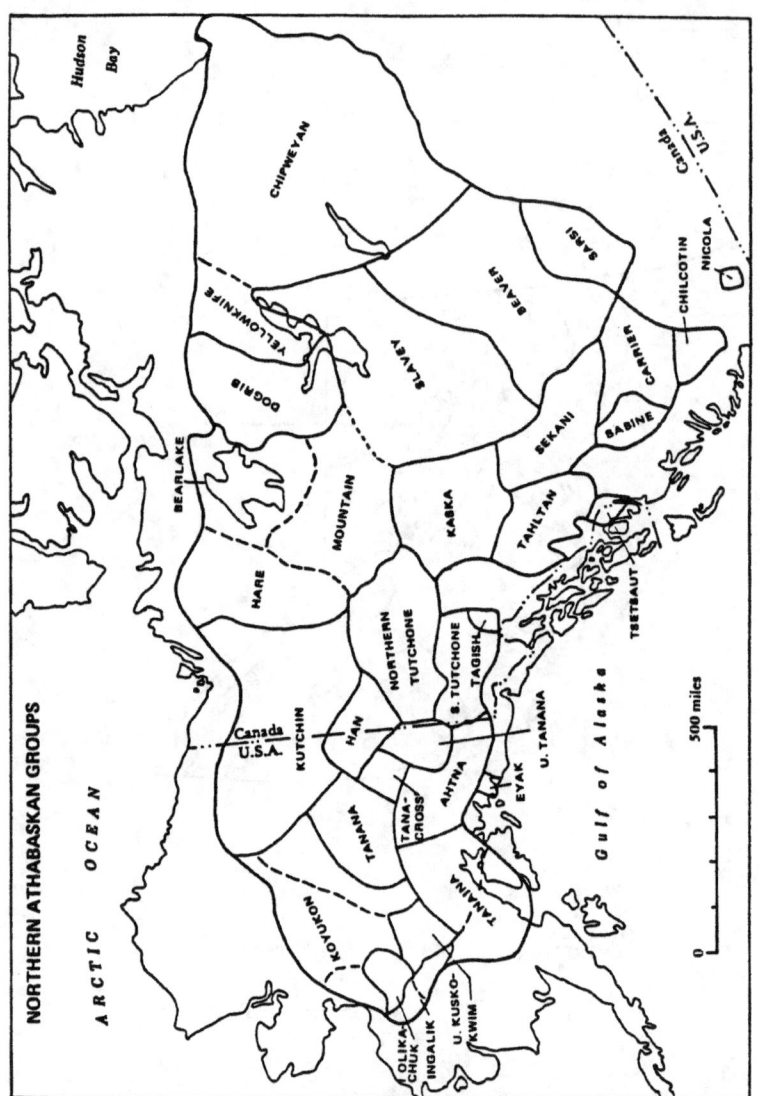

Map 3.

at all mutually intelligible. Research by Story (1979) and Randoja (to appear) on the Doig River and Halfway dialects of Beaver indicate that a close linguistic connection exists between Sekani and Beaver.

Harmon (1957:130, 256) suggested that the Sekanis 'are a small part of a tribe who, but a few years since, came from the east side of the Rocky Mountains...The people who are now called Si-can-nies, I suspect at no distant period, belonged to the tribe called Beaver Indians.'[4] Records from the period of the earliest white-Sekani contacts indicate that Sekani people were forced west of the Rocky Mountains by Beaver and Cree Indians, who obtained firearms before the Sekanis did.

Although it is clear that Sekani and Beaver form a subgrouping within Athabaskan, it is less clear which other languages are closely related to Sekani-Beaver. Jenness (1937) suggested that Sekani belongs to the 'Beaver-Sarcee-Sekani branch' of the Athabaskan family. According to Denniston (1981:433), 'northern Sekani could be called Kaska'. Such statements are, of course, conjectural. As mentioned above, Sekani dialectology is poorly understood. I hope that one contribution of this dissertation will be to provide the beginnings of a better understanding of how McLeod Lake Sekani is related to other Athabaskan languages.

3. Previous studies of Sekani

Very little linguistic research on Sekani has been done, despite the relative geographic accessibility of at least the McLeod Lake community.

A list of manuscripts which contain Sekani vocabulary can be found in Parr (1974) and in Helm and Kurtz (1984). Most of these manuscripts date from the nineteenth and early twentieth centuries. Some anthropological studies of the Sekanis contain lists of Sekani kinship terms; e.g., Jenness (1937), Honigman (1954), and Lanoue (1983).

In 1939, Robert Young and J.P. Harrington collected data from a Sekani woman, Makrit Dominique, at Ft. St. James, B.C. Since Dominique spoke only Central Carrier and Sekani, the interview was conducted in Central Carrier through an individual who was bilingual in Central Carrier and English. The resulting word list, Young (1939), has been regarded by most Athabaskan linguists as the most accurate source of Sekani data. However, perhaps as a result of the trilingual elicitation session, a few of the lexical items on this list more closely resemble Central Carrier than they do current McLeod Lake Sekani.⁵ The forms in (2) are representative. (The orthographic representations from which the phonetic forms in (2) have been interpreted are given below the bracketed representation. Note that [Ṽ] represents a nasal vowel.)

(2)   Hargus   Young (1939)   Carrier Linguistic
               fieldnotes   Committee (1974)

'star'   [sàn]   [sʊ̃m]   [sə̃m]
                              sUm   sum

'one (person)' [ɬàɣí]   [ɪ́ɣṹn]   [ʔɪɬòɣə̀n]
                              ƙIɣUn   ilhoghun

Despite its superiority over previous materials, this list may have resulted in the incorrect attribution to Sekani of certain Central Carrier characteristics. For example, Thompson (1978) lists the human singular relative clause/ nominalizing suffix in Sekani as -Un, rather than -i (cf. Young's ƙIɣUn 'one (person)'). Similarly, Krauss and Leer (1981:67) group Sekani with Babine and Central Carrier as showing a rare reflex of Proto-Athabaskan *m as [m] in 'star'.

In the early 1960s, David and Kay Wilkinson of the Summer Institute of Linguistics did field research on Sekani in McLeod Lake and Ft. Ware. Their work resulted in an unpublished phonemic analysis (Wilkinson and Wilkinson 1965) of the McLeod Lake dialect. A practical orthography and reader

(Wilkinson and Wilkinson 1969a) and a book of bible stories (Wilkinson and Wilkinson 1969b) were developed for the Ft. Ware dialect. Despite this valuable research, however, certain aspects of Sekani have remained a mystery to the Athabaskan linguistic community. For example, Krauss and Golla (1981:72) have noted that the development of the PA vowels in Sekani is unclear, 'due to fragmentary data'.

4. The present study

The fieldwork on which the present study of Sekani is based was conducted at McLeod Lake during 1982-84. Although I refer throughout this dissertation to 'the Sekani language', it should be understood that my remarks are claimed to be true only of the language which is spoken in McLeod Lake.

At McLeod Lake there are about fourteen fluent native speakers of Sekani, ranging in age from approximately 45 to 75 years of age. (Many younger Sekani people understand spoken Sekani but do not speak it fluently.) In this study I worked with eleven of the fourteen speakers at one time or other. However, more frequently I worked with one of three particular speakers. (See Acknowledgements.)

Most of the data in this study are forms which were elicited through translation of English to Sekani. All forms have been checked with more than one speaker.

5. Surface and underlying segments

A phonetic inventory of the consonantal segments of Sekani is given in (3):

(3) Consonants

	lab	alv	alv (lat)	alv	pal	vel	lab-vel	glot
stops:								
voiceless unasp	p_h	t_h	ts_h	$tɬ_h$	$tš_h$	k_h	kw_h	
voiceless asp	p^h	t^h	ts^h	$tɬ^h$	$tš^h$	k^h	kw^h	
ejective		t'	ts'	tɬ'	tš'	k'	kw'	
fricatives:								
voiceless			s	ɬ	ç	x	w̥	
voiced			z	l	y	ɣ	w	
sonorants:	m	n						ʔ
								h

[ç] and [y] are true palatals, whereas [tš tš^h tš'] are palato-alveolar. [p^h] is a rare segment, found only in loan words.

The segment [l] is not a fricative, phonetically, as is [ɬ]. However, the fact that [l] alternates with [ɬ], just as [s] and [z], [ç] and [y], etc. do, indicates that [l] is to be regarded as a fricative phonologically. See Continuant Voicing (Ch. 4, 4.3); Voicing Assimilation (Ch. 3, 3.2.1).

The segments [w̥ w] lack an audible velar component. However, quite apart from pattern congruity, there are reasons for regarding these segments as labio-velar, rather than labial, segments. Several rules of the phonology (w̲ Vocalization and Diphthongization, discussed in Ch. 3, and Nasal Assimilation, discussed in Hargus (to appear (a))) treat these segments as underlyingly labio-velar.

An inventory of the vowels is given in (4):

(4) oral: nasal:

    i   u   į   ų
    e   ə   o   ę   ǫ
        a   ą

[ə] is an abstraction away from the phones [I ə ʌ i]. There is conditioned and sometimes free variation between these phones (see Hargus (to appear (b))).

All Sekani vowels are pronounced on one of two pitches:

(5) Tones

   high: ´   low: `

There are several differences between the underlying and surface inventories of segments and tones, as will become clear in subsequent chapters of this dissertation. For now, I will simply list what I believe to be the inventory of underlying segments:

(6)   Underlying segments

consonants:

$$\begin{array}{llllll} p_h & t_h & ts_h & tl_h & t\check{s}_h & k_h \\ p & t & ts & tl & t\check{s} & k & (kw^h) \\ & t' & ts' & tl' & t\check{s}' & k' \\ \\ & & s & ł & ç & x \\ & & z & l & y & \gamma \\ \\ m & n & & & & ʔ \\ & & & & & h \end{array}$$

vowels:

$$\begin{array}{llll} i & & u & (\mbox{\textsc{u}}) \\ e & ə & o & \\ & a & & \end{array}$$

5.1 Orthographic conventions

For typographical convenience, I will represent some of the segments of Sekani in a slightly modified way in the remainder of this dissertation.

Orthographic representations of the tones and vowel sequences are given in (7):

(7) V́ = high tone vowel
     V   = low tone vowel
     VV = vowel sequence
     V̌V = rising tone vowel sequence
     V̂V = falling tone vowel sequence

The orthographic representations of the consonants are given in (8):

(8) b   d   dz   dl   j   g   gw
     p   t   ts   tl   ch   k   kw
     p'   t'   ts'   tl'   ch' k'   kw'

          s   ł   yh   x   wh
          z   l   y   gh   w

     m   n   ʔ
                                h

As is customary in practical orthographies of Athabaskan languages, I have represented the voiceless unaspirated stops with the usual phonetic symbols for voiced stops, and the voiceless aspirated stops with the symbols for voiceless unaspirated stops. Syllable-finally, there is no three-way contrast between voiceless unaspirated, voiceless aspirated, and ejective stops and affricates, as there is syllable-initially. Instead, only phonetically voiceless unaspirated stops and affricates ([t ts tł tš k]) occur. Accordingly, I use the voiceless unaspirated phonetic symbols for the syllable-final stops and affricates: t̲ t̲s̲ t̲l̲ c̲h̲ k̲.[6] This is summarized in (9):

(9)   phonetic   orthographic

syllable-initially   t_h   d
                       t   t

syllable-finally   t   t

Differences in syllabification result in purely orthographic alterations such as those in (9) and (10):

(9a)   bat̲   mittens
(9b)   sə.bà.d̲e?   'my mittens'

(10a) chok̲   'frog'
(10b) cho.g̲a.zi   'small frog'

Some background information about syllable structure in Sekani may prove useful in subsequent chapters. Aside from a few loan words, neither onsets nor rhymes of phonetic syllables may contain consonant clusters. I assume that underlying representations are devoid of syllable structure and that this is assigned by rule. Following Steriade (1982), I suggest that the syllable structure is assigned by the (universal) core syllable rule in (11a) and by the (Sekani-particular) coda rule in (11b):

(11) Syllabification rules

(a) Core syllable rule:

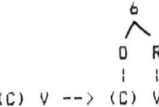

(b) Coda rule:

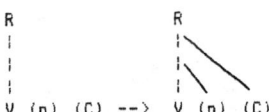

Underlyingly, Sekani rhymes may contain two post-vocalic segments, with the constraint that the first of these must be a nasal. On the surface, this nasal segment appears as nasalization of the preceding vowel (sometimes with accompanying changes in vowel quality as well) (see 5.3 below).

5.2 Labio-velars

The inventory of phonetic segments in Sekani given in (3) includes five labio-velar consonants, each of which is exemplified below:

(12)   [sagwàt]   'my knee'

(13)   [dəkwas]   'he, she coughs'

(14)   [k'was]   'cloud'

(15)   [nàwàt]   'he, she walks fast'

(16)   [whas]   'rose, thorn'

Labio-velars have a highly restricted distribution. They do not occur syllable-finally, unlike velars and other complex segments, such as affricates, and they do not occur before the vowels [o u]. Labio-velars which occur before the vowels [i e a] are rare. In fact, most labio-velars occur before the vowel [a]. Significantly, there is a corresponding gap in the distribution of velar consonants: velar consonants which precede the vowel [o] are very rare.

Alternations between velar + [o] and labio-velar + [a] provide further evidence of a synchronic relation between [o] and [wa]. There are two contexts in which [o] occurs after a velar. (1) Velar + [o] (rather than [wa]) occurs when the segment following [o] is [ɪ], as seen in (16):

(17) -/got-ɪ/   -[goʔ]   'crawl' Prog
(18) -/got-ts/   -[gwats]   'crawl' C

(2) Velar + [o] (rather than [wa]) occurs when [o] is nasal, as in (19):

(19) /gho-n-tsagh/   [ghǫtsagh]   'you (sg) cry' Op
(20) /gho-tsagh/   [watsagh]   'he, she cries' Op

I suggest that labio-velar segments followed by [a] be derived from sequences of velar + /o/ by the rule of Diphthongization, stated informally in (21):

(21) o --> wa / velar ___ (C)

where C ≠ ɪ and [o] is [-nasal]

There are two slightly troublesome aspects to this analysis. First, the stem -[gònè?] 'arm' must be marked as an exception to Diphthongization, since it contains a sequence of velar + [o] in which [o] is oral and not followed by [ɪ]. Secondly, the prefix [wha]- (first person plural object and possessor) fails to obey the blocking condition on Diphthongization:

(22) /who-nka-ya-na-n-zan/ [whįkayanįzan]   'he, she wants us'

Given the rule in (21), the form *[whǫkayanįzan] is expected. The behavior of this form indicates that the output of Diphthongization must be lexicalized in at least this prefix.

5.3 Nasal vowels

Nearly all nasal vowels can be derived from syllable-final /Vn/ sequences by the rule of Nasalization, informally stated in (23):

(23)   Vn --> Ṽ / ___ (C)]$_{syl}$

Nasal vowels and [Vn] sequences are basically in complementary distribution. For example, word-finally, generally only nasal vowels occur:

(24)   [nǫzę]   'skunk'
(25)   -[tsų]   'grandmother'
(26)   [tlį]   'dog'
(27)   [datǫ]   'thick'

Nasalization regularly applies to stem-final sequences of /in en un on/. The nasal vowel [ą] is quite rare: the sequence /an/ does not occur in non-derived forms, and in derived forms, this sequence undergoes a rule of a Raising (Ch. 3, 5.2), surfacing as [ǫ]. (See Hargus (to appear (a)) for more information.) Nasalization systematically fails to apply to word-final /ən/:

(28)   [tən]   'ice'
(29)   [sàn]   'star'

The failure of Nasalization to apply to word-final /ən/ is due to the fact that word-final [ə] does not occur in an open syllable. Some instances of surface [in] occur:

(30)   [dəchin]   'stick, wooden'
(31)   [yhin]   'song'

However, in these forms, the sequence [in] is phonetically [In], and is derived from /ən/. (/ə/ in a closed syllable surfaces as [I] following a palatal consonant.) There are a few stems with surface [on], which must simply be marked as exceptions to Nasalization:

(32) -[ton]   'hold [0]'

(33) [jon]   'up here'

Finally, there are at least two stems that I am aware of that must contain underlying nasal vowels:

(34) /ʔəsk'ų̀è/   [ʔəsk'ų̀èʔ]   'roe'

(35) -/chų̀è/   -[chų̀èʔ]   'son'

Because these stems contain prevocalic, nonalternating [ỹ], I assume that the underlying representations are as given above, rather than /ʔəsk'ùnè/ and -/chùnè/.

In addition to accounting for the near complementary distribution of [Vn] and [ỹ], alternations between [Vn] and [ỹ] provide further evidence for the rule of Nasalization, as will be seen throughout this dissertation.

6. Distinctive features

I provide a distinctive feature analysis of the (non-complex) segments of Sekani in (36) and (37). I have omitted the affricates, ejectives and labio-velars from the table of consonants, and the nasal vowels from the table of vowels, because they are best regarded as combinations of feature matrices.[7]

(36) Distinctive features of the vowels

	i	e	a	o	u	ə
high	+	-	-	-	+	-
back	-	-	+	+	+	+
round	-	-	-	+	+	-
low	-	-	+	-	-	-

14

(37) Distinctive features of the consonants

	b	d	t	s	z	ɣ	l	yh	y
sonorant	-	-	-	-	-	-	-	-	-
continuant	-	-	-	+	+	+	+	+	+
nasal	-	-	-	-	-	-	-	-	-
coronal	-	+	+	+	+	+	+	-	-
anterior	+	+	+	+	+	+	+	-	-
high	-	-	-	-	-	-	-	+	+
back	-	-	-	-	-	-	-	-	-
round	-	-	-	-	-	-	-	-	-
low	-	-	-	-	-	-	-	-	-
lateral	-	-	-	-	-	-	+	-	-
voiced	-	-	-	-	+	-	+	-	+
constricted glottis	-	-	-	-	-	-	-	-	-
spread glottis	-	-	+	-	-	-	-	-	-

	g	k	x	gh	?	h	m	n
sonorant	-	-	-	-	+	+	+	+
continuant	-	-	+	+	-	+	-	-
nasal	-	-	-	-	-	-	+	+
coronal	-	-	-	-	-	-	-	+
anterior	-	-	-	-	-	-	+	+
high	+	+	+	+	-	-	-	-
back	+	+	+	+	-	-	-	-
round	-	-	-	-	-	-	-	-
low	-	-	-	-	+	+	-	-
lateral	-	-	-	-	-	-	-	-
voiced	-	-	-	+	-	-	+	+
constricted glottis	-	-	-	-	+	-	-	-
spread glottis	-	+	-	-	-	+	-	-

To account for the phonetic form of the labio-velar fricatives [w wh], I posit the rule in (38):

(38)   Velar Loss

$$\begin{bmatrix} +cont \\ +round \end{bmatrix} \rightarrow \begin{bmatrix} -high \\ -back \\ -round \\ +ant \end{bmatrix}$$

Notes.

1. In 1968 the construction of W.A.C. Bennett dam at Hudson Hope, B.C., was completed. This dam caused sections of the Peace, Parsnip, and Finlay Rivers to flood, creating Williston Lake.

2. These maps are from Lanoue (1983). I am grateful to Guy Lanoue for allowing me to reproduce them.

3. Map 3 was provided by Jim Kari.

4. Daniel Harmon was a nineteenth century explorer of this area of British Columbia.

5. I recognize that tremendous linguistic diversity exists within and between Athabaskan speech communities, and that some of the discrepancies between Young's and my data may be due to this sort of variation. However, Makrit Dominique was reported to be from McLeod Lake (Mills 1981).

6. In practice, this will be less confusing than it may seem now.

   The syllable-final stops and affricates are traditionally represented with the symbols for the voiceless unaspirated phonetic symbols in Athabaskan practical orthographies, probably because of the influence of English phonetics and orthography.

7. The ejective, affricate and labio-velars consonants are clearly single segments phonologically, rather than sequences of segments, as the following contrasts attest:

(40)   [VC.?V] vs. [V.C'V]

(a) [gat̲.?alè?]   'spruce branch'

(b) [mə.t'ale?]   'his, her zyphoid process'

(41)   [VC.zV] vs. [V.CzV]

(a) [gat̲.zàazi]   'prototypical spruce'

(b) [mə.dzadè?]   'his, her lower leg'

Syllable-initially, there is no contrast between [s z] / t___.

(42)   [C.kuV] vs. [C.kwV]

(a) [?əs.k'ǜè?]   'roe'

(b) [dəghəs.kw'ətl]   'I will stab [O]'

Chapter Two

Lexical Phonology

In this chapter, I present an overview of the theory of Lexical Phonology (LP),[1] and in subsequent chapters, I develop an analysis of Sekani phonology and morphology within this theory.

There are two features of the LP model which most distinguish it from competing models of grammar, such as that presented in Chomsky and Halle (1968) (hereafter, SPE). (1) Analyses in which phonological rule applications precede morphological processes, some of which will be illustrated in section 4, are correctly predicted to occur. (2) As will be discussed in section 5, the theory correctly predicts a significant number of differences between two types of phonological rules: 'lexical' and 'postlexical' rules.

Because Lexical Phonology is a model of the interaction of phonological rules with other types of rules (particularly, morphological processes), it is necessary to clarify the types of morphological derivations which are assumed to be permitted. Nearly all research within the Lexical Phonology framework (including this dissertation) presupposes a rather abstract approach to morphology and the lexicon, due, in large part, to the incorporation of the subtheory of level ordering with its traditionally abstract approach to morphology.

1. The organization of grammar in the Lexical Phonology model

A version of the Lexical Phonology model of grammar is provided in (1) (cf. Stong-Jensen (1987)):

(1)   LP model of the lexicon

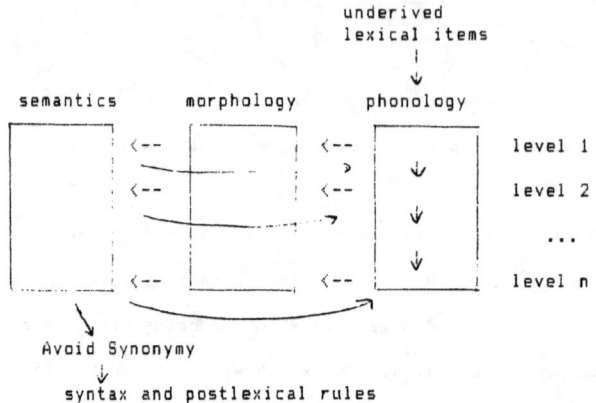

In this model, the lexicon is a component of grammar which is divided into two subcomponents (a list of underived lexical items and a set of rules of morphology). The lexicon overlaps with two other components, the phonology and, in Stong-Jensen's model (following Pesetsky 1985), a semantic component of lexical Logical Form. Lexical items are inserted into structures generated by both the morphology and the syntax. The output of the lexicon is input to the syntactic component, but not vice versa.[2] Phonological rules apply to both morphological and syntactic structures, following lexical insertion.

Most versions of the theory of Lexical Phonology also embrace a theory of morphology known as level ordering (Siegel 1974, Allen 1978), the justification for which will be discussed in 3.2. Briefly, morphological processes are assigned to 'levels' or 'strata' in this theory, which also define the domains of phonological rules. The levels themselves are ordered, but the morphological processes within levels are not generally ordered with respect to each other.

According to the Lexical Phonology version of level ordering, phonological rules are also assigned to particular levels, although, unlike morphological processes, an individual rule may apply on more than one level of the lexicon as well as in the syntax. Phonological rules which apply in the lexicon are 'lexical' rules; 'postlexical' phonological rules apply in the syntax.[3] The phonological rules are predicted to apply cyclically, after each morphological process which applies in the derivation of a word. Semantic interpretation is also assumed to take place cyclically, in conjunction with word formation (Kiparsky 1982, Pesetsky 1985).

Thus, a morphologically complex form like English <u>nationalizers</u> will be derived from a lexical entry [nation] by four distinct suffixation processes: [[[[nation]al]ize]r]s]. The ordered list of phonological rules of level 1 are given a chance to apply following -<u>al</u> suffixation. Similarly, the phonological processes of level 2 may apply after each of the remaining (level 2) suffixes is added. In early research within the Lexical Phonology model, it was observed that this model of the interaction of morphology and phonology predicted that lexical rules are cyclic. Recently, the correctness of this prediction has been questioned; while many lexical rules are cyclic, various analyses have been proposed (Pulleyblank 1986, Mohanan and Mohanan 1984, Mohanan 1986) in which lexical rules do not apply cyclically. In such cases, it is proposed that all of the morphological processes of a given level precede all of the phonological pocesses of that level. I will return to the question of cyclicity of lexical rules in Ch. 7.

2. Comparison with the SPE model of grammar

Lexical Phonology is not the only conceivable model of grammar. For many years, the model of grammar proposed by Chomsky and Halle (1968) in the <u>Sound Pattern of English</u> (hereafter SPE) was widely assumed. This model is schematically represented in (2).

(2)
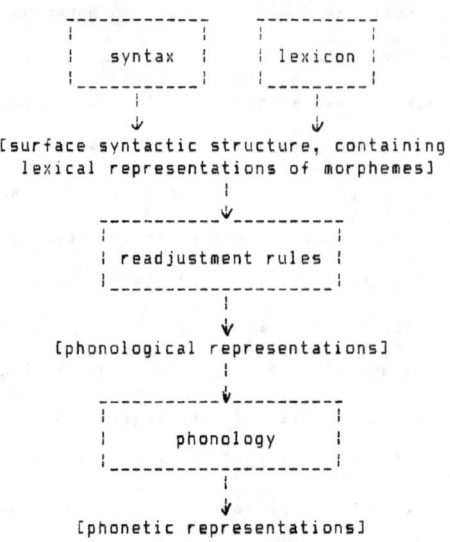

In this model, there is essentially no morphological component: the order of morphemes both within and outside the word is determined by the syntax. Note that the phonological and readjustment rule components follow the lexicon and the syntax: phonological rules only apply after word formation is complete; that is, after fully formed words have been inserted into syntactic structures.

The major difference between the Lexical Phonology and SPE models thus concerns the location of the phonological rule component. In the Lexical Phonology model, some phonological processes are assigned to the lexicon.[4] The fact that phonological rules are allowed to apply in two places in the Lexical Phonology model makes two apparently correct predictions which are unexplained by the SPE model:

1. There are several well-motivated analyses, to be discussed in section 4, found in a variety of languages in which it is necessary for phonological rules to precede morphological rules.

2. Lexical and postlexical phonological rule applications have different characteristics, as discussed in section 5. This correlation between rule ordering and other rule characteristics is unexplained in the SPE model.

3. How abstract is morphology?

As outlined above, Lexical Phonology is a theory of the interaction of phonology with other components of grammar. In this section, I would like to clarify, if not completely justify, the approach to morphology and the lexicon which is widely assumed by nearly all researchers in Lexical Phonology. The best justification for this approach to morphology is found in Kiparsky (1982).

To begin with, I will assume, following Lieber (1980), Kiparsky (1983), and Stong-Jensen (1987), that affixation is largely a process of lexical insertion (regardless of whether affixes are inserted into independently generated word structures, or whether these structures are 'built up' by (e.g.) Percolation conventions (Lieber 1980)). Certainly not all morphological processes can be analyzed as affixation (see Anderson (1988) for discussion of nonaffixational types of morphology; also see section 4), but I see no reason why affixation cannot be regarded as insertion of a lexical entry.

3.1 The Chomsky/Jackendoff approach to morphology and the lexicon

Most speakers of English probably agree that the pairs of words in (3) are in some way related to each other.

(3) arrive   arrival
    decide   decision
    nominate nominee
    negotiate negotiant
    educate   educable
    comfort   comfortable

One of the goals of morphological theory is to account for this sort of linguistic knowledge (cf. Anderson 1988). Independently of speaker intuitions, however, it is possible to argue, as has Chomsky (1970), that a linguistically significant relationship holds between the pairs in (3). For example, apart from their shared elements of phonological shape and meaning, a verb and its corresponding derived nominal, if any, often share certain syntactic properties, such as transitivity or intransitivity:

(4)   John refused the offer
       John's refusal of the offer

       John arrived (*the offer)
       John's arrival (*of the offer)

Ideally, these shared properties should be stated in one place in the grammar, and not, for example, in the lexical entry of <u>arrive</u> as well as in the lexical entry of <u>arrival</u>.

There are basically two ways in which the relation between pairs of words such as those in (3) could be expressed. In a relatively concrete approach to morphology and the lexicon such as that of Jackendoff (1975), nominals in -<u>al</u> and derivatives of <u>educ-</u> would be lexically listed with morphological structure:

(5)   /arrive/   /arriv + al/
       /educ + ate/   /educ + able/
       /decide/   /decid + ion/

Redundancy rules such as that in (6) (from Jackendoff 1975) would express the predictable syntactic, semantic and phonological relation which holds between lexical items such as <u>decision</u> and <u>decide</u>:

(6) $\begin{bmatrix} x \\ /y + \text{ion}/ \\ +N \\ +[NP_1\text{'s} \underline{\quad} (P) \; NP_2] \\ \text{Abstract result of act of} \\ NP_1\text{'s } Z\text{-ing } NP_2 \end{bmatrix}$ (entry number)
(phonological representation)
(syntactic features)

(semantic representation)

$\begin{matrix} \uparrow \\ \downarrow \end{matrix}$

$\begin{bmatrix} w \\ +V \\ +[NP_1 \underline{\quad} (P) \; NP_2] \\ NP_1 \; Z \; NP_2 \end{bmatrix}$

(In this theory, 'entry numbers' are arbitrary indices which permit 'reference to a lexical entry independent of its content' (Jackendoff 1975:642).) While much remains to be worked out in this theory, some fairly specific proposals concerning the mechanics of lexical relatedness in a relatively concrete lexicon have been provided, and in this regard, Jackendoff's work is an improvement over that of Chomsky (1970).[5]

3.2 Level ordering

The Chomsky/Jackendoff abstract approach to morphology and the lexicon contrasts sharply with the approach assumed by researchers within the theory of level ordering (Siegel 1974, Allen 1978, Kiparsky 1982, etc.).

The central claim of the theory of level ordering, as proposed by Siegel (1974) and further modified by Allen (1978), Kiparsky (1982, etc.), Mohanan (1982, 1986) and others, is that there is a correlation between the domains of phonological rules and the order in which word formation rules apply. According to this theory, morphological and phonological rules are assigned to blocks (called 'levels' (or 'strata')). These levels are in turn ordered:

(7)   The Level Ordering Hypothesis (following Pesetsky 1979:19)

       Level n morphology precedes level n+1 morphology.

(Allen's (1978) Extended Ordering Hypothesis is similar.) Thus, with the exception of infixes, level n morphemes occur 'inside of' level n+1 morphemes.

The initial research on level ordering by Allen and Siegel was done within an SPE model of grammar, in which phonological rule applications follow the syntactic component, and thus phonological differences between levels were encoded by boundary symbols. However, it was observed by Pesetsky (1979) that allowing phonological rules to apply in the lexicon along with word formation rules has a striking theoretical consequence. Thus, if phonological as well as morphological rules are assigned to levels, then boundary symbols are not needed to define the domains of phonological rules. This is a welcome theoretical result, given the notorious problems with boundaries (Rotenberg 1978).

There is abundant evidence that phonological rules may apply on more than one level or postlexically as well as lexically (see Mohanan (1982, 1986), Rice (1982), Mohanan and Mohanan (1984)). Many cases of phonological rules which apply on more than one level will be seen in Sekani, most strikingly for levels 2, 3 and 4 (see Ch. 3). This characteristic of phonological rules suggests that the phonological component is a single system of rules, whose domains may overlap between the levels and/or the syntax. Interestingly, the domains of phonological rules are apparently always continuous sets of levels (Mohanan (1982, 1986). Therefore, the following constraint on the domains of phonological rules can be placed:

(8)   Continuous Stratum Hypothesis[6] (Mohanan 1982, 1986)

The domain of a rule may not contain <u>nonadjacent</u> strata.

As far as I know, there are no counter-examples to this hypothesis. Thus to the extent that it is true, the Continuous Stratum Hypothesis is a fact about languages that could not be easily stated without the theory of level ordering.

While phonological rules can be assigned to more than one level, it is not clear whether or not morphological processes such as compounding and affixation are always assigned to unique levels in a language, or whether morphological processes, like phonological rules, may apply on more than one level. (See Mohanan (1986) for a review of this issue.)

3.2.1 A level ordered model of the English lexicon

The model in (9) of the English lexicon is (based on proposals that have been made by Siegel (1974), Allen (1978), and Kiparsky (1983, 1985)) will help illustrate this theory.

(9)

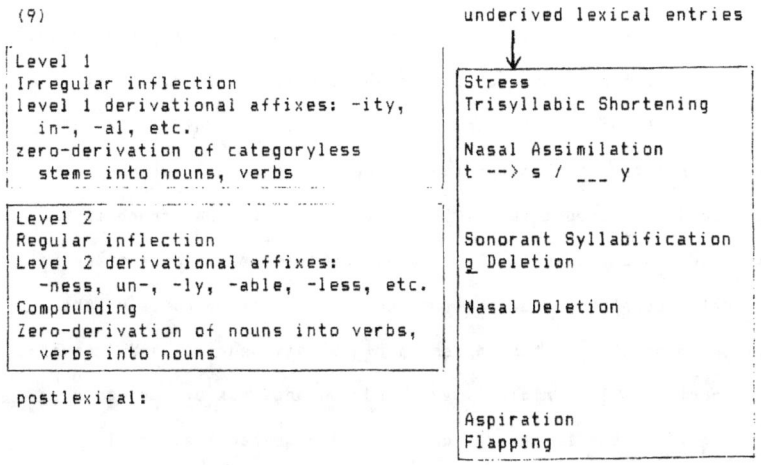

A number of minor differences between the levels of the English lexicon have been proposed. For example, Siegel (1974) and Allen (1978) have both suggested that whereas the level 1 affixes can attach to bound stems (inept, intrepid) or to words (impossible, inedible), the level 2 affixes attach only to words (*unert *unplacable *nontrepid *nonsipid). However, some level 2 affixes apparently do attach to stems (gruesome, winsome, fulsome; hapless, feckless; wilderness, business; uncouth, unkempt, untoward, unruly). Therefore, this difference between levels 1 and 2 morphemes appears to be false.

Allen (1978) has proposed that the phonological and semantic processes of the earliest levels are less compositional than the processes found on later levels. According to Allen's Strong Boundary Hypothesis, content-changing rules (rules which change semantic or phonological properties) cannot operate 'in the environment of' a strong boundary, where # is a strong boundary. Phonologically, this proposal is in accord with Kiparsky's (1984) Strong Domain Hypothesis. However, the admission that the morphology found on earlier levels of the lexicon may not be compositional, semantically, is quite disturbing: this suggests to me that the process in question is in fact not a synchronic process, but one whose outputs have been lexicalized. I return to this point in 3.4. Moreover, it is not clear, even if something like the Strong Boundary Condition turned out to be true, why it would be true.

The most important prediction of the model in (9) is that there is a correlation between phonological rule domains and the derivational potential of morphologically complex forms. One of the most debated aspects of the model in (9) concerns the relative ordering of 'stress-neutral' and 'stress-affecting' morphology. The original level-ordered analysis of the facts as proposed by Siegel is as follows: Siegel (1974) suggested that level 1 suffixes may either cause a rightward shift of main stress on the words to which they attach:

(10) -ion: populate, population
     -ity: toxic, toxicity

or they may occur inside of affixes which cause a rightward shift of stress:

(11) -ism: imperial, imperialism, imperialistic
     -able: recover, recoverable, recoverability
     -ize: terror, terrorize, terrorization

Similarly, Siegel's level 1 prefixes, such as ad- and ex-, are within the domain of stress rules:

(12) ad-:   ádvocate
     ex-:   éxcrement

However, level 2 suffixes are 'stress-neutral': they play no role in the assignment of stress, and never influence the stress contours of the words they attach to:

(13) -al: deny, denial
     -ness: toxic, toxicness
     -less: population, populationless

The level 2 prefixes are also stress-neutral in that they do not influence the stress contours of their bases:

(14) mal-:   adaptation, maladaptation
     pseudo-: assignment, pseudo-assignment
     anti-:   abortion, anti-abortion

In contrast to the level 1 prefixes, the level 2 prefixes have their own stress contours. In fact, Strauss (1982) analyzes words which contain level 2 'prefixes' as compounds. Unlike level 1 affixes or level 2 suffixes, but just like the constituents of compounds, the level 1 'prefixes' can be conjoined. See Strauss or Siegel (1974) for examples.

Kiparsky (1983) has suggested that zero-derived pairs which differ in stress are derived from roots on level 1 (preceding stress assignment), whereas zero-derived pairs of nouns and verbs with identical stress patterns are derived on level 2 (following stress assignment).

However, the correlation of stress placement with levels 1 and 2 morphological processes seems far from well understood. As discussed by Hayes (1984), the rules for stress placement in English are often sensitive to the identity of particular affixes. Moreover, the data in (11) have actually been interpreted by Aronoff and Sridhar (1983) as an argument against level ordering, since in these data, an apparently stress-neutral suffix occurs inside a stress-shifting suffix. I suggest that the properties of stress in English cannot yet be regarded as evidence for or against level ordering.

The negative prefixes in English (3.2.2) and the inflectional characteristics of zero-derived verbs (3.2.3) provide clearer evidence for the model in (9) than does the domain of stress placement.

3.2.2 The negative prefixes in English

The prefixes in- and un- provide an example of the predictions of the theory of level ordering. As discussed by Siegel (1974) and Allen (1978), the phonological properties of these prefixes correlate with their differences with respect to the derivational potential of the words to which they are affixed.

The prefix in- attaches both to nouns (indecision, incertitude, inability, injustice) and to adjectives (illegal, indigestible, inanimate, incoherent, indecisive, inorganic). However, nouns in -ity aside, un- attaches basically to adjectives and not to nouns.

There are certain phonological differences between these prefixes. The final nasal in in- assimilates in place of articulation to a following stop and in manner of articulation to a following liquid:[7]

(15) imbalance
      i[ng]gratitude
      illegal
      irrational

However, the final nasal of un- does not assimilate:

(16) unbalanced
      ungrateful
      unlawful
      unrationalized

in- and un- also differ with respect to stress behavior. In many forms which contain in-, stress falls on the prefix in- itself, whereas it never falls on the prefix un-:

(17) pótent   ímpotent
      píous   ímpious
      fínite   ínfinite

These data could be accounted for by assuming that in- is associated with a weaker boundary (+) than is un- (#), and that the domains of the nasal assimilation and stress placement rules are delimited by the stronger boundary.

Now consider the morphological differences between these prefixes. While in- and un- both attach to adjectives (and do not alter the lexical category of the adjectives to which they attach), an asymmetry exists between in- and un- with respect to the kinds of derived adjectives they may attach to. The prefix in- cannot attach to adjectives which are derived from nouns by 'stress-neutral' suffixes such as -ly, -like, -ful, -worthy, -some, and -ish:

(18)   unfriendly   *infriendly
      unchild-like   *inchild-like
      unfruitful   *infruitful
      unsea-worthy   *insea-worthy
      unwholesome   *inwholesome
      unselfish   *inselfish
      unprecedented   *inprecedented
      undying   *indying

Notice also that when in- and un- co-occur, they always occur in the order unin-, never in the order inun-:

(19)   unillegal, *inunlegal
      unindigestible, *inundigestible
      uninanimate, *inunanimate
      unincoherent, *inuncoherent
      unindecisive, *inundecisive
      uninorganic, *inunorganic

Level ordering provides a way of relating the phonological differences between in- and un- to the the different derivational properties of the words to which they attach: in- is assigned to level 1, as is the nasal assimilation rule, and un- is assigned to level 2, along with other stress-neutral affixes such as those in (18).

3.2.3 Zero-derived verbs

Kiparsky (1983) proposes that there are two sources for zero-derived nouns and verbs in English, categoryless stems and nouns or verbs:

(20) level 1: stems --> nouns, verbs

level 2: nouns --> verbs
verbs --> nouns

The characteristics of level 2 zero-derived verbs are of interest. First note that noun compounds, which supposed to be derived on level 2, can be zero-derived into verbs:

(21) to grandstand, to wallpaper, to quarterback, to stonewall, to roughhouse, to paperclip, to sandbag, to spraypaint,

This fact is predicted by the model in (9), because compounding assigned to level 2.

Secondly, note that verbs in -ing/k usually undergo ablaut (to -ang/k, -ung/k) when inflected for tense:

(22) sing, sang, sung
drink, drank, drunk
ring, rang, rung
sting, stang, stung

However, level 2 verbs which are zero-derived from nouns, according to Kiparsky's analysis, take regular inflection:

(23) ring, ringed, ringed
wing, winged, winged
ink, inked, inked

These facts are accounted for by the model in (9) as follows. Irregular inflection is a level 1 process, but because the zero-derivation of nouns into verbs takes place on level 2, such verbs must take the regular set of inflectional suffixes.

Note also that non-ing/k zero-derived verbs also take regular inflection. The verb to fly out ('to hit a fly ball which is caught and not dropped, thereby forcing the batter out') is presumably zero-derived on level 2 from the noun fly (ball). Thus fly in the verb fly out is also undergo the regular inflectional processes, and this is apparently correct: flied (out) (*flew out).

It is not clear how these facts about the inflection of zero-derived verbs would be accounted for without a level-ordered model of the English lexicon.

3.2.4 Summary

The theory of level ordering has come under attack recently, most notably by Aronoff and Sridhar (1983) and by Sproat (1986), who suggest that it be replaced by a 'word/stem' model in which 'words' and 'stems' are the only two affixal bases/phonological constituents. There are two differences between this theory and that of level ordering. (1) It is a more constrained theory in that only two levels are universally predicted to occur. (2) It is a weaker theory in that the levels are unordered with respect to each other, and this apparently correctly accounts for affix order violations in English (Aronoff and Sridhar) and phenomena which require a 'loop' between levels (Mohanan (1982, 1986); Sproat (1986). However, as will be seen in Ch. 3, there are apparently five levels or domains of phonological rule application in Sekani, and this is problematic for the word/stem model.

3.2.5 The abstractness of level ordering

As may have been observed in the preceding section, the morphological derivations permitted in level-ordered analyses are rather abstract. There are at least two ways in which they could be said to be fairly abstract. First, bound stems (with or without an inherent lexical category) are allowed to be the base of word formation rules. Secondly, derivations in which unproductive affixes are added to bases (whether bound or free) are also permitted. Consider some further examples that have appeared in the literature of these sorts of analyses.

Kiparsky (1982:24) is critical of Aronoff's (1976) truncation analysis of nouns and adjectives derived from verbs in -ate. Aronoff argues that the suffix -ate is deleted (or in his terms, truncated) before certain suffixes, including -ee, -ant and -able:

(24) nominate   nominee
     evacuate   evacuee, evacuant
     negotiate   negotiant, negotiable
     lubricate   lubricant

Rejecting truncation as a possible structural change in morphology, Kiparsky proposes a different analysis of the forms in (24):

> The alternative is to derive both the nouns and the verbs from roots, i.e. nomin-, (e)vacu-, negot-, lubric-. This is a reasonable solution in view of the build of the latinate vocabulary. The roots must be assumed anyway as the base for other level 1 derivatives such as...nominal, vacuous, vacuity, lubricious. And the suffixes -ee, -able, -ant must be allowed to be added to roots anyway in such words as...memorable, lessee, deodorant, innumerable, conferee, obstruent, unconscionable, tenant, sonorant. So we may simply allow the suffixes in question to be added to both roots and verbs.

In other words, Kiparsky assumes that suffixes like -ant are synchronically added to roots like sonor-.

As another example of the abstract approach to generating morphology, consider Strauss's (1982:28) analysis of English adjectives in -y. Strauss has noted that the bases of some of these adjectives are free noun stems (25):

(25) chocolaty   scary
     sugary   salty
     bratty   hairy
     worthy   muddy
     fishy

However, adjectives in -y are also found in which the suffix is attached to bound and apparently categoryless stems (26):

(26) happy   cozy
     zany   pretty
     phony   silly
     puny   wacky
     shabby   rickety
     uncanny   skinny
     lazy   cranky
     skimpy   ready

Strauss suggests that both kinds of adjectives are not only morphologically complex, but synchronically derived. As evidence for this, Strauss notes that neither class of adjective can be suffixed with -ity, -ist, or -ize, but they can both be further derived with -ness, -ish, and -ly:

(27) happiness
      happyish
      happily

(28) *happyity
      *happyize
      *happyist

Strauss provides a level-ordered explanation of the ill-formedness of the words in (28): if -y, -ness, -ish, and -ly are level 2 suffixes, so that all adjectives in -y are derived at level 2, whereas the suffixes -ity, -ist, and -ize are level 1, then the failure of both kinds of adjectives in -y to undergo level 1 suffixation processes is predicted. This requires, of course, that both kinds of adjectives be synchronically derived. While there are problems with this analysis,[8] it is illustrative of the kind of abstract approach to morphology and the lexicon which is often found in the literature.

A quite plausible reaction to the abstract analyses of morphology and the lexicon that have been proposed by Siegel, Allen, Kiparsky, Strauss and others might be that they are overly abstract. Notice that, in terms of accounting for speaker judgments of lexical relatedness, a concrete theory of the lexicon works as well as the more abstract approaches, but only if lexical entries are underspecified and the lexical redundancy rules supply redundant (non-idiosyncratic) information. (Jackendoff argues (but unconvincingly, I think) that lexical entries are fully specified; cf. Stanley (1967).) Of course, if the abstract approach accounts for more than just lexical relatedness (Strauss's analysis of -y is supposed to account for the further derivational potential of these adjectives, for example), then it would have certain advantages over the concrete theory.

In the remainder of this section I will discuss first the advantages of the abstract approach to morphology and the lexicon and then the potential problems with it.

3.3 Advantages of abstract morphology

In 3.3.1 I present evidence that the lexicon must contain bound stems: such stems are the bases of clearly productive morphological processes in language like Latin. In 3.3.2 I present an argument from Kiparsky (1982) that words containing unproductive affixes must be synchronically derived, not lexically listed.

3.3.1 Inadequacy of word-based morphology

Aronoff (1976) has argued that the bases of word formation processes are words, not stems. According to this theory, grammatical is analyzable as the base of -ity in grammaticality because grammatical is a word of English, but educ cannot be the base of educable beause educ- is not a word.

Aronoff's logic is as follows. He assumes (and I agree) that word formation rules derive words which are meaningful. Therefore, all aspects of word formation (not only the word formation rules themselves, but also their bases) must be meaningful. Aronoff argues that it is necessary to recognize the existence of meaningless morphemes, such as -mit.[9] Since meaningless morphemes apparently exist, and meaningless bases must be excluded from participating in word formation processes, then the only class of bases that can participate in word formation processes is that class whose members are always meaningful; i.e. words. Aronoff (1976:22) is quite clear about this aspect of his theory:

> ...I have not specified meaningfulness as a criterion for serving as the base of a WFR. If there are meaningful morphemes, and I have not argued that such entities never exist, the theory as formulated does not permit them to serve as the base of any WFR. This is of course an empirical

claim.

As Aronoff (1976:28) notes, a counter-example to this theory would be 'a case in which there are several words formed from the same stem, but in which the stem never shows up as a word itself'.

Apart from the demonstrable empirical inadequacy of this claim, to be discussed shortly, I suggest that there is a problem with the logic of this argument. Just because some morphemes are not meaningful, why should all morphemes be prohibited from serving as the base of word formation rules? Nonword morphemes participate in other aspects of word formation. Whether conceived of as rules (Aronoff 1976, Kiparsky 1982) or as lexical entries (Lieber 1983, Kiparsky 1983), morphemes can be added to bases. It would make much more sense to specify meaningfulness as the criterion for participating in a morphological derivation.

In any case, as Kiparsky (1982), Anderson (1988 and elsewhere) and others have noted, it is not difficult to demonstrate that there are empirical problems with the word-based hypothesis. In languages in which the members of some lexical category are obligatorily inflected, the base of the inflectional process is often a stem. For example, Latin noun stems are obligatorily inflected for one of six cases:

(29)   singular declension of a Latin (nominal) o-stem /domin/- 'master'

nom	dominus
gen	dominī
acc	dominum
dat	dominō
abl	dominō
voc	domine

Apparently, the base of the preceding nominal paradigm must be the stem /domin/-. Therefore, the lexicon must contain bound stems, and these may serve as the basis for word formation processes.

One might try to argue that stems, rather than words, can serve as the basis for inflectional but not derivational processes. It is true that derivational processes which apply to stems are scarcer, since questions concerning the synchronic viability (productivity) of the process arise more frequently in the case of derivational than inflectional morphology. Latin denominal adjectives (again, from Anderson 1988) are a case in point. As Anderson points out, some of the bases of this derivational process are clearly words:

(30) /vir/:   vir   'man'
               virīlis   'manly'

But in some cases, the base is clearly a stem, not an independently occurring word:

(31) /vulg/   vulgus   'common people'
               vulgāris   'commonplace'
     /reg/   rēx   'king'
               rēgius   'royal'
     /mort/   mors   'death'
               mortālis   'mortal'

But it is not clear from these data how productive the adjectival suffixes are, and thus how viable this derivational process is. A proponent of the word-based hypothesis might argue that there is no synchronic derivational process at work here: the adjectival outputs have all been lexicalized. But regardless of the existence of derivational processes such as (30) and (31), I believe that the inflectional cases suffice to establish the fact that bound stems exist in the lexicon. If <u>domin-</u> is a member of the Latin lexicon, there seems to be no reason not to expect the English lexicon to contain bound stems like <u>educ-</u> and <u>negoti-</u>.

3.3.2 Consequences of lexically listing unproductive affixes in English

Recall that in an abstract approach to morphology and the lexicon, not only bound stems like <u>educ-</u> and <u>negoti-</u> but also unproductive affixes the deverbal nominalizing suffix <u>-al</u> would have lexical entries. In a more concrete theory, there would be no lexical entry for -al or educ-; instead, words like recital, arrival, and educable would be lexically listed.

Like Strauss's argument for an abstract analysis of adjectives in -y, Kiparsky's argument for an abstract analysis of English complex words is based on observations concerning the further derivational potential of morphologically complex forms. Kiparsky (1982:27 ff.) suggests that affixation is often unpredictable for basic lexical entries but predictable for derived lexical items:

> The patterning of derivational suffixes requires...closer study but there seems to be no doubt that derived lexical items do not admit morphological idiosyncracy as freely as basic lexical items do.

Kiparsky argues that if derived forms were lexically listed, they could be lexically marked for idiosyncracies in the same way that underived forms are. However, if derived forms are not lexically listed, but instead derived, then this apparent absence of idiosyncratic marking is predicted.

As an example, consider the properties of the English verb-forming suffix -ize. This suffix attaches to nominal and adjectival bases:

(32)   nouns:

    terrorize   womanize
    moralize   satirize
    scandalize   victimize
    martyrize   lionize
    villainize   oxygenize

(33)   adjectives:

    popularize   fertilize
    spiritualize   humanize
    equalize   westernize
    solemnize   palatalize

-ize is also found on non-word stems:

(34)   baptize   jeopardize
        harmonize   philosophize
        agonize   hypnotize
        epitomize   systematize
        syllogize   propagandize

Clearly, there is much about the bases to which -ize attaches that is idiosyncratic. Not all nouns and adjectives may be suffixed with -ize:

> *horrorize
> *autumnize
> *animalize
> *turtleize
> *heliumize
> *agendize

However, other instances of -ize are more or less predictable. Following Marchand (1966), it seems that -ize attaches fairly productively to adjectives in -al, -ar, -(i)an and -ic:[10]

(35)   territorialize   scripturalize
        nationalize   sphericalize
        naturalize   principalize
        optionalize   secretarialize
        exceptionalize   janitorialize

        linearize
        globularize
        circularize
        tabularize

        Africanize   episcopalianize
        Americanize   presbyterianize
        Canadianize
        Christianize
        Shakesperianize

        rhythmicize
        historicize
        soporificize
        theatricize
        Homericize
        Hellenicize

It could be argued that the derived verbs in (32)-(34) are lexically listed, whereas the verbs in (35) are synchronically derived, since the occurrence of -ize in the latter, but not the former, group of forms is predictable.

However, both groups of forms can undergo a further derivational process, nominalization with -ation:[11]

>   agonization
>   hypnotization
>   womanization
>   popularization
>   fertilization
>
>   soporificization
>   exceptionalization
>   circularization
>   Canadianization

Based on this fact, Kiparsky argues that words like _agonize_ are synchronically derived: if words like _agonize_ in which the occurrence of -_ize_ is unpredictable were all lexically listed, they should be just as idiosyncratic in terms of their further derivational potential (e.g., nominalization) as non-derived verbs are (see Chomsky 1970). However, if _agonize_ is synchronically derived via suffixation of -_ize_ to _agon_-, then its regular derivational potential is predicted: there is no possibility of idiosyncratically marking _agonize_ as, for example, not undergoing nominalization with -_ation_.[12]

To summarize, by not lexically listing apparently unproductively derived forms, the prediction is made that these derived forms cannot be lexically marked for idiosyncracies. If it turns out to be generally true that the further derivational properties of morphologically complex forms are regular, as Kiparsky suggests that it is of English, then this is an argument for not lexically listing, and instead, synchronically deriving, morphologically complex forms.

3.4 Problems with abstract morphology

There are two obvious and well-known problems with the abstract approach to morphology and the lexicon advocated by Kiparsky and others:

How is overgeneration (the generation of ill-formed words) prevented?
How are idiosyncracies (mainly semantic) in derived forms accounted for?

If the abstract approach to morphology and the lexicon is to be taken seriously, solutions to these problems must be available. In this section, I will illustrate these problems, and discuss potential solutions to them.

3.4.1 Overgeneration

If lexical entries may consist of bound stems like <u>educ-</u> and unproductive affixes like <u>-ant</u> (cf. <u>lubricant</u>, <u>defendant</u>, <u>accountant</u>), then the possibility of deriving ill-formed words like *<u>educant</u> arises. However, a number of ways in which overgeneration might be constrained have been proposed.

The first and most obvious line of defense against overgeneration is to refine the subcategorization frames of affixes, thereby generating all and only the well-formed words of a language. For example, the prefix <u>re-</u> (<u>redo</u>, <u>reheat</u>, <u>remarry</u>, etc.) attaches to verbs but cannot be added to just any verb, as ill-formed words like *<u>rehate</u> and *<u>rewalk</u> attest. There are certain semantic conditions on the verbal base of <u>re-</u> which must be met in order for the derivative to be well-formed (see Aronoff (1976) for discussion). If these conditions are omitted from the subcategorization frame of <u>re-</u>, then of course incorrect forms will be generated. Similarly, phonological conditions may have to be included in the subcategorization frames of affixes. The suffix <u>-en</u> which derives causative verbs from (mainly) adjectival bases is a case in point. Marchand (1966:213-4) notes that this suffix has never been productively added to any but stop- and fricative-final stems, and in the last two hundred years, apparently only to adjectives which end in <u>t</u> and <u>d</u>:

(36) greaten   deepen
      harden   cheapen
      deaden   deafen
      gladden   roughen
      lighten   stiffen
      soften   lessen
      sicken   loosen
      blacken   worsen
      quicken   liven

If these phonological conditions are omitted, then the suffixation of <u>-en</u> will obviously create ill-formed words:

(37)   *freeen   *shyen
        *blueen   *newen
        *lowen   *narrowen
        *slowen   *yellowen
        *highen   *steadyen
        *holyen

Level ordering also has the effect of constraining overgeneration, as noted by Allen (1978), Kiparsky (1983), Stong-Jensen (1987), and others. For example, Kiparsky notes that the suffix -ian cannot attach to words containing the suffix -ism (Mendelianism vs. *Mendelismian), and he accounts for this by assigning -ism to level 2 and -ian to level 1. Kiparsky notes that this analysis has the further welcome effect of simplifying 'the statement of combinatorial restrictions on affixes'. Although I believe this analysis of -ism and -ian is vastly oversimplified, it is illustrative of the way in which level ordering assignments can be used to constrain the generative capacity of the lexicon. As seen above in 3.2, Allen (1978) makes use of level ordering to constrain the derivational properties of the negative prefix un- in English.

Another approach is to posit various filters which block the outputs of morphological rules. The existence of such filters is often invoked to constrain word formation but their precise nature is all too often left unspecified (cf. Booij 1981, Halle 1973, Allen 1978). A welcome exception to this trend is Kiparsky's (1983) principle of Avoid Synonymy, which, while not without problems, nonetheless appears to account for the nonexistence of large numbers of words in a very general way.

(38)   Avoid Synonymy

   The output of a lexical rule may not be synonymous with an existing lexical item.

According to this principle, derived forms which are synonymous with a prior derived form or lexical entry are blocked. The derived form fails to surface if entirely synonymous with an existing lexical item:

(39)   men   blocks   *mans
         cattle   *cattles
         oxen   *oxes
         brought   *brang or bringed
         glory   *gloriosity
         guide   *guider
         criticize   *criticalize
         systematize   *(to) system

However, if the meaning of the derived form only partially overlaps with that of an existing lexical item, the derived form is predicted to surface, but it will lack those meanings which already exist in the existing lexical item(s). In this way, Kiparsky accounts for the fact that the meaning of cutter is basically 'any cutting tool that lacks a specific designation of its own.' Thus, the existence of words designating cutting tools which are used for various specific purposes ('knives, scissors, adzes, chisels, axes etc.') blocks only the assignment of those meanings to cutter. That is, the meaning of cutter is basically that of a general tool for cutting, less the meanings of the various specific tools. (However, cutter apparently does not occur outside of compounds like cookie cutter, glass cutter, etc.) Similarly, the the fact that drill means (roughly) 'tool for drilling' blocks only the assignment of this instrumental meaning to the derived agentive noun driller, not the generation of this word. Avoid Synonymy would predict that a word like guider could surface if it meant something other than the meaning assigned to guide. (See Kiparsky 1983 for additional examples.)

The fact that morphological doublets (e.g., lighted and lit are both possible past tenses of light; the plural of fish is fish or fishes) and synonymous words (e.g., billfold and wallet; sofa and couch) do occasionally exist requires further explanation, given this principle. Kiparsky proposes that such synonyms and doublets are simply learned as 'marked exceptions', and in support of this explanation, truly synonymous pairs of words appear to be quite rare.

Kiparsky views Avoid Synonymy as a principle which blocks the actual application of a given morphological process, rather than as a filter on the output of the lexicon. Stong-Jensen (1987) has pointed out that there is a problem with this interpretation of the effect of Avoid Synonymy, because derived stems may surface as bound members of some larger derived structure, as in the following English (40) and Icelandic (41) compounds:

(40)   base stealer, *stealer
       cookie-cutter, *cutter
       theater-goer, *goer
       near-sighted, *sighted
       dark-eyed, *eyed

(41)   /slangur-orð-i/   [slanguryrði]   'slang word'
       slang-word-suffix

       /göfug-mann-i/   [göfugmenni]   'gentleman'
       noble-man-suffix

In Icelandic, the i-stems which appear in the right member of the preceding compounds are structurally identical to free i-stems and would thus appear to be generable by the same rules needed for free i-stems. The problem, of course, is to generate the bound i-stems only as parts of longer words. Stong-Jensen, following Pesetsky (1985), criticizes the morphological structures required by Kiparsky's (1982) direct generation analysis of the English compounds in (40) and argues that (1) morphology overgenerates, as Allen (1978) similarly concludes, and (2) Avoid Synonymy is not a constraint on word formation rules but an output condition on the entire lexicon (and specifically, of 'Lexical Logical Form'). Non-occuring bound stems like -goer, -eyed and -menni must be allowed to be outputs of word formation rules because they are inputs to further word formation processes (compounding).[13]

As mentioned above, there are problems with Avoid Synonymy. Words derived with the deadjectival, noun-forming suffix -ness should fail to exist

if a prior derived nominal exists. However, nouns in -ness do generally exist
regardless of whether there is a prior derivative:

    glory   gloriousness
    decency   decentness
    anxiety   anxiousness

(However, Kiparsky (1983) suggests that words like graciousness and grace may
not be fully synonymous, and that decentness is ill-formed.) Despite the
existence of these forms which are unaccounted for by Avoid Synonymy, it is
fair to say that this principle goes a long way towards constraining
overgeneration in an abstract lexicon.

In still other cases, neither the general refinement of subcategorization
frames nor the positing of some general principle like Avoid Synonymy) is
sufficient to block the generation of ill-formed words. In the cases of
affixes like the deverbal nominalizing suffix -al, there are no obvious
syntactic, semantic or phonological generalizations which govern the bases to
which -al may attach. Generalizations concerning the class of verbs to which
-al attaches have certainly been proposed, but these are problematic. For
example, Ross (1972) suggested that the verbs to which -al may attach must
meet the structural description in (6):

(42) $\begin{bmatrix} +voc \\ +stress \end{bmatrix} \begin{bmatrix} -voc \\ -cons \end{bmatrix} [+cons]_0^1$

But these conditions are insufficient to predict the set of verbs to which -al
can attach:

(43) rental   but   *dental
      trial   *buyal
      arrival   *derival
      burial   *tarryal
      recital   *incital

Marchand (1966:181) is similarly critical of a phonological approach to
refining the subcategorization frame of -al, and proposes instead that this
suffix 'is tacked onto verbs implying a final result'. However, buy, dent and

derive (at least) from the list in (43) all seem to imply a 'final result'
(cf. purchase, dent, and derivation, respectively) as much as rent, try,
arrive, etc., do.

Neither Marchand's nor Ross's attempt to predict which verbs take -al
works. Therefore, in the case of suffixes like -al and -ize (discussed in 2.2
above) it is necessary either to list (1) the bases to which -al attaches in
its lexical entry (either positively (V = rent, bury...) or negatively (V ≠
derive, dent...), or (2) for each verb (or, more generally, for each member of
a lexical category or even for categoryless stems), the derivational affixes
which can or can't attach to that verb:

(44)   arrive, ___ + al]$_N$
        derive, ___ + ation]$_N$
        decide, ___ + ion]$_N$

To summarize, there are basically two ways in which an abstract approach
to morphology can be constrained so as not to generate ill-formed words.
Subcategorization frames can be refined, either in a general way, by placing
semantic, syntactic or phonological conditions on the base, or in an
idiosyncratic way, by simply listing the lexical items that the affix can
attach to. Complementing this, filters on word formation such as Kiparsky's
Avoid Synonymy or general principles of derivation such as level ordering can
account for the nonappearance of large numbers of words which would otherwise
be predicted to occur.

3.4.2 Idiosyncracy of outputs

A much more serious problem for an abstract approach to morphology and
the lexicon concerns the fact that derived words are often phonologically or
semantically idiosyncratic in some way. Various aspects of form or meaning in
derived words are apparently unpredictable from the information contained in
the lexical entries of the parts of these words.

Consider a few examples of semantic idiosyncracy. (1) One of the meanings of recital (from Webster's Third New International Dictionary of the English Language) is 'a homogenous program of vocal or instrumental music usually by a single performer or by a soloist with an accompanist'. This meaning is peculiar to recital and is not to be found among the meanings of recite (or -al). (2) The meaning of review is not simply a function of the meaning of re- and view. To be sure, one of the archaic meanings of review is 'to view or see again', but other meanings of review, such as 'to go over or examine critically or deliberately', are virtually synonymous with those of view, such as 'to examine carefully or officially'. (3) The noncompositionality of the meaning of the derived word is quite obvious in the cases of words which lack meaningful bases altogether: tenant, uncouth, insipid, etc.

Following Di Sciullo and Williams (1988), it would appear that words like recital, review, and uncouth are simply lexical idioms. Like syntactic idioms such as take to task, kick the bucket, etc., such words have regular structures but unpredictable meanings. The most straightforward way to account for the meanings of these words is exactly the same as the generally accepted analysis of syntactic idioms: such words/phrases are lexically listed as a unit together with their idiosyncratic meanings. This is hardly a novel conclusion. Aronoff (1976), for example, uses idiosyncracy as a criterion for listing, although he proposes, somewhat circularly, that listing is the source of idiosyncracy.

This result would seem to provide evidence against abstract morphology. That is, if words like curiosity are idiosyncratic, semantically, and thus lexically listed, it is not clear that this word would need a synchronic morphological derivation, such as the following:

(45)   /curious/

Affix -ity   [[curious] ity]
Trisyllabic Shortening   o

                        curiosity

Kiparsky (1982:26) is aware of the problems involved with idiosyncratic changes in form and meaning in an abstract approach to morphology and the lexicon and it is worth considering his thoughts on this matter:

> It is possible to take an intermediate position and to say that not all actual words are listed but only those which show some idiosyncracy. For example, obesity might be listed because it is an exception to Trisyllabic Shortening and curiosity might be listed because it denotes not only the property of being curious but also a curious thing or property. A priori this is undesirable because it results in considerable redundancy with no compensating gain. It amounts to saying that if a word has one unpredictable feature then everything about it should be treated as unpredictable. The preferable procedure is to list only the unpredictable properties of words. So we may mark obese as an exception to Trisyllabic Shortening, and we may resgister a special meaning for -ity when used after curious, odd, obscene, bestial and a number of other words.

Notice that there is no dispute about the facts: curiousity has an idiosyncratic meaning. Given that fact, then, rather than enormously complicate the lexical entry of -ity, there seems no principled reason not to recognize that curiosity might have its own lexical entry where its special meaning can be located, just like a syntactic idiom.

However, it may also be that a synchronic derivation for morphologically complex but lexically listed words is required. The evidence for this is clearer in languages other than English, although I believe that the structure of lexical entries in human languages is far from understood.

In Athabaskan languages, lexical entries for words are structurall much more like syntactic idioms in that they are often discontinuous. As will be seen in later sections of this dissertation, the basic lexical unit of an Athabaskan language (the 'theme') can be a single stem (46), a stem and adjacent (47)-(48) or nonadjacent prefixes, or simply a string of adjacent

(49) or nonadjacent (50)-(52) prefixes (subscript numbers indicate adjacency; see Ch. 3):

(46)   yhin   'song'

(47)   d   yhin   'sing'
         13   stem

(48)   h   tsùz   'handle clothlike O' (perfective)
         13   stem

(49)   u   'sə   perform motion to a point
         9   10

(50)   ʔə   h   xǫh   'snore'
         7   13   stem

(51)   tà   'sə   'uphill' (used with motion verbs)
         2   10

(52)   ʔədə d   reflexive
         7   13

Given the fact that other prefixes (such as those which productively mark inflectional categories; see Ch. 3) may intervene between the constituents of a theme in a surface form, it is clear that the structure of a lexical entry is not necessarily identical to the phonetic form of that lexical entry. (In order to account for surface positional properties of affixes in Athabaskan languages, the constituents of themes must be lexically associated with positional information, as also proposed by Rice (to appear). Note that Stong-Jensen (1987) similarly concludes that lexical entries for affixes must contain information about level-ordering assignments.)

Languages with nonconcatenative morphology also provide evidence that the elements of a lexical entry are not necessarily associated with each other in the lexical entry, but that association itself is a synchronic generative process. In Yokuts (see Archangeli (1983, 1985), Steriade (1986), Prince (1987) for recent analyses), it appears that vowel and consonant melodies, together with a particular prosodic template with which they will eventually be associated, are present in lexical entries, but the various phonological formatives which are associated with a single meaning are not necessarily underlyingly associated:

(53)   /bnt, i, CVCVVC/   'ask'

(54)   /lk'l, u, CVCC/   'bury'

(55)   /hlṣ, u, CCVVC/   'sit'

In fact, since the prosodic template associated with a given stem may be supplanted by the prosodic template supplied by particular affixes, as demonstrated by Archangeli (1983), it makes more sense from the point of view of Yokuts derivational morphology if lexical entries are structured as in (53)-(55), rather than as in (56)-(58):

(56)   b n t
       | | |
       CVCVVC   'ask'
         \|/
          i

(57)   l k l
       | | |
       CVC C   'bury'
        |
        u

(58)   hl ṣ
       || |
       CCVVC   'sit'
        |/
        u

Semantic idiosyncracy, then, does not necessarily provide an argument against abstract morphology. It is quite possible that the morphemes which comprise the word <u>curiosity</u> are both present in a single lexical entry, but the process of affixing -<u>ity</u> to the stem <u>curious</u> is synchronically performed. That is, there is no reason that <u>curiosity</u> might not have a lexical entry such as:

(59) curious   'marked by desire to investigate and learn, showing interest in finding or searching out information...'
      ___, -ity 'desire to know, desire to investigate, a matter that is curious and ingenious, a curious trait or aspect...'

However, the conclusions reached in this section do run counter to those of Kiparsky (1982) in other ways. Recall that Kiparsky argues that, at least in English, lexically listing unproductive affixes like -ize as parts of lexical entries, together with the stems which they idiosyncratically subcategorize for (e.g., terrorize), makes the apparently incorrect prediction that these sorts of forms might have idiosyncratic derivational potential. For example, there is apparently no verb in -ize which is idiosyncratically marked as undergoing -al, rather than -ation, nominalization. While lexical listing may make incorrect predictions about the idiosyncracy of further derivations, it is a fact that many derived words are idiosyncratic in other ways; namely, semantically.

I suggest that it is useful to distinguish different kinds of idiosycracy when determining whether or not a form is to be listed. My position is that if a word is idiosyncratic in that it fails to undergo a regular process (such as a phonological rule), that word is lexically associated with a feature which indicates that the process in question does not apply to the stem. For example, as is well known, the stressed vowels in season and obese fail to undergo Trisyllabic Shortening in seasonal and obesity, respectively, but this can be accounted for lexically marking season and obese as [-TSS]. Forms which exceptionally undergo regular processes can likewise be handled by marking such forms [+] (see Ch. 3, 5.2.6, for an example). However, where the idiosyncracy is to be found in the nature of the process itself, rather than in the fact that some form has idiosyncratically undergone some process, the output of the putative process must be listed.

3.5 Summary

The picture that emerges of the lexicon and morphology in the modified abstract approach advocated here is as follows:

--The lexicon may contain bound stems.

--Affixes have lexical entries, the length of which is a general reflection of the productivity of the affix. The lexical entries of affixes like -_able_ will contain relatively little information about the sisters which these affixes subcategorize for, as compared to the lexical entries of affixes like -_ize_.

--Morphologically complex words which exhibit semantic idiosyncracies have their own lexical entries, but the constituents of such words are not necessarily arranged in lexical entries in a way which resembles their surface form.

Many more questions concerning the nature of generative morphology and the lexicon arise than are answered here: are there any constraints on what can be a lexical entry or what can be a morphological derivation? For example, if the lexicon of English contains bound stems like /educ/- and affixes like -/ate/, which subcategorizes for particular lexical items as well as classes of lexical items, then is there any reason why _alms_ is not synchronically derived from /alm/ + /s/? Kiparsky (1982, 1983) suggests that this word is lexically listed, rather than synchronically derived, because it can occur compound-internally, a position where inflectional affixes are not normally found (_alms-giving_; cf. *_tolls-paying_). As of yet, however, there is no theoretical reason why _alms_ should be lexically listed while _negotiate_ synchronically derived.

4. Orderings of phonological and morphological processes

Returning now to the phonological side of the Lexical Phonology model, I would like to discuss certain analyses in which phonological rules must precede morphological rules. Such analyses provide the best evidence for the hypothesis that phonological rules apply in two places in the grammar, yet these analyses are relatively rare, hardly as commonplace as Anderson (1988) suggests.[14] It is obvious that some phonological rules must apply to forms in a syntactic context. For example, the structural descriptions of sandhi rules and rules which apply within specific syntactic domains crucially refer to syntactic information. It is less than obvious that phonological rules must also apply in the lexicon, and thus that the extra power of the Lexical Phonology model is required.

The English deverbal nominalizing suffix -al is widely regarded (see e.g. Kiparsky 1982) as supporting the hypothesis that phonological rules may precede morphological rules. However, as discussed above in 3.4.1, the verbal bases to which this affix attaches are lexically specified (probably listed in the subcategorization frame of -al). Clearly, if the bases must be lexically listed, they cannot be predicted as a class from segmental or prosodic conditions. Therefore, the attachment of -al is not crucially preceded by stress assignment.

However, other analyses of phonological and morphological rule interaction can be found which provide better support for the Lexical Phonology model. In this section, I discuss two such cases: Danish Lengthening and imperative formation, and Tagalog Nasal Substitution and Syncope in reduplicative forms. While there are murky aspects to each of these analyses, I believe that they provide better evidence for the hypothesis that phonological rules may precede morphological rules than do English nominals in -al.

4.1 Tagalog Nasal Substitution and Syncope in reduplicative forms

Reduplication processes in which a phonological rule has 'over-applied' or 'under-applied' to both the stem and the reduplicative affix are a notorious problem for the SPE model (Wilbur 1973, Aronoff 1976, Marantz 1982). In this section I discuss the case of overapplication of Nasal Substitution and Syncope in Tagalog reduplicative forms. These rules and their respective ordering are discussed in great detail by Carrier-Duncan (1984), Carrier (1979), and to a lesser extent, by Anderson (1975). I will first present the facts, and then consider various analyses of the data.

As noted by Anderson (1975:44), many Indonesian languages have a rule of Nasal Substitution, according to which a morpheme-final velar nasal (here transcribed as ng) fuses with the initial consonant of a following root, creating a nasal consonant which is homorganic with the original stem-initial consonant. In the Tagalog version of this rule, the following substitutions occur:

(60)   ng + p, b   --> m
       ng + t, d, s   --> n
       ng + k   --> ng
       ng + ?   --> ng

The application of Nasal Substitution can be seen in (61)-(65) (examples are from Anderson (1975), Carrier (1979), and Carrier-Duncan (1984)):

(61) /pang-putul/   [pamutul]   'that used for cutting'
      nom-cut

(62) /mang-bilih/   [mamilih]   'shop'
      subject topic-shop

(63) /mang-sayaw/   [mananayaw]   'dancer'
      nom-dance

(64) /mang-dikit/   [manikit]   'get thoroughly stuck to'
      subject topic-get
      thoroughly stuck to

(65) /mang-ka?ilangan/   [manga?ilangan]   'need'
      subject topic-need

Carrier(-Duncan) (1979, 1984) proposes that reduplication in Tagalog is divided into three types (R1, RA and R2 Reduplication) on the basis of the structural change involved. These reduplication processes are the phonological manifestation of various morphological categories.

Nasal Substitution overapplies in reduplicated forms. Consider Carrier-Duncan's (1984:272) description of the situation:

> If a WFR involving reduplication applies to a form that is subject to Nasal Substitution, the homorganic nasal shows up in both the reduplicated and the original material, although only the nasal in the copy is adjacent to the prefix. This is true for all three types of reduplication...

Carrier-Duncan provides the following forms to illustrate the overapplication of Nasal Substitution. All are apparently derived from the prefix /mang/- and the stem /pulah/:

(66) RA reduplication: [mamu:mulah]   'will turn temporarily red'
(67) R1 reduplication: [pamumulah]   'turning temporarily red'
(68) R2 reduplication: [mamulahmulah]   'turn somewhat red temporarily'

Nasal Substitution is not the only phonological rule which appears to overapply in reduplicated forms. According to Carrier-Duncan (1984:273), 'the vowel in the final syllable of verb roots is deleted before a suffix' by the rule of Vowel Syncope. This rule applies to the stem-final vowel in /sunod/, for example, before the suffix -/in/, creating the form [sundin] 'obey'. The overapplication of Vowel Syncope can be seen in [sundinsundin], which has undergone R2 reduplication (see Carrier-Duncan for discussion of the complicated structural changes involved in this process).

As noted by Anderson (1975), Aronoff (1976), Carrier (1979), Marantz (1982) and others, the overapplication of Nasal Substitution and Vowel Syncope can be straightforwardly accounted for if these phonological rules simply precede the various reduplication processes. Consider a derivation of [pam_u_m_u_tul] 'a cutting in quantity', in which R1 reduplication has applied to the stem /putul/ 'cut':

(69) /putul/

Nominalization   [pang-putul]
Nasal Substitution   [pamutul]
R1 Reduplication   [pamumutul]

The fact that the derived nominal contains two instances of Nasal Substitution is easily accounted for if Nasal Substitution precedes R1 Reduplication. Similarly, the overapplication of Syncope is accounted for if Syncope precedes R2 reduplication:

(70) /sunod-in/

Syncope   [sundin]
R2 Reduplication   [sundinsundin]

Yet Carrier(-Duncan), Aronoff, Marantz, and others, adopting an SPE-type model of grammar, resist this ordering solution. Consider Marantz's (1982:458) comments on such an analysis:

> One problem with this solution is that reduplication has all of the properties of a regular word formation rule and regular word formation rules can be ordered to precede all phonological rules. Ordering reduplication after certain phonological rules implies that one can place a derivational or inflectional affixing rule somewhere in the middle of the phonology, an option that is, apparently, not otherwise needed.

Booij (1981:50), on the other hand, chooses to deny the morphological character of reduplication, arguing instead that reduplication is merely the phonological manifestation of some arbitrary feature such as [+R1]. That is, in his view, the structural change of the various morphological processes is the addition of the feature [+R1]. The strongest argument for this view of reduplication is that the same type of reduplication occurs in several word formation processes. However, it has often been noted that several distinct morphological processes may be associated with a single phonological manifestation (see Kiparsky (1983) concerning German Umlaut, for example).

Clements' (1985) solution is similar in spirit to that of Booij. Clements proposes that reduplication is formally divided into two processes. (1) Adjunction 'in parallel' of a reduplicative affix to the skeletal tier of the base is a morphological operation. (2) Reduplication proper (association of skeletal units, transfer of the base melody to the reduplicative affix, and sequencing of the affix with respect to the base) is a phonological operation.

Carrier-Duncan (1984:274) calls into question the phonological nature of the rules of Nasal Substitution and Sycnope:

> ...a close inspection of Nasal Substitution and Vowel Syncope reveals that they are allomorphy rules in Aronoff's sense...For example, the prefixes and roots involved in Nasal Substitution cannot be specified in purely phonological terms. Not all /ng/-final prefixes and not all obstruent-initial stems participate in the alternation. Thus, the above interactions do not force us to allow morphological rules to follow rules of the phonology.

Apparently, Nasal Substitution and Syncope have lexically marked exceptions. For example, Carrier notes that stems like /basah/ 'read' idiosyncratically fail to undergo Nasal Substitution, as in [mambasah] (*[mamasah]), which contains the subject topic prefix /mang/-. She also notes that the comparative prefix (ka)-sing- and the verbal accidental/result prefix mag-kang- systematically fail to trigger Nasal Substitution ([kasintaliinoh], *[kasinaliinoh] 'as intelligent as').

However, given the Lexical Phonology model of grammar, it is possible to maintain the straightforward ordering analysis. Moreover, lexically marked exceptions to clearly lexical rules like Nasal Substitution and Syncope are expected (cf. section 5).

4.2 Danish Lengthening and imperative formation

The application of Lengthening in imperative forms in Danish, discussed by Anderson (1975), provides another case in which a phonological rule apparently precede a morphological process.

Danish has both long and short vowels and consonants. Length often phonetically manifests itself in the presence of a glottal segment, the stød:

(71)   VV --> [V?]

         CC --> [C?]
          |
         [+voiced]

(The rules in (71) are a rough approximation: the presence or absence of stød is apparently governed by other factors, such as stress.[15] See Basbøll (1985).) The contrast between long and short vowels and consonants can be seen by comparing the nouns in (72) and (73).

long stems:

(72a)   /mæːs/   [mæ?s]   'bother'
(72b)   /spill/   [spil?]   'waste'

short stems:

(73a)   /bað/   [bað]   'bath' (noun)
(73b)   /spel/   [spel]   'game'

Danish also has a rule of Lengthening, whereby stem-final vowels and consonants become long when followed by a vowel-initial suffix. The choice of whether a vowel or consonant undergoes Lengthening is predictable but the conditioning factors are quite complicated (see Anderson (1975) for discussion).

Danish infinitives are formed by the suffixation of -/ə/ to the stem. The phonological requirements of Lengthening are thus satisfied in infinitival forms. If the stem ends in a short vowel or consonant, Lengthening occurs. Compare the infinitive forms in (74)-(77) with the nominal forms in (72)-(73) above, which reflect underlying length:

long stems:

(74)   /mæːs-ə/   [mæːsə]   'to toil'
(75)   /spill-ə/   [spillə]   'to waste'

short stems:

(76)   /bað-ə/   [bæːðə]   'to bathe'
(77)   /spel/   [spellə]   'to play'

The imperative forms of verbs contain no suffix, yet imperatives always contain long vowels or consonants, regardless of whether or not the underlying stem is short or long. Compare the following imperatives with the nominals in (73).

(78)   [bæʔð]   'bathe!'
(79)   [spelʔ]   'play!'

(The **stød** indicates length.) These data suggest that the imperative is derived from the infinitival form by a rule which simply removes the schwa suffix marking the infinitive. The derivation of [spelʔ] given in (80) illustrates this analysis:

(80)   /spel/

infinitive formation   [spel-ə]
Lengthening   [spell-ə]
imperative formation   [spell]
stød insertion   [spelʔ]

The fact that Lengthening precedes imperative formation is a problem for the SPE model of grammar, but easily accommodated by the Lexical Phonology model of grammar.

There is a potential weakness in this analysis, however. While imperative formation is clearly a morphological process, there is some question as to whether Lengthening is a phonological rule. Booij (1981:25) notes that 'Prof. Basbøll has informed me that he holds the opinion that Lengthening is not a purely phonological rule, but morphologically conditioned,' but provides no further elaboration. (Basbøll (1985) does not clarify this point either.)

4.3 Summary

Other cases could be cited in support of the hypothesis that phonological rules precede morphological rules: Luiseño Spirantization in reduplicative forms (Munro and Benson 1973, Anderson 1975, Marantz 1982, Hargus 1988), Abkhaz Epenthesis and agreement (Anderson 1975), Javanese elative formation (Dudas 1974), or the phonological properties of Icelandic action nouns (Kiparsky 1984, Anderson 1988). (I believe that the interaction of ə Deletion and agentive suffix allomorphy in Dutch, discussed by Booij (1981), is subject to reanalysis.) Sekani also provides evidence for this central claim of the Lexical Phonology model. In Ch. 3, 5.2, I will present an analysis in which a phonological rule, ə Raising, must apply before a morphological metathesis process. This example, like the others discussed in this section, is difficult or impossible to account for in an SPE model of grammar, but predicted by the theory of Lexical Phonology.

Clearly the weakest aspect of these analyses is the extent to which the morphological or phonological processes involved are clearly morphological or phonological, respectively. As seen above, it is often difficult to tell the difference, since the structural descriptions of (lexical) phonological rules often refer to morphological information as well as purely phonological information. However, notice that given the Lexical Phonology model, it is not so crucial to determine whether a given lexical process is in fact phonological or morphological.

5. The lexical/postlexical rule typology

Lexical and post-lexical rules are predicted to differ in a number of ways (Kiparsky 1983). I believe that there are basically three characteristics which most distinguish lexical and postlexical phonological rules. (1) Lexical rules are basically restricted to derived contexts, whereas postlexical rules are not. The intricacies of this restriction will be further discussed in 5.2. (2) Lexical rules may have restricted domains (i.e., they may be 'boundary-conditioned') if the lexicon contains more than one level. Postlexical rules, by contrast, are apparently not so restricted. (3) Lexical rules may have lexically marked exceptions. Postlexical rules are automatic.

Other characteristics which distinguish these two types of rules have been suggested (see Kiparsky 1983, for example), but at least two of these hypotheses (that lexical rules are structure-preserving and cyclic) are problematic.[16]

The fact that there is apparently a correlation between rule characteristics and rule ordering is significant. This is a generalization about the phonological structures of languages which would be stated in an at best ad hoc manner in a non-Lexical Phonology model of grammar.

5.1 An example from English

To illustrate the typology, I will consider the characteristics of two rules in English: the lexical rule of Trisyllabic Shortening and the postlexical rule of Aspiration.

The basic alternations accounted for by Trisyllabic Shortening in English are fairly well known (see SPE, Kiparsky (1974), Kiparsky (1982) or Halle and Mohanan (1985) for additional information):

(81) divine, divinity   kinesis, kinetic
     crucify, crucifixion   sane, sanity
     satire, satiric   volcano, volcanic
     hypothesis, hypocrite   nature, natural
     serene, serenity   profound, profundity
     intervene, intervention   pronounce, pronunciation
     verbose, verbosity

Basically, a long vowel is shortened in English if antepenultimate or further from the end of the word (notorious changes in vowel quality also accompany the change in quantity), and if the following vowel is not stressed (note the nonapplication of the rule in <u>hypothesis</u>). See Halle and Mohanan (1985:77) for a formalization of the length alternations expressed by this rule.

Trisyllabic Shortening exhibits the characteristics predicted of lexical rules. (1) TSS is restricted to derived environments. The rule does not apply to the underlyingly long vowels in presumably monomorphemic words such as Ob̲eron, Ro̲tenberg, ro̲sary, i̲rony, i̲vory, ni̲ghtingale, co̲unterfeit, co̲untenance. (2) TSS has a restricted domain. The rule does not apply to words which contain the putative 'stress-neutral' or word-level suffixes in English: bea̲utiful, ma̲idenhood, li̲kelihood, ti̲meliness, co̲ziness, bo̲untiful. In a level-ordered analysis of English, TSS would be analyzed as a level 1 phonological rule. (3) TSS has lexically marked exceptions. The following forms are apparently morphologically complex, but TSS has not applied in these cases: sea̲sonal, obe̲sity, mo̲untainous, hi̲bernate, i̲solate, pro̲bity, ro̲tary, de̲cency, pri̲mary, pa̲pacy, va̲gary, va̲cancy, re̲gency, po̲tency.

Compare TSS with a typical postlexical rule, such as English Aspiration. I follow Kahn's (1976) analysis of this rule. Basically, /p t k/ are aspirated 'if and only if they are both syllable-initial and non-syllable-final' (Kahn 1976:74). The facts are made complicated by the fact that the degree of aspiration of voiceless stops varies according to the degree of stress on the following vowel. Voiceless stops which occur before emphatically or contrastively stressed syllables (marked é) are more aspirated than those which occur before primary-stressed vowels, which are more aspirated than stops which occur before secondarily stressed vowels, which in turn are more aspirated than stops which occur before unstressed vowels:

(82)   most   aspiration continuum   least

         tén   tén   tiptòe   tŏmorrow
         twó   típtoe   Utàh   tĕnacious

(83)   lack of aspiration

         stem
         after

There is no evidence that Aspiration is sensitive to any phonological information other than syllable structure. In particular, (1) Aspiration applies to nonderived forms: pew, ten, kite. (2) Aspiration does not appear to have a restricted domain, although it is difficult to find examples because Aspiration is bled by Flapping in many forms containing level 2 suffixes such as (chocola[D]y), presumably because these suffixes are stress-neutral. (3) There are no exceptions to Aspiration.

Significantly, Trisyllabic Shortening does not follow any phonological rules which have the characteristics of postlexical rules (such as Aspiration) (as might be inferred from the fact that TSS is a level 1 rule), nor does Aspiration precede any rules with the characteristics of lexical rules (such as TSS).

Although it is often the case that a rule applies lexically but not postlexically (or vice versa), as in the case discussed here, it is not necessarily the case that lexical and postlexical rules form disjoint sets. However, the apparently true prediction is that a rule which applies both lexically and postlexically will have different effects when it applies on these two domains in part because the kinds of representations that are found lexically or postlexically are likely to be different, but also because lexical rules are subject to restrictions that postlexical rules are not. Several examples of rules which apply lexically as well as postlexically may be found in Kiparsky (1985), where it is shown that adopting the Lexical Phonology model results in considerable simplification of the grammar.

5.2 The derived-only restriction

The proposal that lexical rules are restricted to derived contexts deserves greater attention, in part because it appears that not all lexical rules are so restricted. In 5.2.1, I elaborate on the definition of 'derived', and in 5.2.2, I discuss attempts to reduce the derived-only restriction to more basic theoretical principles. As will be seen, the exact incorporation of the derived-only restriction in Lexical Phonology is presently a matter of some debate.

5.2.1 A closer look at 'derived'

The hypothesis that there exists a class of rules which are restricted to derived contexts is originally due to Kiparsky (1974), who provides an informal definition of 'derived' as follows:

(84)   I will refer to an input which is created either by combining morphemes
        through derivation or inflection...or by applying a phonological
        rule...as a derived input. (Kiparsky 1974:60)

Notice that the definition of 'derived' in (84) above contains two subcases: a form can be phonologically or morphologically derived. Trisyllabic Shortening in English is clearly blocked from applying morpheme-internally, but there is no phonological process that I am aware of that creates the second kind of derived representation which the rule could apply in. However, the Finnish rule of t --> s (hereafter Spirantization) discussed by Kiparsky (1974:58 ff.) illustrates the need for recognizing both kinds of derived representations.

(85)   Spirantization

        t --> s / ___ i

The rule applies to sequences of [ti] which fall in separate morphemes:

(86)   [halut-a]   'want'

(87)   [halus-i]   'wanted'

The rule does not apply to morpheme-internal [ti]:

(88)   [tila]   'place, room'
       [tili]   'account'
       [kartio]   'cone'
       [tippa]   'drop'
       [vaatia]   'demand'
       [tiivis]   'dense, tight'

Interestingly, however, Spirantization does apply when [i] is phonologically derived, as it is, for example, when the following rule applies:

(89)   e --> i / ___ ##

(90)   [vete-nä]   'water' ess.

(91)   [vesi]   'water' nom.

The proposal that the application of phonological rules to non-derived forms can create derived representations for other phonological rules to apply in has certain problematic side effects, as will be seen below.

5.2.2 Deriving the derived-only restriction

Reducing the derived-only restriction to a more basic theoretical principle has been a popular pasttime in research on phonological theory. As first pointed out by Kiparsky (1974:70) (and whose discussion I summarize), if it is possible to predict which rules are restricted to derived contexts, rule formulations can in some cases be greatly simplified. Consider the application of the rule of Trisyllabic Shortening in the following forms:

(92)   tri+meter
       gran+ular
       penal+ty
       omin+ous

If the locations of the morpheme boundaries must be explicitly mentioned in the formulation of TSS, the context in which the rule applies will be something like (93):

(93)   ___ $\langle+\rangle_a$ C_0 $\langle+\rangle_b$ V $\langle+\rangle_c$ C_0 $\langle+\rangle_d$ C_0

condition: a or b or c or d

Clearly, it would be preferable to be able to predict which rules obey the derived-only restriction, rather than to have to state in the formulation of a rule whether it applies in derived forms. Moreover, while it is possible (even if it requires considerable brute force) to restrict rules to morphologically derived contexts in this way, it is impossible to incorporate the notion 'phonologically derived' into the formulation of a rule.

Kiparsky's (1974) original attempt to define the derived-only class of rules was the Revised Alternation Condition:

(94)   Revised Alternation Condition (Kiparsky 1974:67, 85)

Non-automatic, obligatory neutralization processes apply only to derived forms.

However, as discussed by Kiparsky (1982), this attempt to characterize the derived-only class of rules did not quite work. For example, Velar Softening in English is non-automatic and neutralizing, but it applies morpheme-internally to stems like -ceive.

Mascaró (1976) proposed instead that the derived-only class of rules are those rules which apply cyclically, and that the Revised Alternation Condition is reducible to the Strict Cycle Condition, an independently required condition on the application of cyclic rules first proposed by Kean (1974) and later modified by Mascaró (1976). According to the Strict Cycle Condition, cyclic rules can only apply to derived representations, where, as discussed above in 5.2.1, representations are derived on any given cycle by virtue of containing 'new' morphological or phonological information. An important result of Mascaró's work was the demonstration that various rules of Catalán which obeyed the derived-only restriction were indeed cyclic.

A version of the Strict Cycle Condition (from Kiparsky 1982) is given in

(95):

(95) The Strict Cycle Condition

a. Cyclic rules apply only to derived representations.

b. A representation ⌀ is *derived* with respect to rule R in cycle j iff ⌀ meets the structural analysis of R by virtue of a combination of morphemes introduced in cycle j or the application of a phonological rule in cycle j.

As pointed out by Mascaró, the SCC thus prevents cyclic rules from applying to non-derived representations, and this is clearly necessary, as can be seen from the following example from Polish, discussed by Kiparsky (1985).

The Polish rule of Nominal Strident Palatalization in (96) replaces a stem-final /š/ with a 'prepalatal high fricative' [ç]:

(96) Nominal Strident Palatalization

š --> ç / ___ i

The effect of this rule can be seen in the following pairs:

(97a) kapelusz [š]   'hat'
(97b) kapelusik [ç]   'little hat'

(98a) grosz [š]   'monetary unit'
(98b) grosik [ç]   (diminutive)

According to the rule of First Velar Palatalization, the velar obstruents /k g x/ become palatals [c j s] before the front vowels [i e]:

(99)   k   č
       g --> ǰ / ___ i, e
       x   š

Alternations such as those in (100)-(102) provide evidence for this rule:

(100a) krzyk   'a shout'
(100b) krzyczeć [č]   'to shout'

(101a) strach [x]   'fear'
(101b) straszyć [š]   'to frighten'

(102a) miazga   'squash'

(102b) miażdżyć [ǰ]   'to squash'

Forms like (101b) above and (103b) below indicate that the rules must apply in counter-feeding order:

(103a) gmach [x]   'building'

(103b) gmaszysko [š]   'big building'

A feeding order of the rules derives incorrect phonetic forms:

(104)   gmach

First Velar Palatalization   [š]
Nominal Strident Palatalization   [ç]

                                *gmasysko [ç]

However, if NSP counter-feeds FVP, the right phonetic forms result:

(105)   gmach

Nominal Strident Palatalization   --
First Velar Palatalization   [š]

                                gmaszysko [š]

Kiparsky cites work by Rubach which indicates that these rules are cyclic. The role of the SCC in ensuring the proper derivation of these forms will be apparent when the derivation of forms which contain two or more cycles of affixation are considered. Two cycles will be required in the derivation of gmaszysko 'big hat':

(106)   [[[gmach] ysk] o]

NSP   --
FVP   š

NSP   (blocked by the SCC)
FVP

NSP must precede FVP on the first cycle to prevent the output of FVP from undergoing NSP. Notice that NSP could apply to stem-final [s] on the second cycle of affixation but does not. This fact indicates that a constraint against allowing rules to apply on earlier cycles is needed: enter the Strict Cycle Condition. Since [[gmach] ysk] is not 'derived' on the last cycle in this derivation, NSP cannot apply to the stem-final [s] because it does not make use of information contained on the last cycle.

Despite the promising results achieved by Mascaró, Harris (1983:76) has shown that Mascaró's attempt to predict which rules obey the derived-only restriction does not quite work. In Spanish, stress and syllabification are cyclically assigned phonological properties, yet they apply on the first cycle to non-derived forms. Harris suggested that the nature of the structural operations performed by these rules provided a clue as to their privileged position with respect to the Strict Cycle Condition:

> One characterization of these rules that clearly sets them apart from garden-variety phonological rules is that syllable structure rules do not change features. Rather, they belong to the class of rules that <u>assign</u> features and/or prosodic structure that is lexically <u>unspecified</u>.

In other words, Harris suggested that rules which 'build structure' do not obey the Strict Cycle Condition, where a structure-building rule may be more precisely defined as a rule whose output creates a structure which is non-distinct from its input structure. This, in turn, hinges on the definition of 'distinct', which varies depending on whether a linear or nonlinear approach to phonology is adopted, as pointed out by Clements (1980).[17] Basically, however, two representations are distinct if they contain contradictory feature specifications or contradictory structure.

Returning to the Spanish case, Kiparsky (1982) observed further that some lexical phonological rules apparently apply in nonderived contexts. One such rule discussed by Kiparsky was Depalatalization:

(107) Depalatalization

/ñ/ --> [n] / syllable-finally

This rule is structure-changing, yet it applies morpheme-internally in

/desdeñ+es/ [desdenes] 'disdains' (noun); cf. /desdeñ+a+r/ [desdeñes] 'you (sg.) disdain'.

Kiparsky drew two conclusions from Spanish syllabification and Depalatalization. (1) Lexical rules which build, rather than change, structure are not constrained by the SCC, as suggested by Harris. Given this interpretation of the SCC, this constraint may be viewed as an instance of the Elsewhere Condition. (2) The application of a structure-building phonological rule to a form may create a phonologically derived representation.

Unfortunately, as Kiparsky (1985) observed in later work, the second conclusion makes incorrect predictions. If structure-building rules can create derived environments for structure-changing rules to apply in, then stress should create a derived context for Trisyllabic Shortening to apply in in English. Trisyllabic Shortening applies only to derived representations, and only to long vowels which are followed by an unstressed vowel (cf. hypòthesis, hy̆pocrite). However, if stress is part of the structural description of Trisyllabic Shortening, then the assignment of stress should create a derived environment for TSS to apply in in such non-derived forms as Ro̱tenberg, ni̱ghtingale, etc.

Kiparsky (1985) proposed instead that the SCC (= derived-only restriction) be formulated as in (108):

(108) If W is derived from a lexical entry W', where W' is nondistinct from XPAQY and distinct from XPBQY, then a rule A --> B / XP ___ QY cannot apply to W until the word level

(The 'word level' is the last lexical level.) Basically, this constraint predicts that non-word-level lexical rules (presumably, structure-changing rules) are restricted derived forms, whereas rules which apply on the word level or postlexically do not.[18]

The condition in (108) correctly predicts that English Trisyllabic

Shortening is restricted to derived contexts, since it is a level one rule. Spanish Depalatalization is a word level rule, so its morpheme-internal application is accounted for. (The rule of English which accounts for alternations between dam_n_ing, dam_n_ation and hym_n_al, hym_n_ing is also a word level rule, according to Kiparsky (1985).)

However, Finnish Spirantization is apparently still a problem. Recall from 5.2.1 that there Spirantization applies to morphologically complex forms like /halut-i/ [halu_s_i] 'wanted', but not to morpheme-internal [ti] in (e.g.) [tila] 'place, room'. Spirantization also applies to phonologically derived representations, as in /vete/ [ve_s_i] 'water' (nom.), in which the [i] is phonologically derived by the rule which raises word-final [e] to [i]. Obviously, the latter rule must be a word level rule, since if it applies to word-final [e] it must wait until word formation is complete. Thus, TSS must also be a word-level rule, since it applies to /vete/ following /e/ --> [i]. However, if TSS is a word level rule, then the version of the SCC given in ( ) would incorrectly predict that TSS could apply morpheme-internally in [tila].

To conclude, the question of which lexical rules are restricted to derived contexts is currently unanswered. However, it seems to be true that no postlexical rules are so restricted.

Notes.

1. Other overviews of the Lexical Phonology model can be found in the literature. See, for example, Pulleyblank (1986), Archangeli (1984), Kaisse and Shaw (1985), or Mohanan (1986).

2. I will not attempt to justify the probably incorrect but widely held assumption in Lexical Phonology that all morphological structures are generated within the lexicon.

3. These labels are somewhat misleading, since they imply that phonological rules belong to one of two mutually exclusive domains. However, the same rule may apply lexically as well as postlexically. The term 'lexical phonological rule' thus properly means 'lexical applications of a phonological rule'.

4. Interestingly, this hypothesis was apparently independently arrived at by

several researchers at roughly the same time: Pesetsky (1979), Booij (1981), and Strauss (1982).

5. Chomsky suggests that words like /arrive/ are lexically listed but unspecified with respect to lexical category, and that 'fairly idiosyncratic morphological rules will determine the phonological form of [e.g.] arrive' when it 'appears in the noun position'.

6. Mohanan (1982) refers to this as the Continuous Stratum Hypothesis, but Mohanan (1986) does not give this hypothesis a name.

7. In some dialects, the nasal assimilates obligatorily only to labials, and optionally to velars.

8. For one thing, it is not clear that -ize is a level 1 suffix. Aronoff and Sridhar (1983) and Selkirk (1982), for example, analyze -ize as level 2, given its apparent stress-neutrality. Secondly, as is evident from the discussion in Marchand (1966), -ity, -ist and -ize are limited in productivity. The subcategorization frames of these affixes must refer to particular lexical items, rather than to general lexical categories. The failure of -ity, -ist and -ize to attach to adjectives in -y could just as easily be attributed to their lexical specifications as it could be to their level of attachment. Thirdly, if ity, -ist and -ize did turn out to attach to general lexical classes, it is likely that they would at least be specified as attaching to Greco-Romance lexical items. But -y is a native suffix (Marchand 1966).

9. While it is advisable to consult Aronoff (1976:22) for this argument, it is basically as follows: -mit has an allomorph, -mis, which regularly appears before a certain set of suffixes in all prefix + -mit combinations, such as re-: remit, remission, remissive. This allomorphy rule serves to identify -mit as a morpheme, even if -mit is meaningless in these combinations.)

10. There are systematic (*philologicalize but philologize) as well as idiosyncratic exceptions (alphabetize blocks *alphabeticize, according to Kiparsky (1982)) to this generalization.

11. Either the lexical entry of -ize indicates that it undergoes -ation nominalization, or more likely, the lexical entry of -ation contains a list of bases, including -ize, to which this suffix may attach.

12. To be sure, not all nouns in -ization are in actual use. The noun *recognization is presumably synonymous with recognition, and Avoid Synonymy (see 3.3.1) therefore predicts that the existence of recognition precludes the use of recognization. Along these same lines, agonization is well-formed only only for those speakers for whom it is not synonymous with agony.

13. This result points to the inadequacy of yet another proposed constraint on the generative capacity of the lexicon; namely, Kiparsky's (1982:23) proposal that 'the output of every cycle is a lexical item'. Apart from the fact that this proposal cannot apparently be implemented (how does the grammar determine that something is a lexical item or not?), it is apparently incorrect, if the lexicons of Icelandic and English generate bound derived stems, which are not lexical items.

14. Compare Anderson's earlier (1975:43) observation on this matter:

It is certainly generally the case that, *ceteris paribus*, a morpholexical rule will generally precede a phonological one, and a phonological rule will precede a phonetic one.

15. According to Anderson (1975), stød is predictable. However, according to Clements and Keyser (1983), stød is phonemic.

16. Kiparsky (1983, 1985) has proposed that lexical rules are structure-preserving in that they do not introduce structures or combinations of features which are not found underlyingly. However, this proposal is at best not universal, given the findings of Mohanan and Mohanan (1984) and Hall (1987). Mohanan and Mohanan (1984) argue that Malayalam contains five places of articulation underlyingly, but seven places are derived lexically. Obviously, some underlyingly impermissible combinations of place features are derived in the course of the lexical phonology of Malayalam. Similarly, Hall (1987) points out that German contains no underlying contrast between [x] and [ç], yet the velar fricative is lexically derived.

In early work in the Lexical Phonology model it was hypothesized that all lexical rule applications are cyclic whereas postlexical rules apply noncyclically. However, the correlation between lexical status and cyclic application now appears to be problematic, given the arguably cyclic but postlexical status of tone sandhi in Mandarin (see Kaisse and Shaw (1985) for other examples of possibly cyclic but postlexical rules). Conversely, noncyclic lexical rules may also exist: Dahl's Law in Kikuyu is a fairly convincing case of such a rule. I return to this point in Ch. 7.

17. Compare the definition of 'distinct' in a linear theory of phonology (SPE) with that of Clements (1980):

(109)   Distinctness in a linear theory of phonology (SPE, p. 336)

Two units U1 and U2 are distinct iff there is at least one feature F such that U is specified [aF] and U2 is specified [bF], where a is plus and b is minus; of a and b are integers and a ≠ b, or a is an integer and b is minus (i.e., have contradictory feature specifications). Two strings X and Y are distinct if they are of dif. lengths (differ in number of segments), or if ith unit of X is distinct from ith unit of Y for some i...

(110)   Distinctness in a nonlinear theory of phonology (Clements 1980:54)

Two representations are distinct if there is a segment occuring in one that does not occur (bearing the same relations of order and association) in the other.

18. Notice that if the condition in (108) turns out to be true, it would provide an argument for level ordering. It is perhaps significant that Kiparsky's (1985) analysis of the Icelandic lexicon contains two lexical levels, whereas Kiparsky (1984) apparently analyzes Icelandic as having only one lexical level.

Chapter Three

Level Ordering: The Verbal Prefixes

This chapter presents an analysis of the phonological and morphological properties of the verbal prefixes in Sekani within the theoretical framework discussed in the preceding chapter. The complexity of Sekani phonology and morphology provides a good test of the predictions of Lexical Phonology (and level ordering), and, as will be seen, Sekani supports many of the central claims of the model. Certain phonological rules must precede morphological rules, providing strong support for a model in which some phonological rules can apply in the lexicon. The verbal prefixes of Sekani also yield nicely to a level-ordered analysis: the positional properties of affixes correlate strongly with the domains of phonological rules.

In a traditional (e.g. Hoijer 1971) position-class model of the Athabaskan verb, the verbal prefixes of Sekani would be analyzed as occurring in a fairly rigid order in approximately thirteen prefix positions before the stem:[1]

(1)	position	prefix (abbreviation)
(leftmost)	1	postposition (P)
	2	adverbial (adv)
	3	incorporated stem (N, V)
	4	distributive (dstr)
	5	reversative, customary na (rev, C)
	6	inceptive (incp)
	7	object (O, recp, refl, ar)
	8	subject (S)
	9	derivational (der, thm, asp)
	10	conjugation (cnj)
	11	mode (Imp, Pf, Fut, Op, Prg)
	12	subject (S)
(rightmost)	13	classifier (clf)
		verb stem

Early generative research (Kari 1976, Stanley 1969, 1973) on Athabaskan (largely Navajo) verbal phonology made it clear that the central descriptive problem in the phonology of the Athabaskan verbal prefixes is to formally restrict phonological rules to their proper domains. In early generative analyses, the encoding of morphological (mainly positional) information into phonological rules was usually accomplished by positing boundary symbols of different strengths.[2] However, the standard theoretical inventory of boundaries was inadequate to describe the complexity of the phonological domains encountered in the Navajo verbal prefixes, and ad hoc devices such as readjustment rules, nonstandard morphological features, and even position class labels were often utilized.[3]

As Rice (1982, etc.) has demonstrated for Slave, and as I hope to show in this chapter, level ordering provides a more straightforward characterization of the domains of phonological rules in Sekani (although it is not possible to eliminate reference to morphological features entirely). Five levels may be distinguished, almost exclusively on the basis of phonological evidence. (The morphological evidence for level ordering distinctions in Sekani is not as strong as could be hoped for, involving only surface restrictions on affix order, rather than evidence from the derivational potential of morphologically complex words.) The biggest difference between the lexical phonologies of Athabaskan languages and those of other languages is thus that more lexical levels are required in Athabaskan languages than are usually found in other languages. However, this is a natural extension of the model, not a forced departure from it. Moreover, it is an understandable departure, given the complexity of Athabaskan morphology.

This chapter is organized by level. In each section I provide a brief description of the morphology and phonology that is peculiar to that level, illustrating restrictions on affix order and restrictions on the domains of phonological rules. The final section is an examination of the properties of two rules of the postlexical phonology, and a comparison of these rules with the properties of some of the lexical rules discussed throughout this chapter.

1. A level-ordered overview of the verbal prefixes

In a Lexical Phonology analysis, the verbal prefixes of Sekani can be grouped into five levels, as represented in (2):

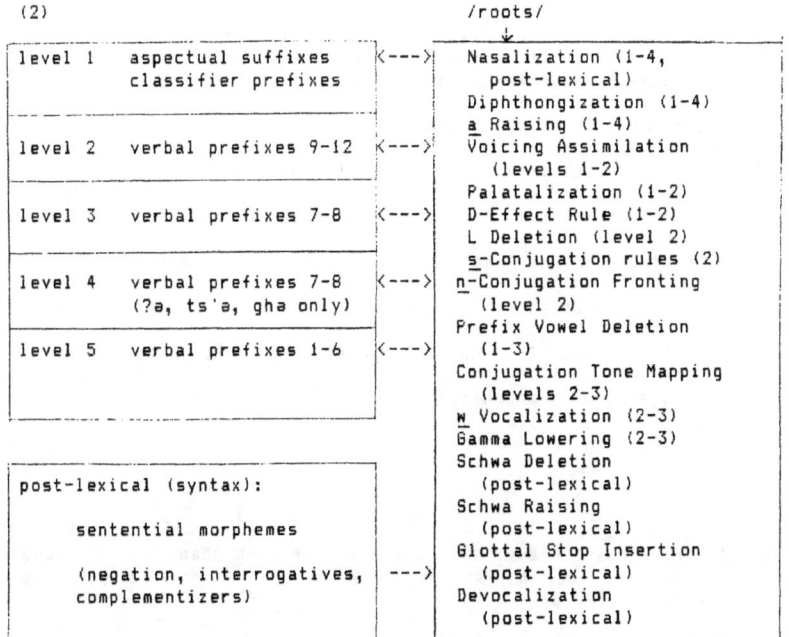

As will be seen in the remainder of this chapter, the verbal prefixes generally occur in a fixed order relative to each other and to the verb stem. This is of some theoretical interest. Pesetsky (1979) has proposed that the word formation rules within a level are unordered with respect to each other, and that level ordering assignments are the sole means of accounting for restrictions on affix order. However, if this were true, it would be necessary to posit 14 lexical levels in Sekani to account for affix order restrictions. Alternatively, if phonological rule domains are made an essential criterion for level ordering, the Sekani lexicon can be reduced to five levels, which is surely a better result.

Before proceeding to present evidence for the level ordering distinctions given in (2), I will first describe the way I will be presenting Sekani data in this and subsequent chapters. The general format is given in (3):

```
(3)     /pfx-pfx-pfx-stem-sfx/    (underlying or intermediate reps)
         asp S  clf      nom      (translation or category)
          9   12  13    stem      (prefix positions)

        [surface form]            translation
```

In some examples, the surface form is identical to the underlying representation, and in those cases I have omitted the surface form. In most examples, I provide intermediate, rather than underlying, representations of the prefixes and stems. I do this to suppress irrelevant phonological complexity, although I realize I do so at the risk of confusing the reader about the underlying shapes of morphemes.

2. Level 1

2.1 Morphology

The verbal morphology of level 1 consists of the verb stem, the aspectual suffixes, and the classifier prefixes.

2.1.1 Aspectual stem suffixation

In this section I provide only a brief summary of aspectual suffixation. For a more complete discussion of aspect in an Athabaskan language see Rice (to appear) for Slave, Kari (1979) for Ahtna, Hardy (1979) for Navajo, or Leer (1979) for Proto-Athabaskan.

Many verb forms are marked with a suffix. The suffixes divide verbs into categories usually described as 'momentaneous', 'durative', 'conclusive', etc., suggesting that the suffixes are aspectual. However, these aspectual categories are not marked solely by suffixation. Equally important is the choice of conjugation prefix (prefix position 10).[4] In some cases, a prefix from positions 2, 4, 5, 6, or 9 occurs as well.

The phonological shapes of the suffixes of each aspectual category vary according to mode (see 3.1.2), and also according to the phonological shape of the underlying verbal stem. Nasal-final and vowel-final stems often require a set of suffixes which is different from that required by obstruent-final stems to mark a given aspect.

Consider the following example. The perambulative aspect/customary mode suffix is -/ts/ when suffixed to obstruent-final stems, but -/h/ when suffixed to vowel- and nasal-final stems:[5]

(4) /xe/   'pack'

```
/k'è-na-n  -d   -ghe -h/
 per C 2sS  clf  pack rep/C
 2   5  12   13   stem
```

[k'èŋǫgeh]   'you [sg] pack [O] around'

(5) /yhot/ 'chase [O]'

```
/k'è-nə -n  -yot  -ts/
 per thm 2sS chase O rep/C
 2   9   12  stem
```

[k'èni̯yots]   'you [sg] chase [O] around'

(In (5), stem-final /t/ is deleted before the suffix -/ts/.) I have illustrated three of the other aspects below using nasal- and vowel-final stems, in which the suffixes are phonologically more transparent.

   Conclusive. This aspect marks verbs with a natural termination point. Typical conclusive verbs are 'shit', 'vomit', 'cook by boiling', etc. The conjugation prefix /'sə/ occurs in perfective forms in this aspect. In (6) I have listed the conclusive stems of the verbal stem /xe/ 'kill [sg O]'. Notice that the phonological shape of the conclusive suffix varies according to mode, as mentioned above:

(6)   Imp   Pf   Fut   Op
suffix: -h   -n   -ɣ   -ɣ
/xe/:   [xeh]   [xį]   [xeɣ]   [xeɣ]

Durative. Inherently durative actions like 'drink', 'eat', 'dance', 'pick berries', 'look at [O]', 'work', etc. require the conjugation prefix /gha/ in the perfective. By far the most common suffixation pattern for nasal- and vowel-final stems is that given in (7):

(7)   Imp   Pf   Fut   Op
         -∅   -/`/     -/`ɣ/   -/`/

Some stems may lexically specify a different perfective suffix instead of /`/, but this is rare. In (8), I have illustrated the suffixation pattern in (7) with the verbs /be/ 'pick berries' and /ta/ 'look at [O]':

(8)   Imp   Pf   Fut   Op
/be/:   [be]   [bè?]   [bèɣ]   [bè?]
/ta/:   [ta]   [tà]   [tàɣ]   [tà?]

Semelfactive. Actions which are normally repeated are marked with the semelfactive aspect if performed exactly once. It is common for verbs such as 'poke', 'kick', 'slap', 'shoot', 'catch', etc., to have a repetitive as well as a semelfactive aspect derivation. Some verbs which inherently denote an action performed a single time, such as 'kindle fire' and 'sneeze', have only a semelfactive aspect derivation. The aspectual prefix /i/ occurs in the non-perfective modes. In the perfective, this prefix is absent and the conjugation prefix /`sə/ occurs instead. I have illustrated the suffixation pattern of the semelfactive aspect in (9), with the verbal stem /k'on/ 'kindle fire':

(9)   -/`h/    -/n/     -/`ɣ/   -/`/
/k'on/   [k'ǫ̀h]   [k'ǫ̀]   [k'ǫ̀ɣ]   [k'ǫ̀?]

Affix order provides little evidence for the place in the lexicon that aspectual suffixation occurs, since, as will be seen, the verbal morphology is mainly prefixing. Moreover, there is no evidence from phonological rule domains that the aspectual suffixes are added on level 1. However, Keren Rice (p.c.) has suggested that these suffixes derive verb stems from stems unspecified for lexical category (see Ch. 4, sec. 1). If this analysis is correct, then the category-assigning role of these suffixes provides the best evidence for their assignment to the earliest level of the lexicon: they must be affixed before strictly verbal prefixes such as the level 2 subject prefixes.

It should be noted that the following data are consistent with an analysis in which these suffixes are added on level 1. The diminutive suffix -/azi/ (Ch. 4, 3.2), which is probably added on level 5, may be suffixed to verbal as well as nominal forms. The aspectual suffixes occur to the left of the diminutive suffix:

(10)   /chu   gho-ìd -d -dǫ   -`   -azi ą/
       water Op 1dS clf drink dur:Op dim Op
             11   12 13 stem

       [chu ghùdǫ̀azi ą]   'we [du] have a little drink' Op

2.1.2 Classifier prefixes (position 13)

The classifier prefixes are the rightmost of the verbal prefixes. They occur immediately to the left of the verbal stem, as will be seen below. Evidence that the classifier prefixes belong on level 1, rather than level 2, is provided by the rule of Conjugation a Deletion (see Ch. 5, 3.1). I will describe the morphology of these prefixes in some detail here, since the form and function of the classifier prefixes is rather complex.

First, the traditional term 'classifier' is actually, as Krauss (1969) puts it, a "blatant misnomer". If anything, these prefixes mark verbal voice rather than noun classification. Secondly, a brief comparative/historical note is in order. In Sekani, the phonetically nonnull classifiers are h and d. In other Athabaskan languages (e.g. Navajo, Chipewyan), there are four classifier prefixes:

(11)   ∅, ɣ, d, l

The classifier prefixes in (11) are generally those reconstructed for Proto-Athabaskan (Krauss 1969). The Sekani h classifier is a reflex of the *ɣ classifier. The *l classifier is phonetically zero in Sekani, but it is useful to think of it synchronically as a voiced segment, as will be seen below.

In Sekani underlying forms, there appear to be only two classifiers, d and h. Many instances of the Sekani reflex of *l are transparently derived from the classifier sequence d+h, which suggests that all instances of synchronic *l can be so derived.[6] In glossing forms, however, I will sometimes use the abbreviation l for this classifier, where I am not illustrating its synchronic derivation from d+h.

2.1.2.1   h

In many forms which contain classifiers, the classifier appears to have no synchronic function, but is simply lexically specified. Compare the pairs in (12), (14), (16), and (17), which differ only in that an h classifier occurs in the (b) forms:

(12a)   [də -k'al]   'he, she is white'
        der be white
        9   stem

(12b)   /də -h -gàs/
        der clf be black
        9   13 stem

        [dahgàs]   'he, she is black'

(In (12b), the rule of Schwa Lowering (13) has applied:

(13) a --> a / ___ h]$_{syll}$

(14a) /ni -də -i -n -?q/
       raise der der Pf handle compact O
       2   9   9   11 stem

       [nidį?q]   'he, she lifted [compact O]'

(14b) /ni -də -i -n -h -tsùz/
       raise der der Pf clf handle cloth-like O

       [nidįhtsùz]   'he, she lifted [cloth-like O]'

(In these latter forms, Prefix Vowel Deletion has applied:

(15) V --> ∅ / ___ [V

See 4.2.1 for a more precise formulation of the rule.)

(16a) [ə -ghq]   'he, she kills [pl O]'
       epen kill pl O

(16b) /za -h -xeh/
       thm clf kill sg O
       9   13 stem

       [zahxeh]   'he, she kills [sg O]'

(17a) /i -gwat/
       asp poke O
       9   stem

       [igwat]   'he, she pokes [O] once'

(17b) /i -h -t'às/
       asp clf shoot O with bow and arrow
       9   13 stem

       [iht'às]   'he, she shoots [O] with bow and arrow once'

In the (b) forms above, the classifier h is simply part of the lexical entry of the verb.

However, in other forms, the occurrence of the classifier h is morphologically predictable. In the (b) forms in (18), (19), (21), and (22), the classifier h derives transitive or causative verbs from intransitive verbs:

81

(18a)   /ts'e-n -zit/
        wake cnj wake up
         2   10   stem

        [ts'ęzit]   'he, she wakes up'

(18b)   /ts'e-n -h -sit/
        wake cnj clf wake up

        [ts'ęhsit]   'he, she wakes up [O]'

(19a)   /nà -nə -n -ghèts/
        down der Pf tree fall
         2   9   11 stem

        [nànighèts]   'a tree fell down'

(19b)   /nà -nə -n -h -xèts/
        down der Pf clf tree fall

        [nànihxèts]   'he, she pushed a tree down'

(The rule of Schwa Raising (20) has applied in (19b):

(20)   ə --> i)

(21a)   /yhęɣ sə -?ǫ/
        trap cnj compact O be in position
                10 stem

        [yhęɣ sə?ǫ]   'a trap is set'

(21b)   /yhęɣ sə -i -h -?ǫ/
        trap cnj 1sPf clf compact O be in position
                10 12 13 stem

        [yhęɣ sih?ǫ]   'I have a trap set'

(22a)   /chu -də -nə -ghə-n -maɣ/
        water thm thm cnj Pf boil
         3   9   9   10 11 stem

        [chudənəghimaɣ]   'water boiled'

(22b)   /chu -də -nə -ghə-n -h -maɣ/
        water thm thm cnj Pf clf boil

        [chudənəghihmaɣ]   'he, she boiled water'

To summarize, in some forms (12, 14, 16, 17), the classifier h has no discernible semantic or grammatical function. In other forms (18, 19, 21,

22), the classifier h has a transitive function.

One rule which affects the h classifier should be mentioned. Phonetically, Sekani has no syllable-final consonant clusters. Syllable-final clusters are simplified according to the rule in (23):

(23) Cluster Simplification

$$C \rightarrow \emptyset / C \_\_\_]_{syll}$$

The effect of this rule can be seen in the following forms:

(24a) /chu -də -nə -s -h -maɬ/
      water thm thm 1sS clf boil
      3   9   9   12 13 stem

      [chudənəsmaɬ]   'I boil water'

(24b) /chu -də -nə -ah -h -maɬ/
      water thm thm 2pS clf boil

      [chudənahmaɬ]   'you [pl] boil water'

Compare (22b) with (24a-b) for evidence that the h classifier is present in these forms.

2.1.2.2 d

When the d classifier is prefixed to fricative- and glottal stop-initial verb stems, the following alternations occur:

(25) clf + stem-initial

      d + ʔ   --> t'
      d + z   --> dz
      d + l   --> dl
      d + y   --> j
      d + gh   --> g

Most of these rules may be collapsed, of course. They are referred to in the Athabaskan literature as the D-Effect Rule (Howren 1971). I will return to this rule in 2.2.2.

When the d classifier is prefixed to stem-initial consonants other than fricatives or glottal stop, it is deleted. Since the form of the classifier is often phonetically zero, it is not always obvious whether a verb contains an underlying d̲ classifier or not. However, several rules of the phonology are sensitive to the presence or absence of the d̲ classifier, and thus serve as diagnostic of its underlying status. These rules will be summarized in 2.1.2.4.

Like the h̲ classifier, many instances of the d̲ classifier are simply lexicalized and apparently functionless in the synchronic grammar. In forms such as (26)-(31), d̲ classifier must simply be analyzed as part of the lexical entry of the verb in which it occurs. (As will be seen in 2.1.2.4, there are good reasons for not assuming that these verb stems are simply /gen/, /ts'at/ etc.)

(26) /yidà -ʔə -nə -s -d -ghį̀/
      inside unspO cnj 1sS clf pack O
      2   7   10 12 13 stem

      [yidàʔənəsgį̀]   'I packed something inside'

(27) /nà -ghə -s -d -ts'at/
      down cnj 1sS clf sg/du fall
      2   10 12 13 stem

      [nàghasts'at]   'I fell down'

(28) /ʔə -ghə-s -d -bà/
      unspO cnj 1sS clf children, animals eat
      7   10 12 13 stem

      [ʔaghasbàʔ]   'I ate something'

(29) /ə -s -d -dli/
      epen cnj clf animate be cold
           10 13 stem

      [asdli]   'he, she is cold'

(30) /ə -s -d -yǫ/
      epen cnj clf grow
           10 13 stem

      [asjǫ]   'he, she is old'

(31)   /gha-s -d -yhan/
       cnj 1sS clf sing
       10 12 13 stem

       [ghasjin]   'I sang'

In other forms, however, the d classifier arguably has some sort of semantic function. Tenenbaum (1978) has suggested that the d classifier can be analyzed as a morpheme which marks action that reverses or turns back on itself; the d classifier is thus perhaps a detransitivizing prefix. The d classifier occurs in the following constructions:

    reflexives
    reciprocal forms
    intransitive forms containing na customary prefix
    intransitive forms containing na 'back, again'
    passive forms

Some examples of the use of the d classifier in such constructions are given in (32)-(41):

    reflexives:

(32a) /ts'e-?ada-na -s -d -zit/
       wake refl cnj 1sS clf wake up
        2   7   10 12 13 stem

       [ts'e?adànasdzit]   'I wake myself up'

(32b) /ts'e-na -s -sit/
       wake cnj 1sS wake up

       [ts'enassit]   'I wake up'

(33a) /Ɣa -gha-ts'a-n -d -tsùz/
       recp P 1pS cnj clf handle cloth-like O
        1   1   8   10 13 stem

       [Ɣats'itsùz]   'we gave each other [cloth-like O]'

(33b) /sa -gha-na -n -h -tsùz/
       1sO P cnj Pf clf handle cloth-like O
        1   1 10 11 13 stem

       [sanihtsùz]   'he, she gave me [cloth-like O]'

(In (33), the gh-initial postposition has undergone the following rule:

85

(34)   Gamma Loss

   gh --> ∅ V [p ___ V

The /ə/ of the object prefix is deleted by Prefix Vowel Deletion.)

   reciprocal forms:

(35)   /ts'e-ɬə -ghə-nə -d -zat/
       wake recp 3p cnj clf wake up
        2   7   8   10 13 stem

       [ts'eɬaghįdzət]   'they woke each other up'

(Cf. (32b).)

(36a) /ʔadə-zə -s -d -h -xį/
       refl thm cnj clf clf kill sg O
        7   9 10 13 13 stem

       [ʔadəzèhghį]   'he, she killed him-, herself'

(36b) /zə -s -h -xį/
       thm cnj clf kill sg O
        9 10 13 stem

       [zèhxį]   'he, she killed [O]'

See 2.1.2.4 and 3.2.1 for a description of the rules which have applied in these forms (in particular, for an explanation of why /h/ but not /s/ surfaces in (36a,b)).

   na 'customary' and na 'back, again'

(37)   /ts'e-na -n -d -sit/
       wake rev cnj clf wake up
        2   5 10 13 stem

       [ts'enǫdzit]   'he, she wakes up again'

(38)   /ts'e-na-s -d -sats/
       wake C 1sS clf wake up
        2   5 12 13 stem

       [ts'enasdzats]   'I wake up habitually'

(In (37), the rule of a Raising (39) (to be further discussed in 5.2) has applied:

(39)   a --> o / ___ n]$_{syll}$)

passive forms:

(40a)   /na -nə -ghə-s -d -ʔagh/
        rev thm cnj 1sS clf fool O
         5   9 10 12 13 stem

        [nanəghəst'agh]   'I was fooled'

(40b)   /dəne na -sə -nə -ghə-n -ʔagh/
        person rev 1sO thm cnj Pf fool O
                5   7   9 10 11 stem

        [dəne nasənaghį?agh]   'somebody fooled me'

(41a)   /tl'uł na -nə -s -d -h -xàl/
        rope rev thm cnj clf clf coil O
               5   9 10 13 13 stem

        [tl'uł nanèhghàl]   'the rope is coiled'

(41b)   /tl'uł na -nə -s -h -xàl/
        rope rev thm cnj clf coil O

        [tl'uł nanèhxàl]   'he, she coiled the rope'

To summarize, the d classifier must be analyzed as part of the lexical entry of some verbs. In other cases, however, d classifier can perhaps be regarded as synchronically derived, serving a 'detransitivizing' function.

2.1.2.3 d+h (*l)

In forms like (39), the classifier sequence d + h is phonetically zero. However, following Rice (to appear), I suggest that a segment which is phonologically [+voiced] is created from this sequence:

(42)   C
        [+voiced]

As noted above, this segment is cognate with the l classifier in certain other Athabaskan languages. In 2.2.1 I will present evidence for the voiced nature of this segment.

Like the classifiers d and h, many instances of the classifier sequence d+h must be regarded as part of the lexical entry of the verb in which it occurs. Some examples of such verbs are given in (43)-(49):

(43)   /i -s -d -h -yòtl/
       asp 1sS clf clf swell up

       [àsyòtl]   'I swelled up'

(The rule of i Lowering (3.1.4) has applied in (43):

(44)   i --> ə / ___ s
                      gh)

(45)   /nà -nə -s -d -h -?į/
       cont der cnj clf clf sneak around
        2   9   10 13 13 stem

       [nànèh?į]   'he, she sneaked around'

(46)   /tà-s -d -h -tla/
       up cnj clf clf sg/du run
        2 10 13 13 stem

       [tàhtla]   'he, she ran uphill'

(47)   /ka-nà -s -d -h -dzàt/
       P cont cnj clf clf hunt
       1   2   10 13 13 stem

       -[kanàhdzàt]   'he, she hunted for [O]'

(48)   /ts'ę u -s -d -h -gèt/
       P   asp cnj clf clf crawl
             9   10 13 13 stem

       -[ts'ę ùhgèt]   'he, she crawled to [O]'

(49)   /?ə -da -s -d -h -gùge/
       unspO thm 1sS clf clf squat
        7   9   12 13 13 stem

       [?ədèhgùge]   'he, she squats'

Like the d classifier, the sequence of d+h classifiers is more often than not phonetically zero. However, it is possible to ascertain whether a verb has underlying d+h from the effect of this sequence on rules whose structural descriptions refer to one or the other of these classifiers. I would now like to turn to these rules.

2.1.2.4 Phonological effects of the classifiers

The surface forms of three prefixes, /s/ first person singular subject,

/ah/ second person plural subject, and /'sə/ conjugation, are determined by the classifier prefix.

The subject prefixes. The first person singular and second person plural subject prefixes /s/ and /ah/ do not occur in the perfective of verbs which contain h or Ø classifier. Instead, prefixes of the shape [i] and [a], respectively, occur:

(50)   s --> i
                    / ___ [(h) stem]
                       [+Pf]
       ah --> a

Compare the perfective forms in (51) and (52) with those in (53) and (54). In (51) and (52), the subject prefixes are uniformly [s] and [ah]:

　　d classifier:

(51a) /ghə-s -d -yhən/
       cnj 1sS clf sing
        10 12 13 stem

       [ghəsjin]   'I sang'

(51b) [ghahjin]   'you [pl] sang'

　　d+h classifiers:

(52a) /ka-nà -sə -s -d -h -dzàt/
       P cont cnj 1sS clf clf hunt for O
       1   2   10 12 13 13 stem

       -[kanàsəsdzàt]   'I hunted for [O]'

(52b) -[kanàsahdzàt]   'you [pl] hunted for [O]'

However, in the Ø and h classifier forms below, the variants [i] and [a] occur instead:

　　Ø classifier:

(53a) /ghə-i -tsègh/
       cnj 1sPf cry
        10 12 stem

       [ghitsègh]   'I cried'

(53b) [ghatsègh]   'you [pl] cried'

h classifier:

(54a) /ghə-i   -h -t'òch/
      cnj 1sPf clf suck on O
      10 12   13 stem

   [ghiht'òch]   'I sucked on [O]'

(54b) [ghaht'òch]   'you [pl] sucked on [O]'

Thus the phonetic shape of the subject prefixes provides evidence about which of the classifiers is present underlyingly.

/'sə/ conjugation prefix. While the occurrence of [s] or [ah] in perfective forms is sufficient to determine that either /d/ or /d+h/ is present underlyingly, the rule in (50) does not determine which of these classifiers is present underlyingly. It is also necessary to consider whether the stem-initial consonant of the verb is a possible output of the D-Effect Rule. If it is not (i.e., if it is a fricative or [?]), this suggests that the underlying classifier is the sequence /d+h/ (*1). However, if the stem-initial consonant is a possible output of the D-Effect Rule, it is not possible to use the stem-initial consonant to determine the underlying classifer. However, the surface form of the conjugation prefix /'sə/ may prove diagnostic in such cases.

The shape of the /'sə/ conjugation prefix is determined in part by which of the classifier prefixes is present. In forms where no prefix intervenes between the conjugation prefix and the classifier (i.e., in third person singular and in first and third person plural forms), the following rules apply to the intermediate representation [s] of the conjugation prefix /'sə/:

(55) Aspiration

$$s \rightarrow h / \underline{\quad} \begin{Bmatrix} h \\ 1 \end{Bmatrix} \text{ stem}$$
[+cnj]

(56) s Voicing

$$s \rightarrow z / \underline{\quad} [\text{ stem }]$$

90

Thus [s] is preserved only before /d/ classifier. These rules are illustrated
in the forms in (57)-(59):

(57)   s --> z

   /ta-da-s -?ǫ/
    lose cnj handle compact O
    2 9   10   stem

   [tadèz?ǫ]   'he, she lost [compact O]'

(58)   s --> h

   /u -za -s -h -ts'ǫ/
    thm thm cnj clf listen to O
    9   9   10 13 stem

   [uzèhts'ǫ]   'he, she listened to [O]'

The rule of Cluster Simplification has also applied in (58):

                            /u-za-s-h-ts'ǫ/

Conjugation Tone Mapping   à
s-Conjugation a Fronting   è
Aspiration   h
Cluster Simplification   ø

                            [uzèhts'ǫ]

(Conjugation Tone Mapping and s-Conjugation a Fronting will be discussed in

4.2.2 and 3.2.1.1, respectively.)

(59)   /nà -na -s -d -h -?į/
         cont der cnj clf clf sneak
         2   9   10 13 13 stem

   [nànèh?į]   'he, she sneaked around'

(60) indicates that [s] is preserved before d classifier:

(60)   /chu -na -s -d -dǫ/
         water term cnj clf drink
         3   9   10 13 stem

   [chunèsdǫ]   'he, she is drunk'

Thus the phonetic shape of the conjugation prefix /'sa/ indicates which of the
classifiers is underlyingly present.

   To summarize, there are three kinds of evidence that determine which of the classifiers is present underlyingly:

    --stem-initial consonant of verb
    --shape of first person singular and second person plural subject prefixes
    --shape of /'sə/ conjugation prefix

Often more than one kind of evidence is required to determine with certainty that the classifier sequence /d+h/, rather than /d/, is present underlyingly. The reader can now verify that the forms in (43) and (45)-(49) do indeed contain /d+h/ classifiers, and that those in (26)-(31) contain the /d/ classifier.

2.2 Level 1 Phonology

In this section I discuss three phonological rules which apply to stems but not to the verbal prefixes:

    Voicing Assimilation
    D-Effect Rule
    Palatalization

These rules therefore suggest that stems and prefixes are separate phonological domains.

2.2.1 Voicing Assimilation

Consider the following contrasts between voiced and voiceless fricatives in stems:

(61a)   -[das̱]   'twist'

(61b)   [daẕ]   'driftwood'

(62a)   -[ʔal̠]   'handle compact O' Fut/Op

(62b)   [ʔal̠]   'branches'

(63a)   [ts'ax̱]   'juniper'

(63b)   -[ts'ag̱h]   'yawn'

It is clearly necessary to posit an underlying contrast between voiced and voiceless fricatives in Sekani. Notice, however, that the contrast is exemplified only by stem-final fricatives in (61)-(63). Stem-initially, voiced and voiceless fricatives are in complementary distribution. This is true of noun and postposition stem-initial fricatives, as well as verb stem-initial fricatives, although, as Rice (1976) first observed, the voicing rule for nouns and postpositions cannot be collapsed with the rule for verbs. I will discuss the rule governing the distribution of voiced and voiceless fricatives in nouns and postpositions in Ch. 4, sec. 4.

Returning to verbs, stem-initial voiceless fricatives occur after voiceless segments, and voiced fricatives, after voiced segments. The following alternations occur:

(64)   s ~ z
       ł ~ l
       yh ~ y
       x ~ gh
       wh ~ w

These can be collapsed into a single rule of Voicing Assimilation:

(65)   Voicing Assimilation

                    C
           | |
       [+voice]   +cont
                  -son

The need for this rule is apparent from consideration of forms like (66)-(70):

(66a)   /ʔònè-də -s -sògh/
         out der 1sS spit
          2   9   12 stem

        [ʔònèdəssògh]   'I spit'

(66b)   [ʔònèdəzogh]   'he, she spits'

Underlyingly, (66b) is identical to (66a) except that (66b) lacks the position 12 subject prefix /s/, and the stem-initial fricative is therefore voiced in this form. Some additional examples of voicing alternations are provided below:

(67a) /ùya ə -s -ɣi̧/
       shy epen 1sS be
              12 stem

       [ùya əsɣi̧]   'I am shy'

(67b) /ùya əli̧/   'he, she is shy'

(68a) /gha-ʔə   -na -ah -yhis/
       P   unspO cnj 2pS scare O
       1   7   10 12 stem

       -[ghaʔanahyhis]   'you [pl] scare [O]'

(68b) /gha-ʔə   -gha-n -yis/
       P   unspO 3pS cnj scare O
       1   7   8   10 stem

       -[ghaʔaghi̧yis]   'they scare [O]'

(69a) /ə -s -xǫ/
       epen 1sS kill pl O
            12 stem

       [asxǫ]   'I kill [pl O]'

(69b) /aghǫ/   'he, she kills [pl O]'

(70a) /nà -s -whàt/
       cont 1sS walk fast
       2   12 stem

       [nàswhàt]   'I walk fast'

(70b) /nàwàt/   'he, she walks fast'

2.2.1.1 Domain of Voicing Assimilation

As seen in the preceding section, stem-initial fricatives participate in this voicing alternation. In prefixes, however, voiceless fricatives occur after a voiced segment. Examples of voiceless fricatives in prefixes of positions 3 and 6-10 are given in (71)-(76):

(71)   /ya -sa -na -ʔàs/
       thm cnj 2sS sneeze
       7   10 12 stem

       [yàsi̱ʔàs]   'you [sg] sneezed'

(72)   /da -ɬa -a -jih   -e/
       Fut thm Fut be sweet Fut
       9   9   11 stem

       [daɬajihe]   'he, she will be sweet'

(73)   /u -sa -na -i -be/
       thm 1dS thm 1dS pick berries
       9   8   9   12 stem

       [usa̱nibe]   'we [du] pick berries'

(74)   /hà -sa -gha-n -ts'i/
       adv 1sO cnj Pf pinch
       2   7   10 11 stem

       [hàsaghi̱ts'i?]   'he, she pinched me'

(75)   /ts'e-whè -sa -na -i -n -h -sat/
       wake incp 1sO der der Pf clf wake up
       2   6   7   9   9 11 13 stem

       [ts'ewhèsani̱hsat]   'he, she started to wake me up'

(76)   /hà -sa -na-da -i -d -ʔah/
       out sun C der der clf compact O habitually be in position
       2   3   5 9   9   13 stem

       [hàsa̱nadit'ah]   'the sun shines habitually'

The fact that voiceless fricatives occur after voiceless segments in prefixes indicates that Voicing Assimilation should apply only to fricatives in stems. Moreover, the data in (61)-(63) indicate that Voicing Assimilation should be restricted to stem-initial fricatives.[7]

(77)   Voicing Assmilation

       $[+\text{voice}] \left\{ \begin{matrix} -\frac{C}{1} \\ \begin{bmatrix} +\text{cont} \\ -\text{son} \end{bmatrix} \dots \end{matrix} \right\}_{\text{stem}}$

I return to the formulation of Voicing Assimilation in Ch. 5, sec. 2.

2.2.1.2 The classifier prefixes

Data in the preceding section indicated that prefixes may provide the context for Voicing Assimilation when it applies to stem-initial fricatives. The classifier prefixes, like other prefixes, serve as a context for Voicing Assimilation:

(80) /a   h   -whàse/
      epen clf   tickle O
            13   stem

      [ahwhàse]   'he, she tickles [O]'

However, the classifier prefixes do not meet the structural description of the rule and thus do not undergo it: d is [-cont]; h is [+cont] but [+son]. Thus Voicing Assimilation does not provide evidence that the classifiers should be grouped with stems, or with the other verb prefixes, for phonological purposes.

As mentioned in 2.1.2.3 above, the classifier sequence d+h gives rise to a segment which is phonologically voiced. Consider the following pairs, which differ in that the (a) forms contain h classifier but the (b) forms, d+h classifiers. (See 2.1.2.3 for underlying forms.)

(79a) [tl'uł nanèhxàl]   'he, she coiled the rope'
(79b) [tl'uł nanèhghàl]   'the rope is coiled'

(80a) [zèhxi]   'he, she killed [sg O]'
(80b) [ʔədəzèhghi]   'he, she killed him-, herself'

The (b) forms appear to be exceptions to the rule of Voicing Assimilation, in that they contain a stem-initial voiced fricative preceded by a phonetically voiceless segment. However, they can easily be accounted for if a phonologically voiced segment intervenes between the [h] (</`sa/; cf. 2.1.2.4) conjugation prefix and the stem-initial fricative.[8] Thus the following rule applies to the classifier sequence d+h:

(81) h Voicing:⁹

    d + h --> C
   [+clf] |
              [+voiced]

A form like (79b) can thus be derived from the intermediate representation in (82) as follows. (I use the segment l as an abbreviation for the segment that results from h Voicing.)

(82) /na -na -s -d -h -xàl/
      rev term cnj clf clf coil O
       5   9   10 13 13 stem

                         /na -na -s -d -h -xàl/

h Voicing   l
Voicing Assimilation   gh
Aspiration   h

eventually   [nanèghàl]

2.2.1.3 Summary

Voicing Assimilation provides evidence that stems and prefixes are separate phonological domains. Even if Voicing Assimilation applies only to syllable-initial fricatives, the rule must still be analyzed as having a restricted domain, since prefixes like /ˋsə/ (conjugation) in position 10, which contain voiceless initial fricatives, are not within the domain of Voicing Assimilation.

In the following sections I will consider additional rules which support the hypothesis that stems and verb prefixes are separate phonological domains.

2.2.2 The D-Effect Rule

Two prefixes, d classifier and id 1d subject, cause the alternations referred to in 2.1.2.2 as the D-Effect Rule. Recall the alternations to be accounted for:

(83)   prefix + stem-initial

$$d + z \longrightarrow dz$$
$$d + l \longrightarrow dl$$
$$d + y \longrightarrow j$$
$$d + gh \longrightarrow g$$
$$d + ? \longrightarrow t'$$

Most of these rules can be collapsed:

(84a) The D-Effect Rule[10]

$$d \longrightarrow \emptyset \, / \_\_ \begin{bmatrix} C \\ -? \\ +cont \\ -son \\ -round \end{bmatrix}$$

(84b)

$$d \longrightarrow \emptyset \, / \_\_ \begin{bmatrix} C \\ -? \end{bmatrix}$$

Some examples of the D-Effect Rule are given in (85)-(89) below:

   d+? --> t'

(85a) /ghuya-gha-ʔa   -sa -na -id -ʔọ/
       3pO   P   unspO 1dS cnj 1dS hire O

       [ghuyaʔasanit'ọ]   'we [du] hired them'

(85b) /ya -gha-ʔa -na -n -ʔọ/
       4sO P   unspO cnj Pf hire O
        1   1   7   10 11 stem

       [yaʔanịʔọ]   'he, she hired him, her'

   d+z --> dz

(86a) /k'è-na-d -zùt/
       per C clf skate
        2 5 13 stem

       [k'ądzùt]   'he, she skates around'

(86b) /nà -sa -zùt/
       cont cnj skate
        2   10 stem

       [nàsazùt]   'he, she skated around'

(The rule of Perambulative Reduction (Ch. 5, 3.2) has applied in (86a).)

d+l --> dl

(87a)   /che -na -na -s -d -làt/
        water rev term cnj clf sink
          2   5   9 10 13 stem

        [chenanèsdlàt]   'he, she sank again'

(87b)   /che -na -s -làt/
        water term cnj sink

        [chenèzlàt]   'he, she sank'

d+y --> j

(88a)   /hà -na -də -`sə-s -ja/
        out rev forth cnj 1sS sg go
          2   5   9   10 12 stem

        [hǫnadèesja]   'I walked back out'

(88b)   /hà -də -`sə-i -ya/
        out forth cnj 1sPf sg go

        [hàdèeya]   'I walked out'

d+gh --> g

(89a)   /sə -ghə-id -ghǫ/
        1sS cnj 1dS kill pl O
         8   10 12 stem

        [saghigǫ]   'we [du] killed [pl O]'

(89b)   /ə -ghǫ/
        epen kill pl O

        [aghǫ]   'he, she kills [pl O]'

Oddly enough, the D-Effect Rule does not apply if the stem-initial consonant is [w]:

(90a)   /sə -id -wàse/
        1dS 1dS itch

        [siwàse]   'we [du] itch'

(90b)   [ə -wàse]
        epen itch   'he, she itches'

Since other rules treat [w] as a labio-velar, one would expect an alternation

[w]~[gw] here. I will return to this curious fact in 2.2.2.2.

2.2.2.1 Domain of the D-Effect Rule

Verbal prefixes which end in /d/ are quite rare. In addition to d classifier and id 1d subject, the only d-final prefix that I know of is the incorporated stem gwàt /gòd/ 'knee':

(91) /nà -gwàd-gha-i -h -ki/
      down knee cnj 1sPf clf wound
       2   3   10 11 13 stem

      [nàgwàtghihki]   'I banged my knee'

(92) /nà -gwàd-gha-n -h -?a/
      down knee cnj Pf clf

      [nàgwàtghįh?a]   'I kneeled down'

The D-Effect Rule has not applied in these forms, even though the final /d/ of the incorporated stem 'knee' is followed by a voiced fricative. This suggests that the D-Effect Rule applies only to stem-initial fricatives and glottal stop. Thus the rule in (84) should be revised:

(93)   The D-Effect Rule

$$t - \begin{bmatrix} C \\ -- \\ \end{bmatrix} \begin{bmatrix} +cont \\ -son \\ -round \end{bmatrix} \dots \Big]_{stem}$$

$$t - \begin{bmatrix} C \\ -- \\ \end{bmatrix} \begin{bmatrix} ? \end{bmatrix} \dots \Big]_{stem}$$

Assuming that rules which refer to morphological bracketing apply on the same level or on a level which is adjacent to that of the bracketed information, the D-Effect Rule applies on levels 1 and 2, but not post-lexically.

2.2.2.2 Order and formulation of the D-Effect Rule

Additional data suggest that the formulation of this rule given in (93) and the proposed analysis of its domain should be revised. The segment that

is the output of the D-Effect Rule is phonetically identical to affricate or
t'-initial stems which do not contain the d classifier or id 1d subject
prefixes. However, certain later rules must distinguish stem-initial
consonants which are genuine outputs of the D-Effect Rule from those which
could be, but are not. For example, the prefixation of perfective /n/
(position 11) does not occur in d classifier forms:

(94)   /k'e   -ts'ə-'nə-n -t'ats/
       in half 1pə cnj Pf cut

       [k'ets'anįt'ats]   'we cut O in half'

(95)   /yidà -na -ts'ə-n -d -ʔats/
       inside rev 1pS cnj clf du go

       [yidǫts'įt'ats]   'we [du excl] walked inside again'

Since the D-Effect Rule would neutralize the contrast between underlying /t'/
and /d-ʔa/, the rule must apply later in the derivation than the point at
which the perfective prefix is added. Accordingly, the D-Effect Rule is
revised as follows:

(96)   The D-Effect Rule: d Delinking

$$\begin{matrix} & C & \\ \cancel{} & | & \cdots \\ d & \end{matrix} \begin{bmatrix} \\ \\ \end{bmatrix}_{stem}$$

On levels 1 and 2, d is simply delinked from its skeletal position by (96).
Post-lexically, this floating [d] is linked to stem-initial fricatives and /ʔ/
by (97).

(97) The D-Effect Rule: d Linking

(a)   C
       x - - -|
       d   ⎛ +cont ⎞
              ⎜{[+cor]}⎟
              ⎝{[+high]}⎠

(b)   C
       x - - -|
       d   ʔ

If d Linking applies after Velar Loss (Ch. 1, 6.3), this will account for the failure of [w] to participate in the D-Effect Rule alternations, as do the other fricatives. Finally, any floating [d]'s will be deleted. This will account for the fact that the final d of the 1d subject and classifier prefixes does not show up on the surface before all stem-initial consonants.[11]

Regardless of how the D-Effect Rule is formally stated, what is of most interest here is its domain. To summarize, the D-Effect Rule lexically links a d-final prefix to an adjacent stem-initial consonant. However, d-final prefixes cannot be linked to prefix-initial consonants. Thus, the D-Effect Rule provides additional evidence that stems and prefixes are distinct phonological domains.

2.2.3 Palatalization

Additional evidence that verb stems and prefixes are distinct phonological domains is provided by the rule of Palatalization. The stem-initial alveolar stops alternate with palatal affricates before the stem vowels [i e u]:

	Imp	Pf	Fut	Op	
(98)	[jèɣ]	[jet1]	[dàɣ]	[jèɣ]	'pl go'
(99)	[jiɣ]	[dəl]	[jiɣ]	[jiɣ]	'handle pl O carelessly'
(100)	[chįh]	[tǫ]	[chįɣ]	[tǫ?]	'handle stick-like O carefully'
(101)	[chès]	[chets]	[tàs]	[chès]	'pl go to sleep'
(102)	[ch'ès]	[ch'əgh]	[t'às]	[ch'ès]	'roast O'
(103)	[ch'ux]	[t'ogh]	[ch'ux]	[ch'ux]	'shoot at O repeatedly'

Palatalization accounts not only for these alternations, but also for the fact that stem-initial coronal stops are restricted in distribution, occurring only before the stem vowels /ə o a/. Thus if palatal-alveolars and alveolars are identically (under)specified underlyingly, Palatalization will apply to non-derived as well as to derived forms:

(104)　/deɣ/

　　　　[jeɣ]　　　　　　　'crane'

(105)　/teh　　-kàɣ -è/
　　　　into water flat psd

　　　　[chehkàɣè?]　　　　'water lilies'

(106)　/t'ès/

　　　　[ch'ès]　　　　　　'charcoal'

In addition to the alternations above in which the verb stem contains an ablauting stem vowel, alternations between t' and ch' also arise through the D-Effect Rule:

(107a)　/k'è -sə -də -i -id -?èts/
　　　　P:on 1dS der der 1dS step

　　　　[k'èsədich'èts]　　　'we [du] stepped on [0]'

(107b)　/k'è -də -də -ghə-id -?əs/
　　　　P:on der Fut Fut 1dS step

　　　　[k'èdədəghit'əs]　　　'we [du] will step on [0]'

The D-Effect Rule thus feeds Palatalization.

Only stem-initial consonants may undergo Palatalization. Palatalization does not apply to stem-final alveolar stops:

(108)　[sə -ləsiet-è?]　　　'my dish'
　　　　1sPsr dish　psd

(109)　[jugheh　　kàdi]　　'apron'
　　　　front side covering

(110)　[sə -bàd -è?]　　　'my mittens'
　　　　1sPsr mittens psd

(111)　/də -ghə-n -tl'èd-e/
　　　　Fut Fut 2sS fart Fut

　　　　[dəghį̀tl'ède]　　　　'you will fart'

Moreover, Palatalization does not apply to /d/-initial verbal prefixes:

(112) /wə-də-i̵ -dlòt/
ar thm thm be steep
7   9   9   stem

[wadidlòt]   '[area] is steep'

(113) /ta-də-s -?ǫ/
lose cnj handle compact O
2   9   10   stem

[tadèz?ǫ]   'he, she lost [compact O]'

(114) /?ònè-də -u -s -sògh ą/
out der Op 1sS spit Op
2   9   11 12 stem

[?ònèdussògh ą]   'I spit' Op

Of course, in all of these forms, the sequences [di], [du], and [de] are derived. The failure of Palatalization to apply here could be a consequence of rule ordering:

/?ònè-də-u-s-sògh/

Palatalization   --
Prefix Vowel Deletion   du

[?ònèdussògh]

However, since Prefix Vowel Deletion is a levels 1-3 rule, Palatalization must also be a lexical rule. As a lexical rule, Palatalization applies to stem-initial coronals:

(115) $\begin{pmatrix} C & V \\ | \text{- - - -} \dashv & \\ [+cor] & [+high] \\ & [-back] \end{pmatrix} \ldots \Big\}$ stem

In keeping with this hypothesis, notice that certain words must be lexically marked as exceptions to Palatalization:

(116) [dèbi]   'Davie'

(117) [dimos dzene]   'Sunday'
       day

One predicted characteristic of lexical rules, as opposed to post-lexical rules, is that they may have lexically marked exceptions. ((116) and (117) are loan words, which might be expected to be exceptional.)

2.3 Level 1: summary

The evidence presented in this section indicates that stems and prefixes constitute separate phonological domains, but there is some uncertainty about which domain the position 12 prefixes belong to. The position 12 first person singular prefix /s/ does not undergo Voicing Assimilation, but the position 12 first person dual prefix /id/ does Palatalize and undergo the D-Effect Rule. However, /id/ could be analyzed as a discontinuous prefix, just like prefixes found in other positions which require the d classifier:[10]

(118)   /ì   d/   1d subject
        12 13

        /?adə d/   reflexive
        7   13

        /na d/   reversative, customary
        5   13

Given this analysis, then only the d classifier triggers the D-Effect Rule, and the prefixes of position 12 do not belong to the same phonological domain as the stem:

(119)   Domains of Voicing Assimilation, Palatalization and the D-Effect Rule

prefix	1	2	3	4	5	6	7	8	9	10	11	12	13	stem
Voicing Assim.		n		n	n	n	n				n			y
D-Effect Rule			n										y	
Palatalization									n				y	

   y = undergoes the rule
   n = may not undergo rule

The rule of L Deletion (4.2.3) will provide additional evidence that the prefixes of position 12 belong to the domain of the prefixes to their left, rather than to that of the classifiers and stems. The rule of Conjugation a Deletion provides evidence that the classifier prefixes belong on level 1, as will be discussed in Ch. 5, 3.1.[13]

3. Level 2

3.1 Morphology

In this section I describe the level 2 prefixes. Although I refer to prefix positions throughout this dissertation, I believe that prefix positions have no formal status in the grammar of Sekani. Affixation is a word formation process, and restrictions on affix order can be accounted for ordering the various word formation processes. However, distinguishing position classes within the verb prefixes provides a convenient way of informally describing the prefix morphology, and of illustrating restrictions on the surface order of the prefixes. My presentation of affix order restrictions will take the form of showing that the prefixes of position n (those discussed in the current section) occur to the left of those of position $n+1$. (Evidence that the prefixes of position n occur to the right of those of position $n-1$ can be found in the next section.)

3.1.1 Subject prefixes (position 12)

Four prefixes occur in this position:

```
[s, i]      1s
[nə, n]     2s
[i]         1d
[ah, a]     2p
```

Examples of these prefixes can be seen in (120):

(120a) /ts'e-nə -s -h -sit/
       wake cnj 1sS clf wake up

       [ts'enəssit]   'I wake up [O]'

(120b) /ts'e-nə -n -h -sit/
       wake cnj 2sS clf wake up

       [ts'enįhsit]   'you [sg] wake up [O]'

(120c) /ts'e-sə -nə -i -d -h -zit/
        wake 1dS cnj 1dS clf clf wake up

        [ts'esənizit]   'we [du] wake up [0]'

(120d) /ts'e-nə -ah -h -sit/
        wake cnj 2pS clf wake up

        [ts'enahsit]   'you [pl] wake up [0]'

As can be seen in the preceding forms, the position 12 subject prefixes occur to the left of the classifier prefixes. Some additional examples which illustrate this ordering restriction are provided below:

(121) /ə -s -d -yhən/
       epen 1sS clf sing

       [asjin]   'I sing'

(122) /i -ah -l -yòtl/
       asp 2pS clf swell up

       [àhyòtl]   'you [pl] swelled up'

3.1.2 Mode prefixes (position 11)

Like 'classifier', the traditional term 'mode' is something of a misnomer. The three non-zero prefixes of the 'mode' position mark most of the major tense/aspect distinctions in Sekani. These prefixes are /gho/ optative, /gha/ future, and /n/ perfective. A fourth category, imperfective, is not phonologically marked. See Rice (to appear) for a discussion of the morphological and semantic characteristics of tense, aspect and mode in Slave, a closely related language.

Optative. The optative prefix /gho/ has a variety of surface forms, which include ghu, u, wə and w as well as gho. These are all derived by regular phonological rules.

The rule of Diphthongization in (123) (together with Velar Loss; Ch. 1, 6.3) creates the sequence [wə] in (124):

(123) o --> wə / velar ___

(124) /gho-s -tsagh/
      Op 1sS cry

      [w̨astsagh]   'I cry' Op

Recall from Ch. 1, 5.2, that Diphthongization is blocked if [o] is nasal. Thus the underlying form of the optative prefix is preserved in second person singular forms:

(125) /gho-n -tsagh/
      Op 2sS cry

      [ghǫtsagh]   'you [sg] cry' Op

In the second person plural form below, Diphthongization creates the sequence [wə]. Then Prefix Vowel Deletion applies to [wə-ah], creating [wah]:

(126) /gho-ah -tsagh/
      Op 2pS cry

      [w̨ahtsagh]   'you [pl] cry' Op

An additional rule of o̜ Raising, given in (127), is required to account for the first person dual form in (128) below.

(127) o --> u / ___ i

(128) /gho-i -d-tsagh/
      Op 1dS clf cry

      [ghùtsagh]   'we [du] cry' Op

                        /gho -i-d-tsagh/
o̜ Raising   u
Prefix Vowel Deletion   ∅

                        [ghùtsagh]

The rules which create the remaining surface form [u] of the optative prefix will be discussed in 4.2.4.

Notice that the preceding forms all indicate that the optative prefix precedes the subject prefixes of position 12.

Future. The future mode is discontinuously marked by position 9 da and position 11 gha. In addition, an optional future suffix -e may also be present.

(129) /?ə -də -ghə-s -h -xǫ̀h/
       unspO Fut Fut 1sS clf snore
       7   9   11 12 13 stem

       [?ədəghəsxǫ̀h]   'I will snore'

(130) /də -ghə-n -dlògh -e/
       Fut Fut 2sS laugh Fut

       [dəghįdlòghe]   'you [sg] will laugh'

Like the optative forms, these future forms also indicate that the mode prefixes occur to the left of the position 12 subject prefixes.

   Perfective. The perfective prefix /n/ occurs phonetically as nasalization of the preceding vowel, as in (131) and (132), in which the perfective prefix is preceded by the conjugation prefixes gha and na. (The rule of ə Raising has also applied in these forms.)

(131) /ghə-n -dlògh/
       cnj Pf laugh
       10 11 stem

       [ghįdlògh]   'he, she laughed'

(132) /che -nə -n -?ǫ/
       water cnj Pf handle compact O

       [chenį?ǫ]   'he, she put [compact O] in water'

The perfective prefix /n/ does not appear in perfective forms which contain the d or *l classifiers. In addition, perfective /n/ is absent in surface forms if a position 12 subject prefix or the position 10 conjugation prefix /'sə/ is present. Thus there are no surface forms in which perfective /n/ and the subject prefixes co-occur. /n/ is assigned to this prefix position because its function is similar to that of the other mode prefixes.

3.1.3 Conjugation prefixes (position 10)

Three prefixes occur in this position: /'nə/, /'sə/, and /ghə/. These prefixes divide the verbs into conjugation classes. As seen in (131) and

(132) above, the conjugation prefixes occur to the left of the perfective mode prefix. I have argued elsewhere (Hargus (to appear (c))), as has Rice (1985), that the conjugation prefixes may also occur with the future and optative mode prefixes. These data also indicate that the conjugation prefixes occur to the left of the future and optative mode prefixes.[14]

I will briefly mention one rule which affects the conjugation prefixes here. In forms in which no prefixes intervene between the conjugation prefix and an optional classifier prefix, the /ə/ of the conjugation and mode prefixes /`sə/, /`nə/ and /ghə/ is deleted. I posit a rule of Conjugation ə Deletion:

(133)
$$ə \longrightarrow \emptyset\ /\ V\ \begin{Bmatrix} n \\ s \\ gh \end{Bmatrix}\ \underline{\quad}\ [\ (clf)\ stem]$$
$$[+cnj]$$
$$[+mod]$$

I return to this rule in 4.2.5, where I present illustrative examples and discuss its domain.

3.1.4 Position 9 prefixes

The following prefixes are found in this position:

(134) ts'ə ghə łə u įdə zə də nə į

Some of these prefixes are 'thematic': they must be analyzed as part of the lexical entry of the verb as they occur in every derivation of the verb. Others have aspectual meanings, and require a particular conjugation prefix and particular set of stem suffixes. Still others are neither thematic nor aspectual, but occur in semi-productive derivations. Historically, many of these prefixes marked noun gender class, as they still do in some of the Athabaskan languages, such as Ahtna (Kari 1979). (The gender system is fairly limited in Sekani.) One of the prefixes of this position, /də/ future, is completely productive.

3.1.4.1 Order of prefixes within position 9.

Unlike the prefixes of most of the other positions, more than one prefix from the derivational position may be present in a given verb form. Given the wide range of functions of the prefixes which occur in this position, as well as the fact that more than one prefix from this position may occur in a single surface form, it is somewhat misleading to think of these prefixes as occurring in a single position. However, the surface order of these prefixes with respect to each other is largely predictable from the phonological shape of the derivational prefix. For example, position 9 gha always precedes na and da:

(135) [k'èghanadah]   'he, she staggers around'
(136) [ghadèsts'èt]   'he, she ate up [O]'

u precedes za and da:

(137) [uzèhts'ǫ]   'he, she listens to [O]'
(138) [jije udanabeɫ]   'he, she will pick berries'

ɫa optionally precedes da:

(139) [ɫadajihe]   'he, she will be sweet'
      =[daɫajihe]

da precedes na and za:

(140) [?adanaghits'įe]   'you [sg] will get sick from eating too much fat'
(141) [dazahxeɫ]   'he, she will kill [sg O]'

na and da precede i:

(142) [whènitsègh]   'he, she started to cry'
(143) [digày]   'it turned white, light'

These ordering restrictions are summarized in (144):

(144)   gh   n
           > d >   > i
        u   z

I assume that (144) is part of the grammar of Sekani, determining the order in which the position 9 prefixes are inserted. (Not all of the prefixes in (134) are to be found in (143), since I have not come across forms in which all possible pairs of position 9 prefixes co-occur.) In the case of da and ya, no ordering restriction is stated; thus these prefixes may be affixed in either order.

In the following sections, I will assume a single position ('position 9') analysis of these prefixes, but will return to the question of the superiority of a single or multiple position analysis of these prefixes in 3.1.4.2.

3.1.4.2 Order with respect to position 8 and 12 prefixes

Some of the position 9 prefixes in Sekani are unstable in position with respect to prefixes of positions to their left and right. Most instances of this instability are accounted for by analyzing the rules which add unstable prefixes as being unordered with respect to other prefix insertion rules. In other cases, howver, it is necessary to posit metathesis rules to account for the positional properties of unstable prefixes.

The vowel-initial position 9 prefixes u and ida optionally precede the position 8 prefix ts'a 1p subject:

(145)   ts'a V
        8   9 --> 9   8   optional

(146a) /?a -ts'a-u -h -ch'às /
         unspO 1pS thm clf hook

        [?ats'uhch'às]

(b)   /?a-u-ts'a-h-ch'às/

        [?uts'ahch'às]   'we go fishing'

(147a) /ts'a-įda-sa -l -?į/
         1pS der cnj clf hide
          8   9   10 13 stem

        [ts'įdèh?į]   'we hide [O]'

(b)   /i̜-ts'ə-də-s-1-ʔi̜/

=[its'adèhʔi̜]

The prefixes da na za optionally precede sə 1d subject:

(148)   sə   da
              na
              za   optional
        8   9   -->   9   8

(149)   /xada sə -za -i̜ -d -h -ghi̜/
        moose 1dS thm 1dS clf clf kill sg O

        [xada səzighi̜]   'we [du] killed a moose'

        =[xada zasighi̜]

(150)   /ni -sə -da -i̜ -i -d -ʔàh/
        raise 1dS der der 1dS clf handle compact O

        [nisadit'àh]   'we [du] lift [compact O]'

        =[nidasit'àh]

(151)   /ji̜je sə -u -na -i -d -be/
        berry 1dS thm thm 1dS clf pick berries

        [usanibe]   'we [du] pick berries'

        =[unasibe]

As can be seen in (151) above and (153) below, position 9 u always occurs to the left of the position 8 1d subject prefix sə.

(152)   sə   u
              ɣə
        8   9   -->   9   8

(153)   /gha-sə -u -i -d -bèh/
        P   1dS asp 1dS clf swim
        1   8   9 12 13 stem

        -[ghausibèh]   'we [du] swim past [O]'

Derivational ɣə also occurs to the left of sə 1d subject:

(154)   /sə -ɣə -i -d -ji̜h/
        1dS thm 1d clf be sweet
        8   9 12 13 stem

        [ɣasiji̜h]   'we [du] are sweet'

113

The derivational prefixes ts'ə ghə also always occur to the left of the subject prefixes of position 8:

(155)   ts'
            gh
         8   9 --> 9   8

(156)   /dah-ts'ə-ghə-a -d   -tlah/
         up 1pS thm cnj clf grab O
         2   8   9   10 13   stem

        [daghats'atlah]   'we grabbed [O]'

(157)   /wə -ghə-ts'ə-də-h -dəne/
         thm 3pS thm pl clf feel negative emotion
         7   8   9   9 13   stem

        [wats'aghədahdəne]   'they are lonesome'

(158)   /dah-na -sə-ghə-i -d   -tl'ų/
         up rev 1dS thm 1dS clf tie
         2   5   8   9   12 13   stem

        [dahnaghasitl'ų]   'we [du] tied up [O]'

Finally, the rightmost of the position 9 derivational prefixes, i, exhibits peculiar positional properties in first person dual optative forms. However, before I can illustrate this, I must first introduce an additional rule:

(159)   i Lowering

         i --> ə / ___ { s }
                         { gh }

This rule applies in forms like the following:

(160)   /i -s -h -t'às/
         asp 1sS clf shoot O with bow and arrow
         9   12 13 stem

        [əst'às]   'I shoot O with bow and arrow'

(161)   /na -i -gho-n -gwət/
         rev asp Op 2sS poke
         5   9   11 12   stem

        [naəghǫgwət]   'you [sg] poke O once again' Op

114

(162)   /i -gho-ah -chut/
        asp Op 2pS take O
         9 11 12 stem

        [àwahchut]   'you [pl] take [O] carefully' Op

Based on these data, one would expect the surface form [aghù...] in first person dual optative forms which contain the prefixes i derivational and i 1d subject. However, instead of *[aghù..], the surface form [ghù..] occurs. Compare (163) with (161), and (164) with (162):

(163)   /na -i -gho-i -d -gwat/
        rev asp Op 1dS clf poke
         5   9 11 12 stem

        [naghùgwat]   'we [du] poke [O] once again' Op

(164)   /i -gho-i-d-chut/
        asp Op 1dS clf take O
         9 11 12 stem

        [ghùchut]   'we [du] take [O] carefully' Op

I suggest that in the optative forms in (163) and (164), the position 9 prefix has metathesized with the position 11 optative prefix position /gho/, as described in (165):

(165)   i gho   i
        9 11 --> 11 9 / ___ 12

Following this metathesis, the vowel sequence /i-i/ is simplifed to [i] by Prefix Vowel Deletion:

(166)   /i-gho-i-d-h-chut/

Metathesis   -gho-i-i
L Deletion   -gho-i-i
o Raising   -ghu-i-i
Prefix Vowel Deletion   -ghu-i
                            -ghù

eventually   [ghùchut]

(See 4.2.3 for a discussion of L Deletion.)

3.1.4.3 Affix order: Summary

In a position class model of the Sekani verbal prefixes, the position 9 prefixes could be analyzed in at least two ways. In the approach taken here, these prefixes are assigned to a single position (9) underlyingly, with (optional and obligatory) metathesis rules determining their surface order both with respect to each other and with respect to certain position 8 and 12 prefixes. Alternatively, surface restrictions on order could be taken much more literally: these prefixes could all be assigned to discreet positions. In this latter analysis, five separate prefix positions would be necessary. A comparison of these analyses is given in (167):

(167) Comparison of two position class analyses

'concrete' positions	4	5	6	7	8	9
'abstract' positions	9	8	9	9	9	9
	ts'a	ts'a	u	ya	na	i
	gha	gha	ida	da	za	
		sa				
	der	subject	der	der	der	der

While the concrete analysis would account for most of the facts about surface order, it would require an additional four prefix positions. Moreover, it would still be necessary to posit rules (145, 148, 152, 165) to account for the instability of the position 9 prefixes with respect to position 8 and 12 prefixes.

3.2 Level 2 (vs. 3) phonology

As will be seen in 4.2, many rules of the phonology distinguish level 5 from levels 2, 3 and 4. In contrast, the evidence for distinguishing levels 2 and 3 is provided by only two rules.

3.2.1 The $\underline{s}$-conjugation rules

The $\underline{s}$-conjugation provides some of the most complicated paradigms in Sekani. First I will illustrate the rules required to account for these paradigms, and then I will consider the domain of these rules. The rules which affect the segmental representation of the conjugation prefix /'sə/ indicate that the prefixes of position 9 are phonologically distinct from those of positions 7 and 8.

3.2.1.1 Formulation of the s-conjugation rules

In (168), I have provided an s-conjugation paradigm in which the position 9 prefix /də/ precedes the position 10 conjugation prefix /'sə/:

(168a) /tse tl'ǫ̀ -də -sə -s -leh/
       rock circle der cnj 1sS handle pl O
         3   9   10 12   stem

       [tse tl'ǫ̀dèesɤeh]   'I put rocks in a circle'

(168b) /tse tl'ǫ̀ -də -sə -n -leh/
       rock circle der cnj 2sS handle pl O
         3   9   10 12   stem

       [tse tl'ǫ̀dèeleh]   'you [sg] put rocks in a circle'

(168c) /tse tl'ǫ̀ -də -sə -ɤeh/
       rock circle der cnj handle pl O
         3   9   10 stem

       [tse tl'ǫ̀dèsɤeh]   'he, she puts rocks in a circle'

(168d) /tse tl'ǫ̀ -də -sə -i -d -leh/
       rock circle der cnj 2sS clf handle pl O
         3   9   10 12 13   stem

       [tse tl'ǫ̀dasiyeh][15]   'we [du] put rocks in a circle'

(168e) /tse tl'ǫ̀ -də -sə -ah -leh/
       rock circle der cnj 2pS handle pl O
         3   9   10 12   stem

       [tse tl'ǫ̀dàahɤeh]   'you [pl] put rocks in a circle'

This paradigm has several unusual characteristics. First, vowel sequences, which are quite rare in Sekani, appear in some of the members of this paradigm.[16] Secondly, the vowel which precedes the conjugation prefix is e, rather than ə, in the first, second and third person singular forms. Thirdly, the s of the conjugation prefix is absent, except in the first person dual and third person singular forms.

Let us first tackle the fact that the prefix which precedes the conjugation prefix contains the vowel [e] in all but first person dual and second person plural forms, although it is underlyingly [a]. Notice that, in all but the first person dual forms, the low tone of the conjugation prefix appears on the preceding prefix. As will be seen in 4.2.3, it is normal for the tone of the conjugation prefixes to be absent in first person dual forms. Thus the rule in (169) will account for the change in vowel quality in all forms in which the low tone of the conjugation prefix is phonetically present:

(169) s-Conjugation a Fronting

$$a \rightarrow e \;/\; \underset{\underset{s}{}}{\overset{L}{|}}$$

Now the third person singular form can be derived as follows:

(170)   /tl'ǫ-da-sa-leh/

Conjugation a Deletion   ∅
a Fronting   e
Voicing Assimilation   ɣ

                         [tl'ǫdèsɣeh]

Although the inclusion of the tone in the context of this rule does not generalize to other Athabaskan languages, it seems to account well for the exclusion of the first person dual form in Sekani.

Next, we need to account for the fact that the s of the conjugation prefix is absent in first and second person singular and second person plural forms. Notice that these forms all contain vowel-initial prefixes. I suggest that the /s/ of the conjugation prefix is deleted intervocalically when it is also preceded by [e]:

(171) Conjugation s Deletion

$$s \rightarrow \emptyset \;/\; e \;\underline{\quad}\; V$$

Since the rule applies only to intervocalic [s], it will not apply to third person singular forms. The inclusion of [e] in the context of the rule will similarly exclude first person dual forms. Thus this rule will apply to a first person singular form as follows:

(172) /tl'ǫ̀-də-sə-s-ɤeh/

a Fronting e
Prefix Vowel Deletion --
Conjugation s Deletion ∅

[tl'ǫ̀dèesɤeh]

Notice that, in order to derive the long vowel in this and other forms, Prefix Vowel Deletion must precede Conjugation a Deletion.

Finally, two vowel assimilation rules are required. One rule will assimilate [e] to a following [a], as required by second person plural forms:

(173) Assimilation to a:

e --> a / ___ a

/tl'ǫ̀-da-sə-ah-ɤeh/

a Fronting e
Prefix Vowel Deletion --
Conjugation s Deletion ∅
Assimilation to a a

[tl'ǫ̀dàahɤeh]

First and second person singular forms similarly require an Assimilation to e rule:

(174) Assimilation to e

V --> e / e ___

The rule in (174) will apply not only to the first and second person singular forms in (168a,b) above, but also to forms in which the perfective allomorph ([i]) of the first person singular prefix is present underlyingly, as in (175):

(175) /tse tl'ǫ̀ -də -sə -i   -la/
       rock circle der cnj 1sPf handle pl O
               2   9   10   12   stem

   [tse tl'ǫ̀dèela]   'I put rocks in a circle'

                  /tl'ǫ̀-də-s-i-la/

a Fronting   e
Prefix Vowel Deletion   --
Conjugation s Deletion   ∅
Assimilation to e   e

                  [tl'ǫ̀dèela]

To summarize, the following rules are required to account for these s-conjugation paradigms:

(176) s-conjugation rules

       s-Conjugation a Fronting
       s Deletion
       Assimilation to a
       Assimilation to e

3.2.1.2 Domain of the s-conjugation rules

The data in the preceding section involved an s-conjugation paradigm in which the conjugation prefix was preceded by a prefix of position 9. All position 9 prefixes of the shape /Cə/ undergo the s-conjugation rules, with the sole exception of the /də/ which occurs in 'kindle fire'.[17]

Now consider a paradigm in which the /`sə/ conjugation prefix is preceded by prefixes of positions 7 and 8. In (177a-e), the /`sə/ conjugation prefix is preceded by position 7 /yə/, and in (177f-g), by the position 8 prefixes /ts'ə/ and /ghə/.

(177a) /yə -sə -i   -?às/
       thm cnj 1sPf sneeze
        7   10 12   stem

   [yàsi?às]   'I sneezed'

(177b) /ya -sə -n -ʔàs/
          thm cnj 2sS sneeze
           7 10 12 stem

      [yàsį̀ʔàs]   'you [sg] sneezed'

(177c) /ya -sə -ʔàs/
          thm cnj sneeze
           7 10 stem

      [yàzʔàs]   'he, she sneezed'

(177d) /ya -sə -i -ʔàs/
          thm cnj 1dS sneeze
           7 10 12 stem

      [yasiʔàs]   'we [du] sneezed'

(177e) /ya -sə -a -ʔàs/
          thm cnj 2pPf sneeze
           7 10 12   stem

      [yàsaʔàs]   'you [pl] sneezed'

(177f) /ya -ts'ə-sə -ʔàs/
          thm 1pS   cnj sneeze
           7   8   10 stem

      [yats'əzʔàs]   'we sneezed'

(177g) /ya -ghə-sə -ʔàs/
          thm 3pS cnj sneeze
           7   8 10 stem

      [yaghàzʔàs]   'they sneezed'

The forms in (177) should be compared with those in (168). Notice that none of the s-conjugation rules in (176) have applied to the forms in (177): the s of the conjugation prefix has not been deleted in the first person singular, second person singular or second person plural forms, and the vowel which precedes the conjugation prefix is a, not e, in the non-first person dual forms.

These data indicate that the domain of the s-conjugation rules should be restricted to include the prefixes of position 9 but not those of positions 7 and 8. The leftmost level 2 prefix position is the derivational position, 9:

```
        level 3         level 2
        subject         derivational
        8               9
```

Since s-Conjugation Fronting applies before the other s-Conjugation rules, such as s-Deletion, one might assume that only the domain of s-Conjugation Fronting needs to be restricted to level 2. The other rules would not apply to the prefixes of positions 7 and 8 because their structural descriptions would not be met:

(178)   /yà-sə-n-ʔàs/

s Deletion   --
Assimilation to e   --

                         [yàsį̀ʔàs]   'you [sg] sneezed'

However, there is some evidence against the hypothetical derivation in (178). Other forms indicate that s Deletion, Assimilation to e and Assimilation to a also have restricted domains; in particular, they do not apply on level 5. In (179) and (180), the vowel which precedes the conjugation prefix /'sə/ is [è], yet s Deletion has not applied:

(179) /ɬè -sə -tl'ų/
        in 2 cnj tie
        2   10 stem

       [ɬèsətl'ų]   'he, she tied a knot'

(180) /na -gǫts'èlè-sə -i -h -kah/
        rev elbow   cnj 1sPf clf wound
        5   3   10 11   13 stem

       [nagǫts'èlèsihkah]   'I banged my elbow again'

In (181) and (182), Assimilation to a and Assimilation to e have not applied:

(181) /ʔədəlè e-ah -kwi/
        blood P 2pS vomit
               1 12 stem

       [ʔədəlèʔ eahkwi]   'you [pl] vomited blood'

(182)   /mə -ghǫh-k'e-įji -nə -n -ts'ats/
         3sO P   adv mind thm 2sS think
         1   1   2   3   9   12 stem

        [mǫhk'ei̯jinįts'ats]   'you [sg] think about him'

I assume that all of the s-conjugation rules given in (176) cease to apply after level 2. In fact, however, there is only evidence that Fronting ceases to apply after level 2; the other rules could apply on levels 2, 3 and 4 (but not on level 5).

3.2.2 n-conjugation ə Fronting

Additional evidence that prefix position 9 forms the leftmost edge of level 2 is provided by the n-conjugation.

An n-conjugation paradigm in which the position 9 derivational prefix /də/ precedes the position 10 conjugation prefix /'nə/ is given in (183):

(183a) /che   -chu -də -'nə-s -l -tla/
        into water water der cnj 1sS clf sg/du run
        2   3   9   10 12 13 stem

       [chechudə̀nastla]   'I ran into the water'

(183b) /che   -chu -də -'nə-n -l -tla/
        into water water der cnj 2sS clf sg/du run
        2   3   9   10 12 13 stem

       [chechudə̀nįtla]   'you [sg] ran into the water'

(183c) /che   -chu -də -'nə-l -tla/
        into water water der cnj clf sg/du run
        2   3   9   10 12 13 stem

       [chechudę̀tla]   'he, she ran into the water'

(183d) /che   -chu -sa -də -'nə-i -l -tla/
        into water water 1dS der cnj 1dS clf sg/du run
        2   3   9   10 12 13 stem

       [chechusədənitla]   'we [du] ran into the water'

(183e) /che   -chu -də -'nə-ah -l -tla/
        into water water der cnj 2pS clf sg/du run
        2   3   9   10 12 13 stem

       [chechudə̀nahtla]   'you [pl] ran into the water'

In the third person singular form in (183c), Conjugation a Deletion has applied, and, as a result, the [n] of the conjugation prefix is syllabified as the coda of the preceding syllable. Syllabification feeds the following rule:

(184)
$$a \rightarrow e\ /\ \underset{\text{syll}}{\underline{\qquad}}\ n]^{L}$$

Because Conjugation a Deletion only applies in third person singular forms, n-Conjugation Fronting only applies to third person singular forms:

(185) /che-chu-də-nə-l-tla/

Conjugation a Deletion	∅
Conjugation Tone Mapping	è
n-Conjugation Fronting	e
Nasalization	ę̀

[chechudę̀tla]

The rule of n-Conjugation a Fronting has a restricted domain. Fronting only applies to the [n] alternant of the n-conjugation prefix when the prefix is preceded by a position 9 prefix, and not when [n] is preceded by a prefix further to the left. In (186)-(189), the conjugation prefix /ˈnə/ is preceded by prefixes of positions 7 and 8, and Fronting has not applied:

(186) /ts'e-ghu-ts'ə-nə -h -sit/
       wake 3pO 1pS cnj clf wake up
       2   7   8   10 13 stem

       [ts'eghuts'į̀hsit]   'we wake them up'

(187) /ts'e-sə -ghə-nə -h -sit/
       wake 1sO 3sS cnj clf wake up
       2   7   8   10 13 stem

       [ts'esəghį̀hsit]   'they wake me up'

(188) /ts'e-sə -nə-h -sit/
       wake 1sO cnj clf wake up
       2   7   10 13 stem

       [ts'esį̀hsit]   'he, she wakes me up'

(189) /yə   -chǫ -ʔə -nə -leh/
       4sPsr guts unspO cnj handle pl O
        3   3   7   10 stem

       [yəchǫʔįleh]   'he, she takes its guts out'

Instead, the rule of ə Raising has applied:

(190) ə --> į

Thus (189) is derived as follows:

                    /yə-chǫ-ʔə-nə-leh/

Conjugation ə Deletion   ∅
Nasalization   ę
ə Raising   į

                    [yəchǫʔįleh]

Actually, my data show some variation with respect to the domain of n-Conjugation ə Fronting. At least two of the position 7 prefixes may undergo the rule:

(191) /kǫh sə -gha-wə-n -ʔàh/
       house 1sO P   ar cnj handle compact O
         1   1   7 10 stem

       [kǫh sawę̀ʔàh]   'he, she gives me a house'

(192) /yə -ghǫh-yə -n -h -tsus/
       4sO P   4sO cnj clf handle cloth-like O
        1   1   7 10 13 stem

       [yǫhyę̀htsus]   'he, she gets [cloth-like O] to him, her'

The domain of n-Conjugation ə Fronting thus provides weaker evidence than that of s-Conjugation ə Fronting that the position 9 prefixes define the left edge of level 2. When the conjugation prefix /ˋnə/ is preceded by a position 9 prefix, Fronting always applies; the rule applies sporadically in other phonological domains.

4. Levels 3 and 4

4.1 Morphology

4.1.1 Subject prefixes (position 8)

Three prefixes occur in this position:

/ghə/   animate plural
/ts'ə/   1p, 1d exclusive; unspecified subject (rare)
/sə/   1d inclusive

These prefixes precede the position 9 prefixes except as noted in 3.1.4:

(193a) /ts'ə-nə -d -dayh/
        1pS thm clf dance
        8   9   13 stem

       [ts'anədayh]   'we dance'

(193b) [ghanədayh]   'they dance'

(193c) /sə -nə -ì -d -dayh/
        1dS thm 1dS clf dance
        8   9   12 13 stem

       [sanìdayh]   'we [du] dance'

The first person dual subject is thus marked discontinuously:

    sə   ì   d
    8   12 13

There is a close synchronic connection between the position 8 prefix /sə/ and the position 10 conjugation prefix /'sə/, as noted by Story (1980) for other languages. In first person dual forms s-conjugation forms, these prefixes do not co-occur. Story suggests that the use of /sə/ in first person dual forms is historically derived from the conjugational use of this prefix.

4.1.2 Object prefixes (position 7)

Several prefixes occur in this position. Most of these are inflectional, serving to inflect the verb for person and number of object.

(194)   sg   du   pl

1   sə   naxə   whə /xo/
2   nə   naxə
3   ghu(yə)
4   yə   ghi(yə)

refl   ?adə
recp   ɬa
area   wə /gho/
unsp   ?ə

As discussed by Saxon (1984 (a, b), to appear), the 'fourth person' category is a third person which is interpreted as obligatorily disjoint in reference to another third person argument (see Ch. 4, 4.1). The prefix wə (/gho/) area is a gender prefix. Its occurrence is obligatory if the theme of the sentence refers to an area.[18]

The object prefixes occur to the left of the position 8 subject prefixes:

(195)   /ɬa   -ghə-d -gak/
         recp 3pS clf massage
         7   8   13 stem

        [ɬaghagak]   'they massage each other'

(196)   /ghu-ts'ə-də -i -ts'agh/
         3pO 1pS   thm thm hear
         7   8   9   9   stem

        [ghuts'adits'agh]   'we hear them'

(197)   /?ə -ghə-a -d -bà/
         unspO 3pS cnj clf children, animals eat
         7   8   10 13 stem

        [?aghabà?]   'they ate something'

(198)   /ghuyə-ghə-s -gwət/
         3pO   3pS cnj poke
         7   8   10 stem

        [ghuyaghəzgwət]   'they poked them'

(199)   /wə-sə -i -d -h -tlagh/
         ar 1dS 1dS clf clf rub with medicine
         7 8   12 13 13 stem

        [wasitlagh]   'we [du] rub [area] with medicine'

4.2 Levels 2 and 3 phonology

Most of the phonological rules of (what I will argue are) levels 2, 3 and 4 are identical. The phonological evidence presented in this section will suggest that prefix position 7 forms the leftmost edge of a phonological domain.

4.2.1 Prefix Vowel Deletion
4.2.1.1 Formulation of Prefix Vowel Deletion

The Sekani rule of Prefix Vowel Deletion reduces sequences of vowels to a single vowel. Prefix Vowel Deletion actually consists of two rules:

(200) Prefix Vowel Deletion[19]

    (a) ə Deletion

        ə --> 0 % ___ V

    (b) i Deletion

        i --> 0 % ___ V

ə Deletion precedes i Deletion.

(201) ə + i --> i

    /ts'ə-i -yòɬ/
    1pS asp swell up
    8   9   stem

    [ts'iyòɬ]   'we swell up'

(202) i + i --> i

    /sə -i -i -d -l -yòɬ/
    1dS asp 1dS clf clf swell up
    8   9   12 13 13 stem

    [siyòɬ]   'we [du] swell up'

(203) u + i --> u

    /ghu-i -d -tsəgh/
    Op 1dS clf cry
    11 12 13 stem

    [ghùtsəgh]   'we [du] cry'

(204) ə + a --> a

/də -ah -bàt/
thm 2pS be hungry
 9   12   stem

[dahbàt]   'you [pl] are hungry'

(205) i + a --> a

/i -ah -yòɪ/
asp 2pS swell up
 9   12 stem

[àhyòɪ]   'you [pl] swell up'

(206) ə + u --> u

/ts'ə-u -tòn/
1pS thm hold O
 8   9   stem

[ts'utòn]   'we hold O'

(207) i + u --> u

/i -u -l -yòɪ/
asp Op clf swell up
 9 11 13 stem

[ùyòɪ]   'he, she swells up' Op

A comparison of (203) and (207) indicates that a mirror-image formulation of these rules is required.

Notice that neither of the vowels in the sequence /ua/ is deleted:

(208) u + a --> ua

/u -ah -tòn/
thm 2pS hold O
 9   12 stem

[uahtòn]   'you [pl] hold O'

The preceding data are summarized in (209). Not all combinations of vowels occur:

(209)   i̲   a̲   u̲

         a̲   i   a   u

         i̲   i   a   u

         u̲   u   ua

There is no need for Prefix Vowel Deletion to refer to /e o/. Most occurrences of [e] in prefixes are derived from /a/ by the rules of s̲- and n̲- Conjugation a̲ Fronting. As for [o], all level 2 and 3 instances of [o] are preceded by velar consonants, and there is no reason that the rule of Diphthongization (210), which creates [ə], cannot precede Prefix Vowel Deletion:

(210) o --> wə / velar ___

This interaction of the rules is illustrated in the derivation of [wahts'it] 'you [pl] tell a lie':

(211) /gho-ah -ts'it/
       ar 2pS tell lie
       7   12 stem

                          /gho-ah-ts'it/

Diphthongization   wə
Prefix Vowel Deletion   ∅
Velar Loss   ∅

                          [wahts'it]

4.2.1.2 Domain of Prefix Vowel Deletion

As discussed in 3.2.1, Prefix Vowel Deletion must precede Conjugation s̲ Deletion, a level 2 rule, and, as will be seen in 4.2.4.2, Prefix Vowel Deletion must precede the lexical rule of w̲ Vocalization. Therefore, Prefix Vowel Deletion must also be a lexical rule of at least level 2.

The following data provide additional support for the analysis of Prefix Vowel Deletion as a lexical rule. In general, vowel sequences formed from prefixes of positions 1-5 are not deleted:

(212) i + i --> ii

/na -tsi -ida-sa -d -?ǫ/
der head der cnj clf compact O is in position
 5   3   9   10 13 stem

[natsiidèst'ǫ]   'he, she holds head in hands'

(213) e + i --> ei

/ma -ghǫh-k'e-iji -na -n -ts'ats/
3sO P   adv mind der 2sS think
 1   1   2   3   9 12 stem

[mǫhk'eijinits'ats]   'you [sg] think about him, her'

(214) e + a --> ea

/?adalè e-ah -h -kwi/
blood P 2pS clf vomit
        1 12 13 stem

[?adalè? eahkwi]   'you [pl] vomit blood'

(215) e + u --> eu

/sa -è-u -da -n -jets/
1sO P der der 2sS talk
 1 1 9   9   12 stem

[sèudijets]   'you [sg] talk to me'

        a + i --> ai

(216) /ma -ghǫh-k'e-na -iji -na -s -ts'ats/
3sO P   adv rev mind der 1sS think
 1   1   2   5   3   9 12 stem

[mǫhk'enaijinasts'ats] 'I think about him, her again'

(217) /na -i -gho-n -d -gwat/
rev asp Op 2sS clf poke
 5   9 11 12 13 stem

[naàghǫgwat]   'you [sg] poke O again' Op

(The rule of i Lowering (3.1.4) has applied in (217).)

(218) a + u --> au

/na -i -u -s -gwat/
rev asp Op 1sS poke
 5   9 11 12 stem

[naùsgwat]   'I poke O again' Op

131

In fact, the only vowel sequence formed from prefixes of positions 1-5 which undergoes a deletion rule is /a-a/:

(219) a + a --> a

/nà -ah -h -chèh/
down 2pS clf handle animate O
 2   12 13 stem

[nàhchèh]   'you [pl] lower [animate O]'

These data are summarized in (220). Again, not all possible combinations occur:

(220)   <u>i</u>   <u>a</u>   <u>u</u>

<u>i</u>   ii

<u>e</u>   ei   ea   eu

<u>a</u>   ai   a   au

To account for the reduction of /a-a/ to [a], I posit the rule of <u>a</u> Deletion in (221):

(221) a --> Ø / ___ a

The fact that Prefix Vowel Deletion has not applied in (212)-(218) suggests that vowel sequences formed from a prefix to the left of position 7 lie outside the domain of this rule:

```
                        position 5      position 7
Prefix Vowel Deletion    no              yes
can apply
```

The domain of Prefix Vowel Deletion thus indicates that the prefixes of position 5 and 7 form distinct phonological domains.

4.2.2 Conjugation Tone Mapping

4.2.2.1 Formulation of Conjugation Tone Mapping

Like Prefix Vowel Deletion, the domain of Conjugation Tone Mapping suggests that prefix position 7 forms the left edge of a level.

As Rice (1985, to appear) and Leer (1979) have shown, the conjugation prefixes /ˋsə/ and /ˋnə/ have a tonal as well as a segmental representation. However, the tone of these prefixes never appears on the vowel of the conjugation prefix, as can be seen from (222)-(223), in which the conjugation prefix /ˋsə/ is word-initial, and in which no low tones are present:

(222) /ˋsə-h -chˋegh/
       cnj clf roast O
       10 13 stem

       [sahchˋegh]   'he, she roasted [O]'

(223) /ˋsə-l -tsəl/
       cnj clf be wet
       10 13 stem

       [sahtsəl]   'he, she is wet'

Instead of associating with the vowel of the conjugation prefix, the low tone of the conjugation prefix appears on the vowel of a prefix to its left, as seen in (224)-(227):

(224) /tà-sə -ˋsə-n -h -chèh/
       up 1sO cnj 2sS clf handle animate O
       2 7 10 12 13 stem

       [tàsə̱s̱i̱hchèh]   'you [sg] carry me uphill'

(225) /kǫh   sə -gha-wə-ˋnə-n -?ǫ/
       house 1sO P ar cnj Pf handle compact O
       1   1 7 10 11 stem

       [kǫh sawə̱ṉi?ǫ]   'he, she gave me a house'

(226) /tsəz   yidà -də -ˋnə-s -ɫeh/
       firewood inside wood cnj 1sS handle pl O
       2   9   10 12 stem

       [tsəz yidàdə̱nəsɫeh]   'I carry wood inside'

(227) /nə -tsˋę̀ u -ˋsə-s -l -gèt/
       2sO P   asp cnj 1sS clf crawl
       9   10 12 13 stem

       [natsˋę̀? ù̱səsgèt]   'I crawled to you [sg]'

These facts suggest that the conjugation prefixes have underlying representations in which the tone is not underlyingly linked to the

133

vowel of conjugation prefix, as in (228):

(228) `sə    `nə

The rule of Conjugation Tone Mapping (229) links the tone of the conjugation prefix to a preceding vowel:

(229)
```
         L              L
         ⁄              ⁄
        ⁄              ⁄
     V   sə         V   nə
```

(In addition to Conjugation Tone Mapping, a rule which deletes any unlinked tones (and which I will leave unformulated) is also required, since the tone does not surface in any form (e.g. as downstep) when the conjugation prefix is word-initial.)

4.2.2.2 Domain of Conjugation Tone Mapping

In (224)-(227), the conjugation prefixes were preceded by prefixes of positions 7 and 9. Now consider forms in which /`sə/ and /`nə/ are preceded by a toneless prefix of positions 1-5. (The only prefixes which occur in prefix positions 4 and 6 have underlying low tone.)

(230) /mə -ghǫh-nə -i   -ya/
        3sO P   cnj 1sPf sg goes
         1   10 12   stem

       [mǫhniya]   'I got to him, her walking'

(231) /tan gha-nə -s -get/
        ice P cnj 1sS poke
         1   10 12 stem

       [tan ghanəsget]   'I chisel through ice'

(232) /dah-sə -h -tsùz/
        up cnj clf handle cloth-like O
         2   10 13 stem

       [dasahtsùz]   'he, she hung up [cloth-like O]'

(233) /ts'e-nə -n -h -sat/
        wake cnj 2sS clf wake up
         2   10 12 13   stem

       [ts'eni̜hsət]   'you [sg] woke up [O]'

134

(234)   /na -sə -s -d -kwi/
        rev cnj 1sS clf vomit
         5 10 12 13 stem

        [nasaskwi]   'I vomited'

(235)   /ts'e-na -na -s -d -zit/
        wake rev cnj 1sS clf wake up
         2   5 10 12 13 stem

        [ts'enanasdzit]   'I wake up again'

In the preceding forms, which contain prefixes of positions 1-5, the tone of the conjugation prefix does not appear on the vowel of the preceding prefix. These data suggest that prefixes to the left of position 7 are not within the domain of Conjugation Tone Mapping, just as positions 1-5 prefixes are outside the domain of Prefix Vowel Deletion:

position	5	7
Prefix Vowel Deletion	no	yes
Cnj Tone Map	no	yes

4.2.3 L Deletion

4.2.3.1 Formulation of L Deletion

Four low tone prefixes are found among the prefixes of positions 7-12:

(236)   i   1d subject   (position 12)
        `sə conjugation   (position 10)
        `na conjugation   (position 10)
        ì   derivational   (position 9)

When two of these low tone prefixes co-occur in a given verb form, only one tone is present in phonetic forms. The leftmost tone is deleted by the rule of L Deletion:

(237)   L Deletion

        L --> ∅ / ___ L

This rule can only be illustrated for forms which contain /ì/ 1d subject and one of the conjugation prefixes /`sə/ and /`na/:[20]

(238a) /kwə̀n na -də -ˋsə-i   -d -h -k'ǫ/
       fire   rev thm cnj 1dS clf clf kindle fire
              5   9   10 12 13 13 stem

       [kwə̀n nadəsik'ǫ]   'we [du] kindled a fire'

      *[kwə̀n nadə̀sik'ǫ]

(238b) /kwə̀n na -də -ˋsə-i   -h -k'ǫ/
       fire rev thm cnj 1sPf clf kindle fire
            5   9   10 12 13 stem

       [kwə̀n nadə̀sihk'ǫ]   'I kindled a fire'

(239a) /che   -chu -sə -də -ˋnə-i   -d -?ats/
       into water water 1dS der cnj 1dS clf du go
       2   3   8   9   10 12 13 stem

       [chechusədanit'ats]   'we [du] walked into the water'
      *[chechusədànit'ats]

(239b) /che   -chu -də -ˋnə-n -ya/
       into water water der cnj Pf sg go
       2   3   9   10 11 stem

       [chechudə̀nįya]   'he, she walked into the water'

The non-occurring forms in (238a) and (239a) are those that would be expected if L Deletion had not applied. The (b) forms given for comparison indicate that there is nothing exceptional about the prefixes which precede the conjugation prefixes in these forms with respect to Conjugation Tone Mapping.

4.2.3.2 Domain of L Deletion

The rule of L Deletion indicates not only that prefixes to the left of position 7 form a distinct phonological domain, but that stems and prefixes form distinct phonological domains.

L Deletion has a restricted domain. This is obvious from the fact that there exist surface forms in which more than one low tone occurs. For example, the tone of the four low tone prefixes in (236) is preserved before a stem which has low tone:

(240) /sə -i -d -jih/
 1dS 1dS clf breathe
 8   12 13 stem

 [sijih]   'we [du] breathe'

(241) /i -h -t'às/
 asp clf shoot O with bow and arrow
 9   13 stem

 [iht'às]   'he, she shoots [O] with bow and arrow'

(242) /kǫh sə -gha-wə-'nə-ʔàh/
 house 1sO P ar cnj handle compact O
       1   1   7 10 stem

 [kǫh sawę̀ʔàh]   'he, she gives me a house'

(243) /tà-sə -'sə-n -h -chèh/
 up 1sO cnj 2sS clf handle animate O
 2 7   10 12 13 stem

 [tàsàsįhchèh]   'you [sg] carry me uphill'

The low tone which precedes the low tone stem has not been deleted in these data, indicating that low tone stems are outside the domain of L Deletion. The revised version of L Deletion in (244) will ensure that no stem tones trigger the deletion of low tones in prefixes:

(244) L Deletion

 L --> ∅ / ___ L [stem]

Only low tones which occur to the left of the stem can trigger L Deletion.

Now consider sequences of low tones in prefixes. Prefixes of positions 1-6 neither trigger nor undergo L Deletion. Forms in which a low tone prefix from positions 1-6 precedes one of the four low tone level 2 prefixes are given in (245)-(247) (and in (243) above):

(245) /tsəz yidà -də -nə -leh/
 firewood inside wood cnj handle pl O
          2   9   10 stem

 [tsəz yidàdęleh]   'he, she carries wood inside'

(246)   /ɣè -sə -i -d -tl'ų̀h/
        in 2 1dS 1dS clf tie
        2 8 12 13 stem

        [ɣèsitl'ų̀h]   'we [du] tie a knot'

(247)   /whè -nə -i -d -yhən/
        incp der der clf sing
        6   9   9 13 stem

        [whènijin]   'he, she started to sing'

The leftmost tone has not been deleted. Next consider the forms (248)-(250), in which two low tone prefixes from positions 1-6 are present:

(248)   /nà -tsi -də-ghəs/
        adv head thm nod?
        2   3   9   stem

        [nàtsidaghəs]   'he, she shakes his, her head "no"'

(249)   /nà -dà -nə -chį̀h/
        down dstr 2sS handle stick-like O
        2   4   12 stem

        [nà̱dànachį̀h]   'you [sg] lower [stick-like Os], one by one'

(250)   /dah-dà -whè -ts'ə-nə -i -n -tl'ų́/
        up dstr incp 1pS der der Pf tie
        2   4   6   8   9   9   11 stem

        [dadà̱whèts'anį̀tl'ų́]   'we started to set snares, one by one'

L Deletion has also not applied to the leftmost tone in these forms.

Both sets of data indicate that prefixes of positions 1-6 are not within the domain of L Deletion:

	prefixes 1-6	9-12	stems
trigger or undergo L Deletion	no	yes	no

4.2.4 Vocalization

4.2.4.1 Formulation of Vocalization

As briefly discussed in 3.1.2, the optative prefix /gho/ has various surface forms. In certain first and third person singular forms, the application of Diphthongization, repeated below in (251), creates the intermediate representation [ghwə]:

(251) Diphthongization

o --> wə / velar ___ (C) ,   C ≠ Y, n

The following examples, in which the optative prefix is word-initial, illustrate Diphthongization. (Recall that the rule of Velar Loss applies to [ghw] and [xw] to produce surface [w] and [wh], respectively.)

(252) /gho-d -yhan/
      Op clf sing

      [wajin]   'he, she sings' Op

                          /gho-d-yhan/
D-Effect Rule   j
Diphthongization   wə
Velar Loss   ∅

                          [wajin]

(253) /gho-s -h -yhòY/
      Op 1sS clf blow on O
      11 12 13 stem

      [wasyhòY]   'I blow on [O]' Op

(254) /gho-s -tsagh/
      Op 1sS cry
      11 12 stem

      [watsagh]   'he, she cries' Op

When preceded by a prefix of positions 7-9, the phonetic form of the optative prefix is not [wə], but [u]. I posit a rule which vocalizes [ghwə] to [u] in such cases:

(255) Vocalization

      ghwə --> u / V ___

(256) /?ə -ghwə-s -h -xǫh/
      unspO Op 1sS clf snore
      7   11 12 1d stem

      [?usxǫh]   'I snore' Op

                              /?ə-gho-s-h-xǫh/

Diphthongization   wə
w Vocalization   u
Prefix Vowel Deletion   ∅

                              [?usxǫh]

(257)   /?adə-də-ghwə-d -ts'àt/
         refl   Op   clf scratch
          7   9   11   13   stem

        [?adaduts'àt]   'he, she scratches him-, herself' Op

(258)   /ts'ə-ghwə-d -yhən/
         1pS   Op   clf sing
          8   11   13   stem

        [ts'ujin]   'we sing' Op

(258)   /ts'ə-ghwə-d -yhən/
         1pS   Op   clf sing
          8   11   13   stem

        [ts'ujin]   'we sing' Op

(256)   /?ə -ghwə-s -h -xǫh/
         unspO Op   1sS clf snore
          7   11   12   1d stem

        [?usxǫh]   'I snore' Op

(259)   /ghə-ghwə-h -yhòY/
         3pS   Op   clf blow on O
          8   11   13   stem

        [ghuhyhòY]   'they blow on [O]' Op

(260)   /zə -wə-s -h -xeY/
         thm Op 1sS clf kill sg O
          9   11 12 13   stem

        [zusxeY]   'I kill [sg O]' Op

(261)   /i -wə-gwət/
         asp Op poke
          9   11 stem

        [ugwət]   'he, she pokes [O] once' Op

The structural description of Vocalization is met only in first and third person singular forms. (These are also the only optative forms in which Diphthongization applies.) Notice that, in the following second person plural

                                140

forms, Vocalization is bled by Prefix Vowel Deletion:

(262) /za -gho-ah -h -xeɣ/
      thm Op 2pS clf kill sg O
      9   11   12 13 stem

      [zawahxeɣ]   'you [pl] kill [sg O]' Op

                /za-gho-ah-h-xeɣ/

Diphthongization   wə
Prefix Vowel Deletion   Ø
w Vocalization   --
Velar Loss   Ø

                [zawahxeɣ]

(263) /nə -ghwa-ah -?įh/
      term Op 2pS steal O
      9   11   12 stem

      [nawah?įh]   'you [pl] steal O' Op

(In first and third person singular forms, Vocalization feeds Prefix Vowel Deletion. See Ch. 7.)

4.2.4.2 Domain of Vocalization

    Vocalization has a restricted domain. In examples (256)-(261) above, the optative prefix is preceded by a prefix of positions 7-9. However, in (262)-(265), a vowel-final prefix of positions 1-5 precedes the optative prefix, and in these forms, Vocalization does not apply:

(262) /?ədalè e-ghwa-h -kwi/
      blood P Op clf vomit
           1 11   13 stem

      [?ədalè? ewahkwi]   'he, she vomits blood' Op

(263) /nà -ghwa-s -h -chèɣ/
      down Op 1sS clf lower animate O
      2   11   12 13 stem

      [nàwaschèɣ]   'I lower [ani-mate O]' Op

(264) /ts'ah t'à -tsi -wa-l -?atl/
       hat inside head Op clf compact O be in position
              1   3   11 13 stem

       [ts'ah t'àtsiwa?atl]   'he, she wears a hat on his, her head'

(265) /na -wa-s -d -kwi/
       rev Op 1sS clf vomit
        5   11 12 13 stem

       [nawaskwi]   'I vomit' Op

The optative prefix is phonetically [wə] in these forms, just as in forms where it is word-initial. These data suggest that the prefixes of positions 1-5 and those of positions 7-9 belong to different phonological domains:

                         position 5   position 7
Vocalization can apply   no   yes

4.2.5 Conjugation a Deletion

The domain of this rule also suggests that prefix position 7 marks the left edge of a phonologically-defined level. However, while the domain of this rule as applied to /ghə/ is unproblematic, the application of the rule to the conjugation prefixes /'sə/ and /'nə/ is quite a bit messier.

4.2.5.1 Formulation of Conjugation a Deletion

As mentioned in 3.1.3, the vowel of the conjugation and mode prefixes /'sə 'nə ghə/ is deleted by the following rule:

$$(266) \quad ə \rightarrow \emptyset / V \begin{Bmatrix} s \\ n \\ gh \end{Bmatrix} \_\_\_ [\,(clf)\,stem]$$

Evidence for the rule in (266) is provided by the following alternations: [sə]~[s], [nə]~[n] and [ghə]~[a]. As the following examples will show, Conjugation a Deletion fails to occur if a position 11 (mode) or 12 (subject) prefix is present: the rule only applies in forms in which no prefix intervenes between the conjugation or mode prefix and the optional classifier prefix.

First consider alternations which involve the conjugation prefix /'sə/. In (267) and (268), this prefix is preceded by a prefix of positions 7-9. In (267a,b) and (268a), Conjugation ə Deletion has applied. However, in (267c) and (268b), Conjugation ə Deletion cannot apply because a subject prefix (1s /s/ and 2p /ah/, respectively) is present.

(267a) /chu -na -ʔə -'sə-d -k'àts/
　　　　water rev unspO cnj clf wash O
　　　　 3   5   7   10 13 stem

　　　　[chunaʔəsk'àts]　　　'he, she washed [O]'

(267b) /chu -na -ʔə -ts'ə-'sə-d -k'àts/
　　　　water rev unspO 1pS cnj clf wash O
　　　　 3   5   7   8   10 13 stem

　　　　[chunaʔats'əsk'àts]　　'we washed [O]'

(267c) /chu -na -ʔə -'sə-s -d -k'àts/
　　　　water rev unspO cnj 1sS clf wash O
　　　　 3   5   7   10 12 13 stem

　　　　[chunaʔəsəsk'àts]　　'I washed [O]'

(268a) /ts'ę̀ u -'sə-l -tleh/
　　　　P asp cnj clf sg/du run
　　　　 9   10 13 stem

　　　　-[ts'ę̀ʔ ùstleh]　　'he, she runs to [O]'

(268b) /ts'ę̀ u -'sə-ah -l -tleh/
　　　　P asp cnj 1sS clf sg/du run
　　　　 9   10 12 13 stem

　　　　-[ts'ę̀ ùsahtleh]　　'you [pl] run to [O]'

An alternative explanation for the failure of Conjugation ə Deletion to apply in forms like (268b) might be as follows: Conjugation ə Deletion, like w Vocalization, might be bled by Prefix Vowel Deletion. However, while this will account for second person plural and first person dual forms, it will clearly not explain why Conjugation ə Deletion fails to apply in first person singular forms (cf. w Vocalization).

Alternations between [nə] and [n], illustrating the application of this rule to the conjugation prefix /'nə/, are given in (269)-(270):

(269a) /sa -gha-wa-'na-?àh/
   1sO P ar cnj handle compact O
    1 7 10 stem

   [sawe̲?àh]   'he, she gives me [areal O]'

(269b) /ma -gha-wa-ts'a-'na-?àh/
   3sO P ar 1pS cnj handle compact O
    1 1 7 8 10 stem

   [mawats'i̲?àh]   'we give him, her [areal O]'

(269c) /sa -gha-wa-'na-n -?o̲/
   1sO P ar cnj Pf handle compact O
    1 7 10 11 stem

   [sawàni̲?o̲]   'he, she gave me [areal O]'

(270a) /yidà -da -'na-leh/
   inside wood cnj handle pl O
    2   9 10 stem

   [yidàde̲leh]   'he, she carries [pl wooden O] inside'

(270b) /yidà -da -'na-n -leh/
   inside wood cnj 2sS handle pl O
    2   9 10 12 stem

   [yidàdàni̲leh]   'you [sg] carry [pl wooden O] inside'

Conjugation ə Deletion has not applied in (269c) because the perfective prefix /n/ intervenes between the conjugation prefix and the stem. Similarly, in (270b), the presence of the second person singular subject prefix [n] prevents the rule from applying.

  Alternations between [ghə] and [a] are illustrated in (272)-(273). The additional rule of Gamma Lowering in (271) applies to [gh] following the application of Conjugation ə Deletion:

(271) Gamma Lowering

   gh --> a / ___ [(clf) stem]

(272a) /ʔə   -ghə-d -bà/
       unspO cnj clf children, animals eat
       7   10 13   stem

       [ʔabà?]   'he, she ate something'

                    /ʔə-ghə-d-bà/

Conjugation a Deletion   ∅
Gamma Lowering   a
Prefix Vowel Deletion   ∅

                    [ʔabà?]

(272b) /ʔə   -ts'a-ghə-d -bà/
       unspO 1pS cnj clf children, animals eat
       7   8   10 13   stem

       [ʔats'abà?]   'we ate something'

(272c) /ʔə   -ghə -s -d-bà/
       unspO cnj 1sS clf children, animals eat
       7   10   12 13   stem

       [ʔaghasbà?]   'I ate something'

(273a) /də -i -ghə-l -yòɤ/
       Fut thm Fut clf swell up
       9   9   11 13   stem

       [dàyòɤ]   'he, she will swell up'

(273b) /də -i -ghə -n -l -yòɤ/
       Fut thm Fut 2sS clf swell up
       9   9   11 12 13 stem

       [dàghiyòɤ]   'you [sg] will swell up'

I will return to the formulation of this rule in Ch. 5, 3.1.

4.2.5.2 Domain of Conjugation a Deletion

First I will illustrate the domain of Conjugation a Deletion as applied to the prefix /ghə/. Then I will discuss the more complicated facts involving /`sə/ and /`nə/.

4.2.5.2.1 /ghə/

Conjugation a Deletion does not apply when /ghə/ is word-initial (as in

274-275) or preceded by a prefix of positions 1-5 (276-279).

(274) [sas ghə-ʔį]   'he, she sees a bear'
     bear cnj see
          10 stem

(275) [ghə-beɫ]   'he, she is swimming'
     Prg swim
     10 stem

(276) /yə -tʼà -ghə-1 -goɫ/
     4sO P:inside Prg clf crawl
     1   1   10 13 stem

     [yatʼàghagòɫ]   'he, she is crawling inside it'

(277) /nà -ghə-d -tsʼət/
     down cnj clf sg/du fall
     2   10 13 stem

     [nàghatsʼət]   'he, she fell down'

(278) /tsʼah tʼà -na -tsi -ghə-d -ʔatl/
     hat   inside rev head cnj clf handle compact O
               2   5   3   10 13 stem

     [tsʼah tʼǫ̀tsighətʼatl] 'he, she put a hat back on'

(279) /na -ghə-d -daɫ/
     rev Prg clf sg go
     5   10 13 stem

     [naghədaɫ]   'he, she is going back'

In (276)-(279), the surface form of this prefix is [ghə], not [a], although it is preceded by a vowel-final prefix. These data suggest that prefixes of positions 5 and further to the left are outside the domain of Conjugation ə Deletion.

4.2.5.2.2 /ˊsə/ and /ˊnə/

The data which illustrate the domain of Conjugation ə Deletion as applied to /ˊsə/ and /ˊnə/ are quite a bit more complicated. When /ˊsə/ and /ˊnə/ are preceded by a prefix of positions 1-5 or are vowel-initial, Conjugation ə Deletion sometimes applies. The circumstances under which this may occur are not entirely clear, but the available data indicate that at least the following factors are relevant:

    choice of mode: imperfective or perfective
    choice of classifier prefix
    segmental shape of level 5 prefix (vowel- or consonant-final)

The significance of the latter factor is particularly unclear, due to my incomplete data. Thus, in what follows, I will only illustrate the surface forms of the conjugation prefixes /`sə/ and /`nə/ taking into consideration the first two factors.

First consider /`sə/. In perfective, ∅- or h-classifier forms in which the conjugation prefix is word-initial or preceded by a level 5 prefix, Conjugation a Deletion does not apply:

(280) [sə -ch'ǫ]   'he, she shot [O] dead'
     cnj shoot O dead
     10 stem

(281) /sə -h -ch'egh/
     cnj clf roast
     10 13 stem

     [sahch'egh]   'he, she roasted [O]'

(282) [Yè -sə -tl'ų]   'he, she tied a knot'
     in 2 cnj tie
     2 10 stem

(283) /dəltsogh e-sə -h -kwi/
     bile   P cnj clf vomit
            1 10 13 stem

     [dəltsogh esahkwi] 'he, she vomited bile'

These data are just as predicted by the analysis: Conjugation a Deletion has not applied in these forms.

However, in s-perfective forms which contain the /d/ classifier, application of Conjugation a Deletion occurs when the conjugation prefix is word-initial or preceded by a level 4 prefix:

(284) /ə -s -d -ji/
     epen cnj clf breathe
         10 13 stem

     [asji]   'he, she breathed'

(285) /na -s -d -kwi/
       rev cnj clf vomit
        5 10 13 stem

       [naskwi]   'he, she vomited'

If the classifier is */l/ (/d-h/) instead of /d/, deletion fails to occur if the conjugation prefix is word-initial, and is optional if the conjugation prefix is preceded by a level 5 prefix:

(286) /sə -l -tsəl/
       cnj clf wet
       10 13 stem

       [sahtsəl]   'he, she is wet'[21]

(287) /ka-nà -sə -l -dzàt/
        P cont cnj clf hunt
        1 2   10 13 stem

       -[kanàhdzàt]   'he, she hunted for [O]'
   =   -[kanàsədzàt]

The s-perfective forms in (280)-(287) are summarized below:

(288) | word-initial /'sə/ | /'sə/ preceded by level 5 prefix | classifier |
       |--------------------|----------------------------------|------------|
       | sə | sə | ∅ |
       | sə | sə | h |
       | s | s | d |
       | sə | s~sə | l |

The facts concerning the application of Conjugation a Deletion in s-imperfective forms are slightly less complicated because there are no s-imperfective forms in my data in which the conjugation prefix /'sə/ is word-initial.

Conjugation a Deletion applies to s-imperfective forms in which /'sə/ is preceded by a prefix of positions 1-5 and which contain ∅, h, or d classifier prefixes:

(289) [tà-s -kèh]   'he, she goes ashore'
       up cnj travel by boat
        2 10 stem

148

(290) /tà-s -h -tsus/
       up cnj clf handle cloth-like O
       2 10 13 stem

       [tàhtsus]   'he, she carries [cloth-like O] uphill'

(291) /tǫ-na -s -d -dah/
       up rev cnj clf sg/du go
       2 5 10 13 stem

       [tǫnasdah]   'he, she goes back uphill'

However, in forms which contain the *l classifier, no deletion occurs:

(292) /tà-sə -l -tleh/
       up cnj clf sg/du run
       2 10 13 stem

       [tàsətleh]   'he, she runs uphill'

These data are summarized below:

(293) /'sə/ preceded by: classifier
       level 5 prefix |
       ------------------- | ------------
       s | ∅
       s | h
       s | d
       sə | l

The application of Conjugation a Deletion to /'na/ is similarly complicated. Just as for /'sə/, Conjugation a Deletion tends to apply in ∅, h or d classifier forms, but not in l classifier verbs. I have no examples of n-conjugation forms in which the conjugation prefix is word-initial.

∅- and h-classifier n-perfective forms are not possible inputs to Conjugation a Deletion because the perfective prefix /n/ is present. (Cf. (269c) above.) However, in d and l classifier verbs, the perfective prefix is absent and thus Conjugation a Deletion is potentially applicable. In d classifier verbs, Conjugation a Deletion is optional:

(294) /Ɨàts'ę̀ nè -na -d -ji/
       cease adv cnj clf breathe
                 2 10 13 stem

       [Ɨàts'ę̀? nęji]   'he, she stopped breathing'

     = [Ɨàts'ę̀? nènaji]

149

In l classifier verbs, Conjugation a Deletion does not apply:

(295)   /yidà -nə -l -tla/
        inside cnj clf sg/du run
        2   10 13 stem

        [yidànatla]   'he, she ran inside'

In n-imperfective forms, Conjugation a Deletion occurs if the verb contains a 0 or h classifier:

(296)   /yhèɬ nè -nə -leh/
        trap ground cnj handle pl O
                    2   10   stem

        [yhèɬ nèleh]   'he, she sets traps'

(297)   /ts'e-nə -h -sit/
        wake cnj clf
        2   10 13 stem

        [ts'ęhsit]   'he, she wakes up [O]'

If the classifier is d, deletion is optional:

(298)   /ts'e-nə -na -d -zit/
        wake rev cnj clf
        2   5   10 13 stem

        [ts'enanadzit]
    =   [ts'enǫdzit]   'he, she wakes up again'

If the classifier is l, deletion does not occur:

(299)   /yidà -nə -l -tleh/
        inside cnj clf sg/du run
        2   10 13 stem

        [yidànatleh]   'he, she runs inside'

The n-imperfective and -perfective data are summarized below:

(300)

imperfective	perfective	classifier
n	--	0
n	--	h
n~nə	n~nə	d
nə	nə	l

4.2.5.2.3 Domain of Conjugation a Deletion: Summary

The data presented in 4.2.5.2.2 indicate that Conjugation a Deletion sometimes applies when the conjugation prefix /`sə/ or /`nə/ is preceded by a level 4 prefix or is word-initial. These complicated facts contrast with the completely regular application of Conjugation a Deletion to forms containing /ghə/ in which this prefix is preceded by a prefix of positions 7-9, as illustrated in 4.2.5.1. In any analysis, one would need to distinguish the levels 2-4 and level 5 applications of Conjugation a Deletion as applied to /`sə/ and /`nə/. In the analysis proposed here, I have simply collapsed the regular levels 2-4 application of Conjugation a Deletion to /`sə/ and /`nə/ with that for /ghə/. A separate (set of) Conjugation a Deletion rule(s) (which I have left unformulated) is needed to describe the complicated facts which result from level 5 and word-initial applications of this rule to /`sə/ and /`nə/.

4.2.6 nə Absorption

Within the verbal prefixes of positions 7-12, there are two prefixes of the shape /nə/ which alternate with [n] when preceded by vowel-final prefixes of certain positions. The distribution of this alternation provides evidence that the prefixes of position 5 and 7 belong to two separate phonological domains.

The position 12 second person singular subject prefix is phonetically [nə] when word-initial:

(301) [nə -wə̀se]   'you [sg] itch'
       2sS itch
       12   stem

(302) /nə -d -jih/
       2sS clf breathe
       12 13 stem

       [najih]   'you [sg] breathe'

Similarly, one of the position 9 derivational prefixes is phonetically [nə] when word-initial:

(303)   [nə -tsį?]   'he, she is bad'
         der bad
         12 stem

(304)   /nə -tsə̀dlazi/
         der small
         12 stem

         [nətsə̀dlazi]   'he, she is small'

These data suggest that these prefixes are underlyingly /nə/.

When these prefixes are preceded by vowel-final prefixes of positions 5-9, they surface as nasalization of the preceding vowel. In such cases, the rule of nə Absorption in (305) has applied, creating syllable-final [n] from the prefixes /nə/:

(305)   nə Absorption

         ə --> ∅ / V n ___

nə Absorption then feeds Nasalization (and may also feed Raising if the preceding vowel is /ə/). Data in which the [n] alternants of these prefixes occur are provided in (306)-(316):

    /nə/ 2s subject

(306)   /?ə -nə -d -bà/
         unspO 2sS clf children, animals eat
         7   12   13 stem

         [?įbà?]   'you [sg] eat something'

                             /?ə-nə-d-bà/

Absorption   n
Nasalization   ə̨
ə Raising   i
D-Effect Rule   ∅

                        [?įbà?]

(307)   /na -nə -d -kwi/
        rev 2sS clf vomit
         5   12 13 stem

        [nǫkwi]   'you [sg] vomit'

(308)   /sə -nə -h -whàse/
        1sO 2sS clf tickle O
         7   12 13 stem

        [sįhwhàse]   'you [sg] tickle me'

(309)   /ya i -nə -tsèɬ/
        sky der 2sS handle compact O carelessly
             9   12 stem

        [ya itsèɬ]   'you [sg] throw [compact O] into the air'

(310)   /sə -nə -d -dli/
        cnj 2sS clf animate be cold
        10   12 13 stem

        [sidli]   'you [sg] are cold'

(311)   /də -ghə-nə -tsaz/
        thm cnj 2sS be shaky
         9 10 12 stem

        [dəghitsaz]   'you [sg] were shaky'

(312)   /gho-nə -tsagh/
        Op 2sS cry
        11 12 stem

        [ghǫtsagh]   'you [sg] cry' Op

(313)   /mə -è-də -ghə-nə -tsaɬ -e/
        3sO P Fut Fut 2sə chase O Fut
         1   1 9 11 12 stem

        [mèdəghitsaɬe]   'you [sg] will chase [O]'

        /nə/ derivational:

(314)   /gho-nə -chà/
        ar thm big
         7   9 stem

        [ghǫchà?]   '[area] is big'

153

(315) /ts'ə-nə -tsį́/
       1pS thm bad
        8   9   stem

       [ts'įtsį́?]   'we are bad'

(316) /ghə-nə -tsə̀dlazi/
       3pS thm small
        8   9   stem

       [ghį̀tsə̀dlazi]   'they are small'

   In the preceding examples, /nə/ is preceded by a prefix of positions 5-
11. However, when /nə/ is preceded by a prefix of positions 1-4, <u>nə</u>
Absorption does not apply:

(317) /xəda ka-nə -l -dzə̀t/
       moose P 2sS clf hunt
               1 12 13 stem

       [xəda kanədzə̀t]   'you [sg] hunt down a moose'

(318) /xəda ka-nà -nə -l -dzə̀t/
       moose P cont 2sS clf hunt
               1   2   12 13 stem

       [xəda kanə̀nədzə̀t]   'you [sg] hunt for a moose'

(319) /ɫè -nə -tl'ų́h/
       in 2 2sS tie
        2   12 stem

       [ɫènətl'ų́h]   'you [sg] tie a knot'

(320) /chu sə -gha kà   -nə -ya/
       water 1sO P   contained O 2sS sg go
                       3   12 stem

       [chu sa kànəya]   'you [sg] fetch water for me'

(321) /xa -nə -dzis/
       hair 2sS pluck
         3   12 stem

       [xanədzis]   'you [sg] pluck out [O]'

(322) /nà -dà -nə -chį̀h/
       down dstr 2sS handle stick-like O
         2   4   12 stem

       [nà dà nachį̀h]   'you [sg] lower [stick-like O's], one by one'

These data suggest that prefix positions 1-4 and 5-12 form separate

154

phonological domain for the purposes of this rule. The inclusion of prefix 5 with the prefixes of positions 7-12 comes as a surprise, given the other data that have been presented throughout 4.2, in which prefix position 5 has patterned with prefixes to its left, rather than to its right. One way to account for the application of this rule to the position 5 na prefixes would be to formulate a level 5 rule of Absorption, which would be triggered only by na in position 5.

Two additional complications to the rule of Absorption must be mentioned. The first complication is easily accommodated. If the derivational prefix u precedes na, Absorption does not apply:

(323) [u   -na -tòn]
       der 2sS hold O
       9   12   stem   'you [sg] hold [O]'

(324) /u   -na -h   -ch'às/
       thm 2sS clf hook
       9   12   13   stem

       [unahch'às]   'you [sg] go fishing'

Absorption is accordingly revised:

(325) na Absorption

       a --> ∅ / V n ___ V ≠ u

The second complication is more messy. The prefixes which undergo the rule of na Absorption must be distinguished from other derivational and conjugation prefixes with the segmental underlying representation /na/ which do not alternate with n. I propose to do this by means of an arbitrary feature [+A(bsorption)].[22]

I leave open the question of whether or not Conjugation a Deletion and na Absorption should be collapsed.

4.2.7 Levels 2, 3 and 4 phonology: Summary

Many rules whose structural descriptions specify that a vowel precede the focus of the rule fail to apply when the vowel belongs to a prefix of positions 1-5. A summary of the domains of these sorts of rules is provided below:

(326) Domains of levels 2-4 phonological rules

prefix position:	1	2	3	4	5	6	7	8	9	10	11	12
level:					5		4-2					
Conjugation Tone Mapping	no	no	no	-	no	-	y	y	y	y		
L Deletion	no	no	no	no	no	no	-	-	y	y	-	y
w Vocalization	no	no	no	no	no	-	y	y	y	-	y	
na Absorption	no	no	no	no	y	-	y	y	y	y	y	y
Conjugation a Deletion	no	no	no	-	no	-	y	y	y	y	y	

    no = not within domain of rule

    y = within domain of rule

    - = does not meet structural description of rule
        or no available example

The domains of the rules of Conjugation Tone Mapping, w Vocalization and Conjugation Tone Mapping suggest that a major phonological boundary or, in present terms, difference in level assignment separates the prefixes of positions 1-5 from those of positions 7-9. The domain of L Deletion indicates that prefix position 6 patterns with positions 1-5. Thus the phonological evidence presented here suggests that prefix positions 6 and 7 belong to different levels.

    Some data which are problematic for this analysis have been encountered. The prefixes of position 5 pattern with those of positions 7-11 with respect to the application of na Absorption. Conjugation a Deletion sometimes applies on level 5 to the conjugation prefixes /`sa/ and /`na/. Thus in these cases, affix order and phonological rule domains fail to match up. But given the overwhelming evidence from the other rules for the proposed level ordering distinction, it seems clear that these are to be treated as exceptions.

4.3 Level 3 vs. 4 phonology

The position 7 prefix ?ə unspecified object and the position 8 prefixes ts'ə and ghə share certain phonological properties with adjacent positions 7-9 prefixes, but they appear to constitute their own phonological domain, level 4, as they fall outside the domain of Conjugation Tone Mapping, a rule which normally applies to the position 7-9 prefixes.

4.3.1 Similarities of ?ə, ts'ə and ghə to other positions 7-9 prefixes

As seen in previous sections, the prefixes ?ə, ts'ə and ghə have a number of phonological characteristics in common with the other position 7-9 prefixes which clearly distinguish them from prefixes further to the left. For example, they are within the domains of Vocalization (327)-(328), Conjugation ə Deletion (329), and Prefix Vowel Deletion (330)-(331):

(327)   /ts'ə-ghwə-d -yhən/
         1pS   Op   clf sing
          8   11   13 stem

        [ts'ujin]   'we sing' Op

(328)   /?ə -ghwə-s -h -xǫh/
         unspO Op   1sS clf snore
          7   11   12 1d stem

        [?usxǫh]   'I snore' Op

(329)   /chu -na -?ə -ghə -'sə-d -k'ə̀ts/
         water rev unspO 3pS cnj clf wash O
          3   5   7   8   10 13 stem

        [chunə?əghəsk'ə̀ts]   'they washed [O]'

(330)   /ts'ə-ł -yòł/
         1pS asp swell up
          8   9 stem

        [ts'iyòł]   'we swell up'

(331) /ts'ə-u -tòn/
       1pS thm hold O
        8   9   stem

       [ts'utòn]   'we hold O'

The prefixes ?ə, ts'ə and ghə appear to pattern phonologically like the position 7 object prefixes, in that they are outside the domain of s-Conjugation ə Fronting:

(332) /xwə-ghə-'sə-ch'ǫ/
       1pO-3pS-cnj-shoot
        7   8   10 stem

       [whaghazch'ǫ]   'they shot us dead'

(333) /wə-ts'ə-'sə-h-tləgh/
       ar-1pS-cnj-clf-lubricate
        7   8   10 13 stem

       [wats'ahtləgh]   'we rubbed area [with medicine]'

These data suggest that the deictic subject and the direct object prefixes constitute a single phonological domain; namely, one on which Fronting does not apply.

Positional evidence seems to confirm this analysis. The prefixes ?ə, ts'ə and ghə do not constitute their own position class, but appear in the midst of positions 7-9 prefixes. The unspecified object prefix ?ə occurs in the direct object prefix position (7), and the deictic subject prefixes ts'ə and ghə occur to the right of the direct object prefixes in prefix position 8, (although, in surface forms, the deictic subject prefixes ts'ə and ghə are separated from the direct object prefixes by the homophonous thematic prefixes ts'ə and ghə). Given the strong correlation between affix order and phonological rule domains which exists in Sekani, it would be expected that ?ə, ts'ə and ghə would behave phonologically like the prefixes which surround them.

4.3.2 ʔə, tsʼə, ghə and the domain of Conjugation Tone Mapping

However, ʔə, tsʼə and ghə differ from the other level 3 prefixes with respect to the domain of Conjugation Tone Mapping.[23] As illustrated above in 4.2.2, only positions 7-9 prefixes can bear the tone of the conjugation prefixes /ˈnə/ and /ˈsə/; the tones of these conjugation prefixes do not surface if a positions 1-5 prefix precedes the conjugation prefix. However, unlike other prefixes of positions 7-9, ʔə, tsʼə and ghə are not possible conjugation tone bearers:

(334)   /ghə-ˈsə-chʼo̜/
       3pS cnj shoot
       8   10 stem

       [ghəzchʼo̜]   'they shot (O) dead'

(335)   /chu -na -ʔə -ˈsə-d -kʼə̀ts/
       water rev unspO cnj clf clean
       3   5   7   10   13   stem

       [chunaʔəskʼə̀ts]   'he, she washed (O)'

(336)   /yidà -tsʼə-ˈnə-l -tla/
       inside 1pS cnj clf sg/du run
       2   8   10 13 stem

       [yidàtsʼitla]   'we (du.) ran inside'

The prefixes ʔə, tsʼə and ghə cannot simply be marked as impossible tone bearers (or perhaps analyzed as underlyingly linked to high tone) because conjugation tone does appear on the deictic subject prefixes if a direct object prefix other than ʔə occurs to the left of the deictic prefix:

(337)   /ghu-tsʼə-ˈse-chʼo̜/
       3pO 1pS cnj shoot
       7   8   10 stem

       [ghutsʼə́zchʼo̜]   'we shot them dead'

(338)   /xwə-ghə-ˈsə-chʼo̜/
       1pO 3pS cnj shoot
       7   8   10 stem

       [whaghə́zchʼo̜]   'they shot us dead'

(339) /ghuyə-gha-wə-ts'ə-`nə-n -ʔǫ/
      3pO   P   ar 1pS cnj Pf handle compact O
      1   1   7   8   10 11 stem

      [ghuyawəts'ə̀nį́ʔǫ]   'we gave them areal O'

(340) /xwə-gha-wə-gha-`nə-n -ʔǫ]
      1pO P   ar 3pS cnj Pf handle compact O
      1   1   7   8   10 11 stem

      [xwawaghə̀nį́ʔǫ]   'they gave us areal O'

However, if the leftmost conjunct prefix is the indefinite prefix ʔə,
conjugation tone does not appear when the deictic subject prefix precedes the
conjugation prefix:

(341) /mə -chǫ -ʔə -ts'ə-`nə-n -la/
      3pPsr guts unspO 1pS cnj Pf handle pl O
      3   3   7   8   10 11 stem

      [məchǫʔəts'ə̀nįla]   'we took its guts out'

(342) /mįɣ dah-ʔə -ghə-`sə-tl'ų/
      snare up unspO 3pS cnj tie
      2   7   8   10 stem

      [mįɣ daʔaghə̱ztl'ų]   'they set a snare'

Recall that ʔə-, like ts'ə- and ghə- and unlike the other object prefixes,
does not surface with the tone of the conjugation prefixes when it immediately
precedes the tonal conjugation prefixes.

The domain of Conjugation Tone Mapping is summarized in (343).

(343) Domain of Conjugation Tone Mapping

preceding prefix				conjugation prefix	
1-5	7-9			tone	segments
	7	8	9		
1-5				∅	sə, nə
			9	`	s, n
	DO (not ʔə)			`	s, n
		ts'ə, ghə		∅	s, n
	ʔə			∅	s, n
	DO (not ʔə)	ts'ə, ghə		`	s, n
	ʔə	ts'ə, ghə		∅	s, n

Thus conjugation tone is one area in which the prefixes ʔə, ts'ə and ghə
distinguish themselves from other conjunct prefixes. Unlike other conjunct

prefixes, the prefixes ?a, ts'a and gha cannot surface with the tone of the s- and n-conjugation prefixes unless another conjunct prefix which can appears with conjugation tone occurs to the left. Because ?a, ts'a and gha pattern like the prefixes of positions 1-5, which are clearly outside the domain of Conjugation Tone Mapping, I suggest that are assigned to a phonological domain which is intermediate to levels 3 and 5; namely, level 4. Notice, then, that the subject prefixes ts'a and gha are infixed within the level 3 domain, rather than prefixed to the left of the affixes of the earlier level, unlike all other prefixes in Sekani.

Two additional characteristics of the prefixes ?a, ts'a and gha which provide further evidence for this analysis are discussed in Hargus (1987).

5. Level 5

Kari (1975) has noted that the prefix-internal boundary or level ordering distinction which separates position 7-9 prefixes from prefixes to their left exists in most of the Athabaskan languages. (The main exceptions appear to be the Pacific Coast Athabaskan languages.) Just as in Sekani, this boundary is quite prominent in the other languages: many phonological rules refer to it. In fact, this boundary has long been recognized in the Athabaskan languages. Li (1933, 1946), in his study of Chipewyan, was the first to propose that a 'disjunct' boundary exists within the verb prefixes, corresponding to the level 5 vs. levels 2-4 distinction motivated above. He labelled the prefixes which occur to the left of the disjunct boundary 'disjunct prefixes', and those which occur to the right of this boundary, 'conjunct prefixes'.

According to Krauss (1969), there is both internal and external evidence that the leftmost verbal prefix position in Proto-Athabaskan was that of the direct object prefixes. In Eyak, the direct object position (cognate with Sekani prefix position 7) is the leftmost verbal prefix position (Krauss

1965). Moreover, many of the disjunct prefixes in the Athabaskan languages are stems, whereas there are no stems in the conjunct prefixes. Krauss has suggested that the process of incorporating the disjunct prefixes had only begun in Proto-Athabaskan prior to the dispersement of the speakers of this language, and that the disjunct prefixes were fully incorporated into the verb prefixes in the daughter languages. In support of this hypothesis, there is greater cross-linguistic diversity in the inventory and positions of the Athabaskan disjunct prefixes than there is in the conjunct prefixes.

5.1 Morphology

In Sekani the disjunct prefixes form a unified phonological domain, level 5. As will be seen, many of the level 5 prefixes are actually stems. Six disjunct prefix positions can be distinguished.

5.1.1 Inceptive prefix (position 6)

The inceptive prefix /xò/ (phonetically whè) in position 6 forms a discontinuous constituent along with the position 9 prefixes na and i. Some examples of inceptive verbs are given below:

(344)   /whè -na -i -i   -tsègh/
         incp der der 1sPf cry
          6   9   9   12   stem

        [whènitsègh]   'I started to cry'

(345)   /lèdi ?a -whè -na -i -n -là/
         tea adv incp der der Pf make O
              2   6   9   9   11 stem

        [lèdi ?awhènįlà?]   'he, she started to make tea'

(346)   /nà -whè -na -i -n -h -chǫ/
         cont incp der der Pf clf rain
          2   6   9   9 11 13 stem

        [nàwhènįhchǫ]   'it started to rain'

(347) /k'è-whè -nə -i -s -d -dah/
       per incp der der 1sS clf sg go
        2   6   9   9   12 13 stem

       [k'èwhènəsdah]   'I start to walk around'

The inceptive prefix occurs to the left of the position 7 object prefixes:

(348) /whè -ya -nə -i -n -ʔàs/
       incp thm der der Pf sneeze
        6   7   9   9   11 stem

       [whèyanįʔàs]   'he, she started to sneeze'

(349) /kǫh whè -wa-da -nə -i -i -tl'às/
       house incp ar thm der der 1sPf paint
              6   7 9   9   9   12 stem

       [kǫh whèwadənitl'às]   'I started to paint the house'

(350) /ts'e-whè -sə -nə -i -n -h -sət/
       wake incp 1sO der der Pf clf wake up
        2   6   7   9   9   11 13 stem

       [ts'ewhèsənįhsət]   'he, she started to wake me up'

Because of the obligatory co-occurrence of position 6 [whè] and position 9 [nə i], many of the rules discussed in 4.2 do not provide evidence as to whether the inceptive prefix belongs on level 5 or on level 4. However, evidence for its assignment to level 5 is provided by the rule of L Deletion (4.2.3). It is also worth noting that all instances of the vowel [e] on levels 2-4 are derived: there are no prefixes with underlying /e/ in this domain. In contrast, both /ə/ and /e/ occur in the disjunct prefixes. The inceptive prefix [whè] patterns like the prefixes to its left, rather than those to its right, in this respect.

5.1.2 The na prefixes (position 5)

Two homophonous prefixes, na 'reversative' and na 'habitual, customary', occur in this position. Both prefixes require the d classifier.

5.1.2.1 Reversative na

na 'reversative' is often translated as 'again'.

(351) /chu -na -ts'ə-nə -sə -d -dǫ/
      water rev 1pS term cnj clf drink
      3   5 8   9   10 13 stem

    [chunats'anèsdǫ]   'we are drunk again'

(352) /ts'e-na -na -s -d -zit/
      wake rev cnj 1sS clf wake up
      2   5   10 12 13 stem

    [ts'enanəsdzit]   'I wake up again'

With motion verbs, reversative na is often translated as 'back (returning)':

(353) /įdǫ̀ -na -ts'ə-nə -n -d -ʔats/
      inside rev 1pS cnj Pf clf du go
      2   5 8   10 11 13 stem

    [įdǫ̀nats'anįt'ats]   'we [du excl] went back inside'

(354) /na -də -sə -d -ya/
      rev der cnj clf sg go
      5 9 10 13 stem

    [nadèsja]   'he, she went back'

5.1.2.2 Customary, habitual na

Unlike reversative na, the customary/habitual prefix requires an aspectual suffix (-h or -ts), as discussed in 2.1.1. Compare the following pairs with (353)-(354) above:

(355) /chu -na-ts'ə-nə -s -d -jį -h/
      water C 1pS term 1sS clf drink C
      3   5 8   9   12 13 stem

    [chunats'anəsjįh]   'we are habitually drunk'

(356) /chu -ts'ə-nə -sə -d -dǫ/
      water 1pS term cnj clf drink
      3   8   9   10 13 stem

    [chuts'anèsdǫ]   'we are drunk'

(357) /ts'e-na-s -d -zət -ts/
       wake C 1sS clf wake up C
       2   5 12 13   stem

       [ts'enasdzəts]   'I wake up habitually'

(358) [ts'e-nə -s -sit]
       wake cnj 1sS wake up
       2   10 12 stem   'I wake up'

Unlike reversative na, customary na also requires a null conjugation prefix in the imperfective, as can be seen by comparing (357) and (358).

5.1.2.3 Positional properties of the na prefixes (I)

Both na prefixes occur to the left of the inceptive prefix whè:

(359) /na -whè -na -i -n -h -xę/
       rev incp der der Pf clf thaw, melt
       5   6   9   9 11 13 stem

       [nawhènihxę]   'he, she started to thaw out [O]'

(360) /chəmįł hà -na -whè -na -i -n -la/
       fishnet out rev incp der der Pf handle rope-like O
              2   5   6   9   9 11 stem

       [chəmįł hǫnawhènįla]   'he, she started to take the fishnet back out'

(361) /na -whè -na -i -d -kwi/
       rev incp der der clf vomit
       5   6   9   9 13 stem

       [nawhènikwi]   'he, she started to vomit again'

In other Athabaskan languages, such as Slave and Ahtna, the reversative and customary/habitual prefixes do not occur in the same position:

(362) Ahtna disjunct prefixes (Kari 1979)

       Adverbial   Iterative   Incorporate Distributive

       na rev   na C

(363) Slave disjunct prefixes (Rice (to appear))

Adverb   Postposition Adverbial Distributive Customary Incorp.
         and object   stem

                      na rev   na C

However, in Sekani there is no evidence that they do not occur in the same position. (These prefixes apparently do not co-occur.) Perhaps the difference between Sekani and other languages with respect to the position of the na prefixes is due to the fact that these prefixes are unstable in position, as will be seen below. I will return to the question of their underlying position in 5.2.

5.1.3 Distributive prefixes (position 4)

The distributive plural prefix marks actions that are performed (a) separately rather than collectively, or (b) on separate objects, or (c) by separate subjects, or (d) in separate places. There are two alternates of this prefix, dà and yàdà, the choice of which is probably not determined by the phonology but by morphological factors. See Rice (to appear) for some discussion of what those factors might be.

Some examples of the distributive prefixes in Sekani are given in (364)-(369):

dà

(364) /mįɬ   dah-dà -ʔə   -s -tl'ųh/
      snare up dstr unspO 1sS tie
              2   4   7   12 stem

[mįɬ dadàʔəstl'ųh]   'I set snares, one by one'

(365) /che -dà -nə -n -h -bets/
      water dstr cnj 2sS clf boil O
       2   4   10 12 13 stem

[chedànįhbets]   'you [sg] boil separate [Os]'

(366) /ya dà -i -n -tsèɬ/
      sky dstr der 2sS handle compact O
           4   9   12 stem

[ya dàįtsèɬ]   'you [sg] throw [compact Os] into air, one by one' yàdà

(367) /yàdà-yə -ts'ə-sə -?às/
    dstr thm 1pS cnj sneeze
    4   7   8   10 stem

  [yàdàyəts'əz?às]   'we sneezed separately'

(368) /yàdà-ts'ə-nə -ɨ -d -dày/
    dstr 1pS thm der clf dance
    4   8   9   9   13 stem

  [yàdàts'ənidày]   'we danced separately'

(369) /chu -yàdà-ts'ə-nə -ɨ -d -jįh/
    water dstr 1pS term der clf drink
    3   4   8   9   9   13 stem

  [chuyàdàts'ənijįh]   'we customarily get drunk separately'

Evidence that the distributive prefixes occur to the left of reversative and customary na will be presented in 5.2. For now, note that the distributive prefix occurs to the left of the inceptive prefix:

(370) /dah-dà -whè -ts'ə-nə -ɨ -n -tl'ų/
    up dstr incp 1pS der der Pf tie
    2   4   6   8   9   9 11 stem

  [dadàwhèts'ənitl'ų]   'we started to set snares separately'

5.1.4 Incorporated stems (position 3)

Most of the noun and verb stems that may be incorporated into the verb prefixes occur in prefix position 3. Some examples are given below:

incorporated noun stems

(371) /hà -sa -də -ɨ -dlat/
    out sun der der shine
    2   3   9   9   stem

  [hàsadidlat]   'the sun is shining'

(372) /mə -ghǫh-k'e-įji -nə -s -ts'əts/
    3sO P   adv mind der 1sS think
    1   1   2   3   9   12 stem

  [mǫhk'eįjinəsts'əts]   'I think about him, her'

incorporated verb stems

(373) [k'è-tsi -da -tsih]   'he, she sniffs around'
      per sniff der sniff
       2   3   9   stem

(374) [łè -ts'agh-da -?ah]   'he, she yawns'
      adv yawn   der handle compact O
       2   3   9   stem

The incorporated stems occur to the left of the distributive plural prefixes in position 4:

(375) /je -gwàt-dà -ts'a-s -h -kah/
      adv knee dstr 1pS cnj clf wound
       2   3   4   8   10 13 stem

      [jegwàtdàts'ahkah]   'we banged our knees separately'

(376) [chu -dà -ya]   'Tudyah Lake'
      water dstr sg go
       3   4   stem

(377) /chu -yàdà-ts'a-na -s -d -dǫ/
      water dstr 1pS term cnj clf drink
       3   4   8   9   10 13 stem

      [chuyàdàts'anèsdǫ]   'we got drunk separately'

I will return to a discussion of the underlying order of the incorporated stems, distributive plural, and na prefixes in 5.2.

The incorporated stems may themselves be prefixed:

(378) /ma -chǫ -?a -na -s -łeh/
      3sPsr guts unspO cnj 1sS handle pl O
        3   3   7   10 12 stem

      [machǫ?anasłeh]   'I take its guts out'

(379) /k'è-uyuz -e -da -d -dah/
      per whistling vb der clf sg go
       2   3   3   9 13 stem

      [k'èuyuzedadah]   'he, she walks around, whistling'

In (378) and (379), the possessive prefix ma- and the thematic prefix u- occur. This suggests that the incorporated stems are formed on earlier levels of the lexicon and incorporated as units into the level 5 prefixes.

5.1.5 Adverbial prefixes (position 2)

Most of the prefixes of this position have clear spatial, temporal, aspectual or other adverbial meanings. Some examples are given below:

(380) /dàghe nè   -nə -n -kàh/
      ground to ground cnj 2sS handle contained O
              2   10 12 stem

      [dàghe nènįkàh]   'you [sg] put [contained O] on the ground'

(381) /ːa-də-'s -kį/
      lost cnj rope-like O be in position
      2   9   10   stem

      [tadèzkį]   '[rope-like O] is lost'

(382) /ts'e-də -n -h -tsus/
      into fire 2sS clf handle cloth-like O
      2   9   12 13 stem

      [ts'edįhtsus]   'you [sg] put [cloth-like O] in the fire'

(383) /k'è-ghə-l -ghəs/
      per 3pS clf pl run
      2   8   13 stem

      [k'èghaghəs]   'they run around'

The adverbial prefixes occur to the left of the position 3 incorporated stems:

(384) /tà-tsi -sə -s -l -ʔatl/
      up head cnj 1sS clf handle compact O
      2   3   10 12 13 stem

      [tàtsisəsʔatl]   'I wear [O] on my head'

(385) /įdà -yhən-e -də -'nə-i -ya/
      inside sing vb der cnj 1sPf sg go
      2   3   3   9   10   12 stem

      [įdàyhinedəniya]   'I walked inside, singing'

See also (370)-(374) and (378) in 5.1.4 above.

Since many of the adverbial prefixes are stem-like (a few are clearly stems), and since the adverbial and incorporated stem positions are adjacent, one might consider collapsing these prefix positions (cf. prefix position 9). However, the data presented in 5.2 suggest that these are two distinct prefix positions.

5.1.6 Incorporated postpositions (position 1)

An incorporated postposition, together with its object, if pronominal, is the leftmost verbal prefix. The incorporated postpositions precede the adverbial prefixes of position 2:

(386)   /tlį è-k'è-də -ghə-s -tsəts/
        dog P per Fut Fut 1sS chase O
         1 2   9   11 12 stem

        [tlį èk'èdəghəstsəts]   'I will chase the dog around'

(387)   /xədə ka-nà -sə -l -dzàt/
        moose P cont cnj clf hunt for O
          1   2   10 13 stem

        [xədə kanàhdzàt]   'he, she hunted for a moose'

(388)   /mə -è-ne -s -jit/
        3sO P adv 1sS be afraid
         1 1 2   12 stem

        [mènesjit]   'I'm afraid of [O]'

(389)   /mə -t'à   -hà -ghə-i -ya/
        3sO P:inside out cnj 1sPf sg go
         1   1   2   10 12 stem

        [mət'àhàghiya]   'I took [my clothes] off'

Incorporated postpositions are phonologically distinguishable from unincorporated postpositions: the former undergo phonological rules that the latter do not. For example, the vowel inserted by Epenthesis (Ch. 6, sec. 2) is deleted if it follows a vowel-final incorporated postposition, but not if it follows an unincorporated postposition. Compare (390)-(392) with (393)-(395):

    incorporated postpositions

(390)   /xədə ka-ə -s -l -dzàt/
        moose P epen cnj clf hunt O
          1   10 13 stem

```
                    /ka-ə-s-l-dzàt/

Aspiration            h
ə Deletion            ∅

            [xəda kahdzàt]    'he, she hunted down a moose'
```

(391) /tən gha-ə -n -get/
       ice P   epen cnj poke, chisel
            1   1O stem

       [tən ghǫget]   'he, she chisels through the ice'

(392) /sə -gha-ə -h -ʔa/
       1sO P   epen clf
       1   1   13 stem

       [sah?a]   'he, she hires me'

unincorporated postpositions

(393) /ʔə -nka ə -ch'į/
       unspO P   epen be, do

       [ʔįka ach'į]   'he, she is trapping'

(394) Peter [la ə -ch'į]   'he, she helps Peter'
              P epen be, do

(395) [bàt   ka ə -ch'į]   'he, she is cooking'
       stomach P epen be, do

Thus phonological evidence indicates that at least some preverbal postpositions are genuine verbal prefixes, not independent words.

5.2 Level 5 phonology: a Raising

Phonological evidence for distinguishing the level 5 prefixes from the level 2-4 prefixes was presented in 4.2. In this section I discuss the rule of a Raising, which applies throughout the lexicon. This rule provides evidence concerning the underlying position of the na prefixes with respect to other disjunct prefixes. The analysis of these forms provides an argument for the theory of Lexical Phonology: the phonological rules of a Raising and Nasalization must precede the application of morphologically restricted rules of na Metathesis and na Deletion.

5.2.1 Formulation of a̱ Raising

The rule of a̱ Raising is informally stated in (396):

(396)   a --> ǫ / ___ n]$_{syll}$

Alternations between [a] and [ǫ] provide evidence for this rule:

(397a) /chu -na -s -d -k'às/
        water rev 1sS clf wash O
        3   5   12 13 stem

        [chunask'às]   'I wash [O]'

(397b) /chu -na -n -d -k'às/
        water rev 2sS clf wash O
        3   5   12 13 stem

        [chunǫk'às]   'you [sg] wash O'

(398a) [?a -s -ɫà?]   'I made [O]'
        adv 1sS make O
        2   12 stem

(398b) /?a -n -là/
        adv Pf make O
        2   11 stem

        [?ǫlà?]   'he, she made O'

(399a) /k'è-na-d -lits/
        per C clf float
        2   5 13 stem

        [k'ạdlits]   'he, she floats around'

(399b) /k'è-na-n -d -lits/
        per C 2sS clf float
        2   5 12 13 stem

        [k'ènǫdlits]   'you [sg] float around'

In (399a), a̱ Raising must precede the rule of Perambulative Reduction,
informally stated in (400):

(400) Perambulative Reduction

      k'è+na --> k'an / ___ (C) [(clf) stem]

```
                         /k'è-na-d-lits/
a Raising                    --
Perambulative Reduction      k'an
Nasalization                 k'ą

                         [k'ądlits]
```

Perambulative Reduction is a morphologically restricted rule, applying only to the sequence of position 2 /k'è/ and position 5 /na/. I will return to the formulation of this rule in Ch. 5, 3.2.

5.2.2 Domain of a Raising

a Raising also applies on level 1 of the lexicon, as can be seen in the following alternations between [a] and [ǫ] in stems:

(401a) /chu   k'è-na-d -ka   -h/
       water per C clf handle contained O C

       [chu k'ąkąh]   'he, she carries [container of] water around'

(401b) /nà -sə -ka   -n/
       cont cnj handle contained O Pf

       [chu nàsəkǫ]   'he, she carried [container of] water around'

(402a) /na -n -ʔa   -'h/
       rev 2sS handle compact O Imp

       [sįdlogh nǫʔąh]   'you [sg] give me back [compact O]'

(402b) /na -ghə-n -ʔa   -n/
       rev cnj 2sS handle compact O Pf

       [sįdlogh naghįʔǫ]   'you [sg] gave me back [compact O]'

If a Raising applies on levels 1 and 5 of the lexicon, one would also expect to find forms in which it has applied on levels 2-4. However, a-final prefixes (and nasal-initial stems) are rare in Sekani. In the few cases where the combination arises, the syllable-final restriction on a Raising is not met:

(403)   /chu də -a -nįɣ -e/
        water Fut Fut high Fut

        [chu danįɫe]   'there will be high water'

(404)   /chè-nə -a   -na/
        adv cnj 2pPf move

        [chènana]   'you [pl] moved'

Thus, the structural description of a Raising is only met on levels 1 and 5.

5.2.3 Positional properties of the na prefixes (II)

The rule of a Raising provides evidence that the na prefixes should be assigned to prefix position 5, as has been assumed, but not demonstrated, in preceding sections.

Note that level 5 [a]-final prefixes undergo a Raising when followed by /na/:

(405a) /nà -ghə-d   -ts'it/
        down 3pS clf sg/du fall
        2   8   13   stem

        [nàghats'it]   'they [du] fall down'

(405b) /nà -na-ghə-d   -ts'əts/
        down C 3pS clf sg/du fall
        2   5 8   13 stem

        [nǫnaghats'əts]   'they [du] fall down customarily'

(406a) [tà-sə -ya]   'he, she went uphill'
        up cnj sg go
        2 10 stem

(406b) /tà-na -s -d -ya/
        up rev cnj clf sg go
        2 5   10 13 stem

        [tǫnasja]   'he, she went back uphill'

The fact that a Raising has applied to the sequence /ana/ (syllabified [a.na]) in these forms seems very strange, because in other forms, a Raising fails to apply if the [an] sequence is not syllable-final. However, notice that the vowel of the prefix which precedes /na/ has not only undergone a Raising, but is also nasalized. These data suggest that /na/ in these forms has undergone a morphologically restricted rule, n Insertion:

(407) n Insertion

∅ --> n / a ___ na

The alternative to positing the rule of n Insertion would be to hypothesize that the na prefixes have underlying representations of the shape /nna/. However, this representation ought to cause the vowel of any preceding prefix to be nasalized, and this is apparently not the case:

(408) /ni-na-ts'ə-də -ì -d -ʔah/
```
      up C  1pS  der der clf handle compact O
      2  5   8    9   9  13  stem
```
[ninats'ədit'ah]   'we customarily lift [compact O]'

(409) /mə -k'e-na-sə -də -ì -d -t'əs/
```
      3sO on C   1dS der 1dS clf move foot
      1   1  5   8    9  12  13 stem
```
[mak'enasədit'as]   'we [du] customarily step on it'

(410) /che -chu -na -də -'n -d -ya/
```
      in water water rev der cnj clf sg go
      2      3     5   9  10  13 stem
```
[chechunadę̀ja]   'he, she walks into the water again'

Thus I assume the existence of a rule of n Insertion. Clearly n Insertion must precede a Raising, as illustrated in the following derivation of (406b):

/tà-na-s-d-ya/

```
n Insertion        tàn-na
a Raising          tòn-na
Nasalization       tǫ̀-na

                   [tǫ̀nasja]
```

na is optionally deleted after a Raising and Nasalization have applied:

(411) na Deletion

na --> ∅ / ǫ ___   optional

The optional nature of this rule is indicated by the following variants:

175

(412a) /dà -na -da -na -n -chįh/
adv rev der cnj Pf handle stick-like O
2   5   9   10   11 stem

[dàdętǫ dǫnadànįchįh]   'you [sg] close the doog again'
=
(412b) [dàdętǫ dǫ̀dànįchįh]

(413a) /hà -na -ah -ɫeh/
out rev 2pS handle rope-like O
2   5   12 stem

[chamįɫ hǫnahɫeh]   'you [pl] take the fishnet back out'
=
(413b) [hǫahɫeh]

Form (413b) indicates that Nasalization must precede na Deletion:

/hà-na-ah-ɫeh/

n Insertion   hàn-na
a Raising   hòn-na
Nasalization   hǫ̀-na
na Deletion   hǫ̀

[hǫahɫeh]

Otherwise *[hònahɫeh] would result; [hǫahɫeh] would not be a possible surface form. Notice that, if na Deletion is a lexical rule, Nasalization must also apply in the lexicon. I will return to a discussion of this form in (430) below.

The na prefixes may occur either to the right or the left of the incorporated stems, as the following free variant forms indicate:

(414) /nà -chu -na -da -s -ts'at/
cont water rev der 1sS sg/du stand
2   3   5   9   12 stem

(a)   [nǫnachudasts'at]   'I stand in the water again'

(b)   =[nàchunadasts'at]

(415)   /nà -xeɬ -na -də -i -n -d -ʔàh/
        down pack rev der der 2sS clf handle compact O
         2   3   5   9   9   12 13 stem

(a)   [nàxeɬnadįt'àh]   'you [sg] put your pack down again'

(b)   =[nǫ̀naxeɬdįt'àh]

(416)   /tà-tsí -na -ghə-d -ʔǫ/
        up head rev cnj clf handle compact O
         2   3   5   10 13 stem

(a)   [tàtsínaghət'ǫ]   'he, she put [O] on his, her head again'

(b)   =[tàtsínaghət'ǫ]

(417)   /ɬughe chǫ -na -ʔə -da -ghə-s -ɬeɬ/
        fish guts rev unspO Fut Fut 1sS handle pl O
                    3   5   7   9   11 12 stem

(a)   [ɬughe chǫnaʔədəghəsɬeɬ]
        'I will take the guts out of another fish'

(b)   =[ɬughe nachǫʔədəghəsɬeɬ]

(418)   /dlògh-na -yə -ghə-nə -n -zən/
        laugh rev thm 3pS face Pf have made?
          3   5   7   8   9   11 stem

(a)   [dlòghnayəghənįzən]   'they smile again'

(b)   =[nadlòghyəghənįzən]

To account for this positional instability, I suggest that, unlike the other verbal prefixation rules, the insertion of the na prefixes and the incorporated stems are unordered with respect to each other.

Notice that the na prefixes cannot occur to the left of the adverbial prefixes (position 2):

(419)   /ts'e-na -yə -də -ghə-n -ʔǫ/
        fire rev 3sO fire cnj Pf handle compact O
          2   5   7   9   10 11 stem

        [ts'enayədəghį̀ʔǫ]   'he, she put it in the fire again'

        *[nats'eyədəghį̀ʔǫ]

177

(420) /yidà -na -n -d -ya/
       inside rev cnj clf sg go
       2   5   10 13 stem

   [yidònoja]   'he, she went back inside'

   *[nayidòja]

(421) /che -na -ghə-nə -d -jetl/
       water rev 3pS cnj clf pl go
       2   5   8   10 13 stem

   [chenaghį jetl]   'they ran into the water again'

   *[nacheghį jetl]

These data suggest that the incorporated stem and adverbial prefix positions are in some way formally distinguished in the grammar of Sekani.

We have seen that the na prefixes may optionally precede the incorporated stems. It is now possible to determine more precisely the position of the na prefixes with respect to the other disjunct prefixes. We have seen examples in which (a) incorporated stems occur to the left of the distributive prefixes (375-377), (b) the distributive prefixes occur to the left of the inceptive prefix (370), and (c) the na prefixes occur to the left of the inceptive prefix (359-361). Thus there is evidence for the following surface order of the rightmost disjunct prefixes:

(422)   stems   distributive   inceptive
        ↑   ↑
        na   na

As noted above, na may occur either to the left or the right of the stems in phonetic forms. This suggests that the na prefixes might also either precede or follow the distributive prefixes. I have postponed presenting forms in which the distributive and na prefixes co-occur until now, because in order to make sense of the facts, it is necessary to know that (1) there is a rule of a Raising, (2) there is a rule of n Insertion, and (3) na is unstable in position in some forms.

Consider the following forms, in which na and dà co-occur:

(423) /che   -dà -na-ghə-l -ghəs/
       into water dstr C 3pS clf pl run
       2   4   5   8   13 stem

       [chenadǫ̀ghaghəs]   'they habitually run into the water separately'

(424) /ni   -dà -na-ts'a-də -i̧ -?ah/
       raise dstr C 1pS thm thm handle compact O
       2   4   5 8   9   9   stem

       [ninadǫ̀ts'ədi̧?ah]   'we habitually lift [compact O] separately'

(425) /dà   -na-ah -d -kwi/
       dstr C 2pS clf vomit
       4   5 12 13 stem

       [nadǫ̀ahkwi]   'you [pl] habitually vomit separately'

In these forms, na occurs to the left of the distributive prefix, which has undergone a Raising. To account for these forms, I suggest that, following the application of n Insertion, na has undergone the metathesis rule in (426):

(426) Distributive-na metathesis

       dà n na   -->   na dà n
       4   5   5 4

This analysis is illustrated in a derivation of (425):

                    /dà-na-ahkwi/

n Insertion   dàn-na
a Raising   dòn-na
Nasalization   dǫ̀-na
Metathesis   na-dǫ̀

                    [nadǫ̀ahkwi]

Unless na is to the right of dà at some point in the derivation, the fact that the vowel of the prefix dà has become [ǫ] cannot be accounted for by the rules of n Insertion and a Raising.

Additional support for this metathesis analysis comes from consideration of forms which contain na and the yàdà allomorph of the distributive prefix:

(427) /yàdà-na-ts'ə-i -d -kwi/
dstr C 1pS der clf vomit
4   5 8   9 13 stem

[yànadǫ̀ts'ikwi]   'we vomit again separately'

(428) /yàdà-na-ts'ə-i -tsǫ̀/
dstr C 1pS der shit
4   5 8   9 stem

[yànadǫ̀ts'itsǫ̀?]   'we shitted again separately'

In these forms, na occurs to the left of dà but to the right of yà. Only the vowel of dà, however, has become nasalized and undergone a Raising. These forms are predicted by an analysis in which na occurs to the right of the distributive prefixes prior to n Insertion. Moreover, they support the formulation of the Distributive-na Metathesis rule given above. na can only move to the left of the rightmost syllable (dà) of the yàdà allomorph of the distributive prefix.

The derivations required to account for second person plural forms like (413b) [hǫ̀ahɁeh] and (425) [nadǫ̀ahkwi] are of considerable interest for Lexical Phonology. na Deletion and na Metathesis are arguably 'morphological' rules, since they apply only to the position 5 prefixes na reversative and na customary, never to position 2 adverbial prefixes such as nà continuative. In In contrast, the rules of Nasalization and a Raising are general phonological processes in Sekani. Note that in the derivations of these forms, the phonological rules of Syllabification, Nasalization and a Raising must precede the morphological rules of na Metathesis and na Deletion. Otherwise, the [n] inserted by n Insertion would be resyllabified with the following vowel. This resyllabification would bleed a Raising and Nasalization, resulting in incorrect phonetic forms:

(429)   /dà-na-ahkwi/

morphological rules:

n Insertion   dàn-na
Metathesis   na-dàn

phonological rules:

Syllabification   na.dà.na
a Raising   --
Nasalization   --

                         *[nadànahkwi]

(430)   /hà-na-ah-ɤeh/

morphological rules:

n Insertion   hà-n-na
na Deletion   hà-n

phonological rules:

Syllabification   hà.nah.ɤeh
a Raising   --
Nasalization   --

                         [hànahɤeh]

The analysis of these forms requires a model of grammar in which phonological rules may precede morphological ones. In other words, these forms provide strong support for the Lexical Phonology model and against an SPE-type model of morphology-phonology interaction.

6. Postlexical phonology

As discussed in Ch. 2, section 5, there are a number of hypothesized differences between lexical and postlexical rules. For example, lexical rules are generally restricted to derived contexts, often apply in restricted, morphologically-defined domains, are usually structure-preserving, and they may have lexically marked exceptions. Postlexical rules, on the other hand, have none of these characteristics, but are typically low-level, allophonic, boundary-insensitive rules. Moreover, lexical rules are predicted to precede postlexical rules. This is an important prediction: in another model, these differences between rule types could only be regarded as incidental.

Kiparsky (1985:94) proposes that postlexical rules may either assign gradient or categorical values of features, and he suggests further that it may be possible to predict which rules function in which ways from the formulation of the rule:

> Context-sensitive rules which override lexical marking conditions have gradient outputs...Rules (usually context-free) which assign default values have categorical outputs...Rules which assign lexically markable feature values are normally categorical.

In Sekani, most of these kinds of postlexical rules occur. An example of a rule which assigns a lexically markable feature value is Nasalization. This rule applies on all levels of the lexicon as well as postlexically. However, its postlexical application is not gradient and variable: the sentential morpheme hą negative interrogative does not vary between [hą] and [han], for example. Another postlexical rule which I will discuss in 6.2, Glottal Stop Insertion, is also a rule of this sort. Neither rule violates structure-preservation.[24]

The postlexical rule of Devocalization, discussed in 6.1, is a type of rule which overrides lexical marking conditions: in this case, conditions on possible syllable onsets. The output of this rule is variable, as the application of the rule depends on rate and style of speech.

6.1 Devocalization

The round vowels /o u/ are devocalized to [w] before another vowel. This rule applies in normal- to fast-paced speech:

(431) Devocalization

$$u, o \longrightarrow w / \_\_\_ V$$

(432a) [ʔaskʼųèʔ]   'roe'

(b)   =[ʔaskʼwęʔ]

(433a) [dək'ǫazi]   'he, she is midget-sized'

(b) =[dək'wązi]

The (a) forms in each pair represent a slow or careful pronunciation. In slow speech, the quality of the devocalized vowel as well as its underlying tone and nasality are recoverable. In the fast speech forms in (b), the low tone is deleted, whereas nasality is stable, appearing on the vowel which triggers Devocalization.[25]

Devocalization has many of the predicted characteristics of postlexical rules. First, its output is gradient and variable: the devocalized version of /u/ may be any segment on a syllabicity cline from [w] to [u], depending on rate of speech. Secondly, this rule does not appear to have any lexically marked exceptions, unlike other rules in Sekani, such as Palatalization. Thirdly, the formulation of Devocalization does not require morphological conditioning: the level 2 derivational prefix u- and the level 1 plural suffix -hu undergo this rule just like the stem-final round vowels in (432) and (433) above.

(434) [uahtòn]   'you [pl] hold [O]'

~[wahtòn]

(435) [uahch'eh]   'you [pl] shoot [O] repeatedly'

~[wahch'eh]

(436) [ts'ùdahuazi]   'children'

~[ts'ùdahwazi]

Finally, Devocalization is clearly not structure-preserving. Devocalization often results in syllable-initial consonant clusters of the form [Cw], which are not possible underlying clusters. (As discussed in Ch. 1, there are no underlying onset clusters in Sekani, and the only possible underlying syllable-final clusters are sequences of /nC/.)

(437) jeyǫ̀è   'bullmoose'
     =jeywę̀

(438) [ʔət'ǫazi]   'small leaf, flower'
     =[ʔət'wązi]

(439) [dəch'ue]   'porcupine'
     =[dəch'we]

(440) [dlǫazi]   'mouse'
     =[dlwązi]

(441) [jèzʔǫazi]   'gun'
     =[jèzʔwązi]

The fact that Devocalization creates underlyingly impossible consonant clusters suggests that it is not a lexical rule. Although, as discussed in Ch. 2, there is some empirical evidence against the universality of this principle as a constraint on lexical rules, it is generally true that the outputs of lexical rules are structure-preserving.

Devocalization thus has many of the predicted characteristics of post lexical rules. While it can apply to the output of lexical rules such as a Raising, there are no lexical rules that it must precede, as predicted by a post-lexical analysis of this rule.

6.2 Glottal Stop Insertion

Most of the Athabaskan languages, including Sekani, are tone languages. Krauss (1964) has proposed that tone in the Athabaskan languages developed historically from the presence or absence of a glottal segment in the nucleus of Proto-Athabaskan syllables. The contrast between glottalized and non-glottalized nuclei yielded to a tonal contrast when nucleus glottalization was lost. The glottal segment has led to the development of high tone in some languages (these are the 'high-marked' languages), but low tone in others (the 'low-marked' languages).[26]

Sekani is a low-marked language: syllable-final glottalization has yielded to low tone. Knowing the historical situation, it would not be surprising to find that either low tone or post-vocalic glottal stop is predictable in the synchronic phonology.

6.2.1 Underlying tone or glottal stop?

Synchronically, low tone and syllable-final glottal stop are in complementary distribution except word-finally, as the alternations in (442)-(446) indicate. In the following pairs, a low tone stem is word-final in the (a) forms, but word-internal in the (b) forms. The pronunciation of the unincorporated stem in the (a) forms contains a word-final glottal stop, whereas the pronunciation of the same stem in the (b) forms, where it is not word-final, lacks the stem-final glottal stop.

(442a) [sətsi?]   'my head'

(442b) /nà -tsi -də -ghəs/
       cont head thm
       2   3   9   stem

       [nàtsidəghəs]   'he, she shakes his, her head "no"'

(443a) [sətl'à?]   'my buttocks'

(443b) /tl'à   -na -ghə-da -i -ts'əts/
       buttocks rev 3pS der der
       3   5   8   9   9· stem

       [tl'ǫnaghədits'əts] 'they slide down again'

(444a) [sagǫ̀ts'ḛ̀lḛ̀ʔ]   'my elbow'

(444b) /gǫ̀ts'ḛ̀lḛ̀-sə -i   -h -kah/
       elbow   cnj 1sPf clf wound
       3   10 12 13 stem

       [gǫ̀ts'ḛ̀l̰ḛ̀sihkah]   'I banged my elbow'

(445a) [mət'à?]   'inside it'

(445b) /nat'əne t'à -ghə-i -ya/
       clothes inside cnj 1sPf sg go
                       1   10 12 stem

       [nat'əne t'àghiya]   'I put some clothes on'

(446a) [whək'à?]   'by us'

(446b) /whə-k'à-sə -n -da/
       1pO by cnj 2sS sg sit
       1   1   10 12 stem

       [whək'às̰ida]   'you [sg] stay with us'

Clearly, low tone and syllable-final glottal stop are still synchronically related. But these data do not indicate whether low tone is predictable from glottal stop, or whether word-final glottal stop is predictable from low tone.

Consider the rules that would be required by either analysis. If low tone were present underlyingly, the following postlexical rule would be needed:

(447) Glottal Stop Insertion

$$\emptyset \longrightarrow ʔ\ /\ V\overset{L}{\underset{|}{\underline{\quad}}}\ ]$$

However, if low tone were derived from glottal stop, a more complicated analysis would be required. A rule creating low tone would be needed, along with an additional rule deleting syllable-final glottal stop everywhere but word-finally:

(448) Low Tone Insertion

$$\emptyset \longrightarrow L \:/\: \underset{V}{\_\_\_} \: ? \: (X) \:]_{syll}$$

(449) Glottal Stop Deletion

$$? \longrightarrow \emptyset \: \_\_\_ \:]_{syll} \: X$$

Alternatively, these two rules could be collapsed into a slightly less phonetically plausible rule of Glottal Stop Absorption, which would apply word-finally as well as word-internally:

(450) Glottal Stop Absorption[27]

$$? \longrightarrow L \:/\: \_\_\_ \:]_{syll}$$

Under this analysis, postlexical Glottal Stop Insertion would still be required.

To summarize, if low tone is present underlyingly, the phonology requires fewer rules, but the complementary distribution of low tone and syllable-final glottal stop in underlying representations is unaccounted for. An analysis which posits underlying /?/ accounts for the distribution of /?/, but requires more rules.

The /?/ analysis is certainly attractive. Although the /'/ analysis requires only one rule, and the /?/ analysis requires two, positing a rule of Glottal Stop Absorption/Insertion would simplify the phonology in other ways. The rule of Conjugation Tone Mapping (4.2.2) is repeated below in (451):

(451)
$$\overset{L}{\underset{sə}{V'}} \qquad \overset{L}{\underset{nə}{V'}}$$

If the underlying representations of these conjugation prefixes are not /'sə/ and /'nə/, but /?sə/ and /?nə/, then Conjugation Tone Mapping can simply be regarded as an instance of Absorption/Insertion.

Moreover, the /?/ analysis would account for certain facts about aspectual stem variation that would be unaccounted for in the /'/ analysis.

As discussed in 2.1.1, the typical durative aspectual suffixation pattern for vowel- and nasal-final roots is that given in (452):

(452)   Imp   Pf   Fut   Op
        -∅   -`      -`ɣ   -`

This pattern is illustrated below with the roots /da/ 'pl eat' and /t'in/ 'work':

(453)   -[da]   -[dà?] -[dàɣ] -[dà?]
(454)   -[ch'į] -[ch'į?] -[ch'įɣ] -[ch'į?]

Obstruent-final roots usually exhibit no stem variation in the durative aspect, as can be seen with /daɣ/ 'play cards' and /sogh/ 'shave':

(455)   -[dàɣ] -[dàɣ] -[dàɣ] -[dàɣ]
(456)   -[sogh] -[sogh] -[sogh] -[sogh]

Now consider the following stems sets:

(457)   -[?į?] -[?į?] -[?į?] -[?į?]   'hide'
(458)   -[bà?] -[bà?] -[bà?] -[bà?]   'children, animals eat'

Notice that no aspectual suffixes are present in (457)-(458). If these roots are underlyingly vowel- or nasal-final (/?in/ and /bà/), they would be expected to pattern like those in (453)-(454). However, the fact that the typical durative suffixes for vowel- and nasal-final roots are not added is easily accounted for if the roots in (457)-(458) are underlyingly consonant-final: /?in?/ and /ba?/, respectively.

An additional argument for deriving low tone from glottal stop is provided by the following stem set. The non-imperfective stems in (459) suggest that the durative aspect non-imperfective suffix is underlyingly /?/, rather than /`/:

(459)   -[sən] -[sį?] -[sįɣ] -[sį?]   'smile'.[28]

As illustrated in Ch. 1, it is normal for Nasalization to fail to apply to word-final /an/. However, notice that in the non-imperfective stems, the stem vowel /ə/ has become nasalized and has undergone a_Raising. If a consonantal suffix /?/, rather than a suprasegmental one /`/, has been added in the non-imperfective modes, then the nasalization and raising of /ə/ to [į] is predicted. However, if the durative suffix is /`/, it would be necessary to list two allomorphs of the stem for 'smile': /san/ (imperfective); /sin/ (nonimperfective).

While the /?/ analysis has a lot going for it, it is suspiciously abstract, and in fact, additional evidence indicates that this analysis is untenable. First, given the historical development of tone in Sekani, one would predict that no sequences of high tone vowels followed by syllable-final glottal stop ([V́?]) exist in the synchronic phonology of Sekani. However, there are a small number of such syllables in Sekani, an exhaustive list of which is given in (460)-(464):

(460) [bo?]   'kiss'

(461) /na -də -s -d -zo?/
       rev thm cnj clf kiss
       5   9   10 13 stem

       [nadèsdzo?]   'he, she kissed [O]'

(462) [na?]   'here, take [O]' voc

(463) [je?]   'give [O] to me' voc

(464) [bùs-azįį?]   'baby kitten'
       cat ddim

If low tone is present in underlying representations, then the forms in (460)-(464) are predicted, not exceptional. However, given an underlying /?/ analysis of tone, the forms above would have to be listed as exceptions to Absorption/Insertion. However, since other lexical rules, such as Palatalization, have marked exceptions, this cannot be considered a serious objection to a /?/ analysis, especially given the small number of such forms.

The problem is that low tones exist where the /?/ analysis would predict [?]. Consider the low tone position 9 prefix [i]. This prefix occurs to the left of the vowel-initial position 12 second person plural subject prefix in certain forms:

(465) /ì -ah -l -yòtl/
      thm 2pS clf swell
       9   12 13 stem

  [àhyòtl]   'you [pl] swelled up'

(As discussed in 4.2.1, the rule of i Deletion has applied in this form.) If the thematic prefix were /i?/-, it would be impossible to derive the low tone. Since Insertion/Absorption are syllable-based rules, syllabification must precede their application. However, nothing would prevent the putative prefix-final /?/ from resyllabifying with the following vowel-initial prefix, and Absorption/Insertion would be bled:

(466)   /i?-ahyòtl/

Syllabification   i.?ah.yòtl/
Absorption   --
i Deletion   --

                   *[i?ahyòtl]

Tonogenesis is apparently complete in Sekani: a synchronic analysis of low tone as /?/ is not warranted after all, despite its superficial attractiveness. Thus there is simply a rule of Glottal Stop Insertion in Sekani.

6.2.2 Characteristics of Glottal Stop Insertion

As discussed above, Glottal Stop Insertion must be a postlexical rule: it applies to word-final low-tone vowels, and so must apply after all word formation is complete. Like Devocalization, this rule has many of the characteristics that postlexical rules are predicted to have. First, the application of Glottal Stop Insertion varies according to rate of speech.

Consider the following forms:

(467) [nǫ̀gha   unaghùgǫ̀   ą]
       wolverine we du behave like Op

(a)   [nǫ̀gha unaghùgǫ̀ ą]   'we [du] behave like wolverines' Op[29]

(b)   =[nǫ̀gha unaghùgǫ̀? ą]

(468) [nàts'aduyà   ą]
       we stand around Op

(a)   [nàts'aduyà ą]   'we stand around' Op

(b)   =[nàts'aduyà? ą]

The variants in (a) represent fast speech forms: in fast speech, glottal stops are not inserted word-finally. The variants in the (b) forms which contain stem-final glottal stop are heard in slow or careful pronunciations. Although rate of speech determines whether or not word-final glottal stops are inserted, note that the rule never applies word-internally even in slow speech:

(469) /?a   -s-k'ų̀-è/
       unspPsr ? roe psd

       [?as.k'ų̀.è?]   'roe'

Glottal Stop Insertion only applies to word-final low tone vowels.

Secondly, the formulation of Glottal Stop Insertion does not require morphological conditioning: it applies to the possessive suffix -/è/ as well as to low-tone vowel-final stems:

(470) /tsà/
       [tsà?]   'beaver'

(471) /sa-tsà-è/
       [satsàè?]   'my beaver'

Thirdly, also like Devocalization, Glottal Stop Insertion does not appear to have lexically marked exceptions. Fourthly, Glottal Stop Insertion is not structure-preserving in the sense that it creates phonetic sequences which are not found in underlying representations: [V?]. Finally, Glottal Stop Insertion exhibits the predicted ordering relationship to other rules of Sekani: no lexical rules can be shown to follow Glottal Stop Insertion.

7. Summary

In many ways, the Sekani verbal prefixes behave as predicted by the theory of Lexical Phonology.

There is a strong correlation between the surface order of the prefixes and the domains of phonological rules. This was perhaps most dramatically illustrated in 4.2, where many rules of the phonology indicated that the prefixes of position 7 form the left edge of a major phonological domain, level 3.

Five levels of affixation/phonological rule domains can be distinguished in Sekani. As noted in Ch. 2, the existence of languages like Sekani which contain more than two phonological rule domains is problematic for theories which propose to limit the number of phonological rule domains universally to two, as in the word/stem models proposed by Aronoff and Sridhar (1983) and Sproat (1986).

In 5.2.1 I presented an analysis in which it was crucial that the phonological rules of a Raising and Nasalization precede the arguably morphological rules of na Deletion and Metathesis. Such analyses provide the strongest possible evidence that phonological rules must be allowed to apply in the lexicon.

Finally, Sekani supports the lexical/postlexical rule typology. As illustrated in section 7, the rules of Round Vowel Devocalization and Glottal Stop Insertion are gradient and variable, are arguably non-structure-preserving, do not have lexically marked exceptions, and do not precede any clearly lexical rules.

Notes.

1. Kari (1988) provides an overview of the strengths and weakness of these models.

2. For example, Stanley posited seven boundaries of different strengths within the verb prefixes. Because his theory required that all boundaries had to be present in the representations that served as input to the phonological component, the representations that he posited were unnecessarily baroque.

3. Kari, while correctly rejecting the boundary hierarchy proposed by Stanley, was forced to encode positional information in other ways which were equally non-standard. Many of his rules make use of the symbol [(marking the division between the classifiers and other prefixes), although Kari explicitly remarks that this symbol should not be interpreted as a boundary. Other rules are restricted to their proper domain by direct reference to prefix positions: STEM, ASPECT, etc.

4. The conjugation prefixes had aspectual functions historically. See Krauss (1969) for discussion.

5. Following Kari (1979), I use the term 'perambulative' for the combination of morphemes k'e in the adverbial position 2 and na customary in position 5 which can be used to derive verbs which denote repeated, undirected motion. I will return to perambulatives in Ch. 5, 3.2. I use the term "repetitive" to denote a derivation which requires position 9 u (and the conjugation prefix gha in the perfective). See Semelfactive later in this section.

6. In departing from the traditional Athabaskan analysis of four synchronic classifiers (∅, h (<*ł), d and *l), I follow the analysis first proposed by Stanley (1969) for Navajo. Stanley suggested that all instances of the l classifier in Navajo could be derived from /d+ł/.

7. In support of this, stem-final fricatives do not undergo Voicing Assimilation in suffixed stems:

(472) /nà -h -chįł -azi/
      cont clf rain dim
       2   13 stem

      [nàhchįłazi]   'it is raining a bit'

(473) /k'e -da -a -yis -e/
      break Fut Fut break Fut
       2   9   9 stem

      [k'edayise]   'he, she will break [O] in two'

8. In languages like Navajo which have a phonetic [l] classifier, exceptions to Voicing Assimilation which are parallel to these arise from rules which delete the l classifier interconsonantally.

9. h Voicing provides weak evidence that the voiceless unaspirated stops are voiced underlyingly.

10. As Howren notes, an additional rule is required to convert:

```
    C                    C
   / \       into        |
  d   gh                 g
```

11. This floating [d] analysis was suggested to me by Bruce Hayes. In an earlier analysis I had proposed that the levels 1-2 rule causes [d] to be doubly linked to classifier and stem-initial consonant positions. However, such an analysis needlessly violates structure-preservation.

12. Of course this move undermines the hypothesis that derivations in which d classifier occurs are semantically 'detransitivizing'. However, I am not aware of any other problems that this analysis would lead to.

13. I present the argument for assigning the classifiers to level 1 in Ch. 5 because it is somewhat theory-dependent.

14. The interested reader is referred to the above sources for exemplification. These data are especially complicated and the rules required to account for these paradigms are complicated and not really relevant to the discussion of level ordering.

15. As in other Athabaskan languages, the stem-initial consonant of 'handle pl O' irregularly changes from l to y in the 1d.

16. The vowels transcribed [èe] and [àa] in (168a,b,e) of these paradigms are actually phonetically short: [e] and [a]. The rising tone on these vowels suggests that these vowels are phonologically long until quite late in the derivation. There is no evidence that (default) high tone insertion is anything but a late, postlexical process.

17. Consider the first person singular perfective form in (474):

(474)   [kwàn nadàsihk'ǫ]   'I kindled a fire'

   *[kwàn nadèehk'ǫ]

This instance of the prefix /də/ must be exceptionally marked as not undergoing the s-conjugation rules.

18. Some of the nouns that require the areal prefix are listed below:

            [ya]   'sky'
            [mįghe]   'lake'
            [sahghè?]   'river'
            [tse k'eh]   'mountain'
            [yhis]   'hill'
            [dachin tah]   'bush, forest'
            [keyih]   'town'
            [kǫh]   'house'
           -[t'adzè?]   'back'

Some examples of this prefix in verb forms are given below:

(475a) [mət'adzę̀? wə̀sch'ǫ]   'he was shot in the back'

(475b) [mətsì? asch'ǫ]   'he was shot in the head'

(476a) [mįghe tawədəch'e]   'three lakes'

(476b) [ghadi tadəch'e]   'three animals'

(477a) [sahghè? ghochà?]   'the river is big'

(477b) [ts'ęlį nəchà?]   'the creek is big'

19. This particular formulation of the rule was suggested by Bruce Hayes.

20. The prefix i does not occur with either of the conjugation prefixes na or sə, requiring instead a null conjugation prefix. There are also no surface forms in which this prefix occurs with the first person dual subject prefix i in which they are separated by some prefix. In optative forms, where this would be expected, the derivational prefix i occurs to the right of the first person dual subject prefix i (see 3.1.4).

21. The fact that the *l classifier is phonetically non-zero ([h]) in this form is quite unusual. It is clear from other members of this paradigm that this verb has l classifier. Compare the second person singular and first person plural forms in (478a) and (b):

(478a) /sə -n -l -tsəl/
       cnj 2sS clf wet

       [sįtsəl]   'you [sg] are wet'

(478b) /ts'ə-sə -l -tsəl/
       1pS cnj clf wet

       [ts'ahtsəl]   'we are wet'

In the first person plural form, the vowel of the conjugation prefix has been deleted by Conjugation ə Deletion and Aspiration has converted [s] to [h]. Although this form is consistent with either an l or an h-classifier analysis, if 'wet' were an h classifier verb, the second person singular form would be [sįhtsəl] instead.

22. Historically, the two sets of prefixes were distinguishable phonetically: the prefixes which undergo Absorption are historically derived from *ń (a palatalized or 'front' velar), whereas those that do not are historically derived from *n (Krauss and Leer 1981). I do not believe that the synchronic phonology of Sekani still sufficiently distinguishes the reflexes of these segments to justify the positing of an abstract underlying segment /ń/.

23. As discussed in 4.1.1, there is an additional position 8 subject prefix, /sə/, which occurs with /i/ and /d/ in first person dual forms. This prefix and the conjugation prefix /`sə/ do not co-occur; moreover, in n-conjugation

forms, the low tone of the conjugation prefix /ˋnə/ is deleted by the rule of L Deletion. Thus this prefix provides no evidence about the domain of Conjugation Tone Mapping. In the absence of evidence against this analysis, I will simply assign it to level 4 with the other position 8 prefixes.

24. While most nasal vowels in Sekani are derived, it is apparently necessary to recognize a few underlying nasal vowels, as discussed in Ch. 1.

25. Notice that the deletion and automatic reassociation of autosegments is not as predicted by Clements and Ford (1979).

26. See Krauss (1978) or Leer (1979) for further information about tone in the Athabaskan languages.

27. Keren Rice suggested this rule to me.

28. This stem is exemplified with the following third person singular form:

(479)   /dlògh-ʔə   -nə   -n -zən/
         laugh unspO face Pf make
           3   7   9   11 stem

        [dlògh?ənįzən]   'he, she smiles'

29. Wolverines behave in a destructive or sabotaging manner.

Chapter Four

Level Ordering: Nominals and Postpositions

In this chapter I present a level-ordered analysis of nouns and postpositions in Sekani.[1] Evidence from affix order and phonological rule domains suggests the following model of the nominal and postpositional morphology:

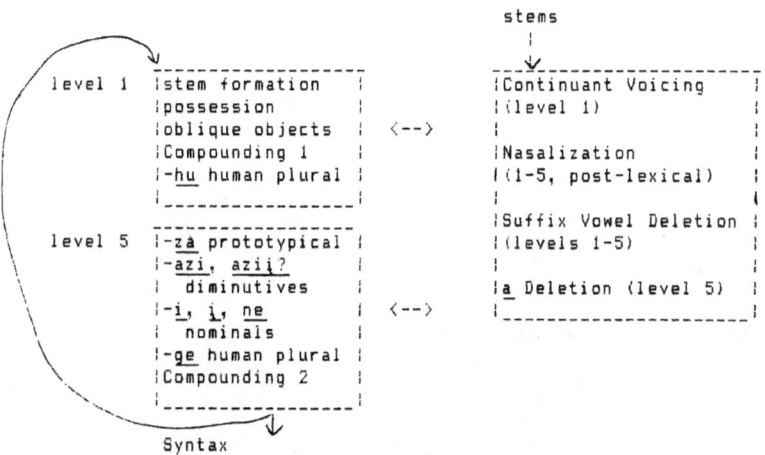

Notice that only two levels can be distinguished on the basis of evidence from phonological rule domains. Moreover, as will be seen, nouns and postpositions present a problem for the theory of level ordering in that possessed derived nominals and compounds appear to require a loop from level 5 back to level 1. The properties of nouns and postpositions thus apparently support the proposals of Aronoff and Sridhar (1983) and Sproat (1986) that (1) there are universally two domains of lexical phonological rule application, and (2) these domains are not ordered with respect to each other.

This chapter is organized as follows. In section 1 I illustrate the fact that the lexicon of Sekani apparently contains stems which are not assigned to a lexical category. In section 2 I discuss the level 1 suffixes, and in section 3, the level 5 suffixes. In Section 4 I illustrate compounding and the possessive and oblique object prefixes.

1. Stems

Many stems in Sekani can be inflected with either nominal or verbal morphology. Some examples are given in (1)-(14) below, with nominal stems listed in (a) and verbal stems in (b):

(1a)	-[bət]	'stomach'
(b)	-[bət]	'be hungry'
(2a)	[t'oghəs]	'paddle'
(b)	-[h -t'oghəs] clf stem	'paddle O'
(3a)	[uyuz]	'whistling'
(3b)	-[h-yhùs]	'whistle'
(4a)	[yhin]	'song'
(4b)	-[jin] (</d-yhin/)	'sing'
(5a)	-[gha-?]	'hair'
(5b)	-[gha -n]	'be hairy'
(6a)	[xatl'e]	'nighttime'
(6b)	-[h-xatl]	'become dark, night'
(7a)	-[ghẹ?]	'grease'
(7b)	-[h-xẹ]	'melt O' (x~gh]
(8a)	-[dəl]-	'blood'
(8b)	-[dəl]	'be red; raw'

198

(9a)   [tsǫ?]   'shit'
(9b)   -[tsən, tsǫ?]   'shit'

(10a)   [tas]   'cane'
(10b)   -[tas]   'walk around with a cane'

(11a)   [t'as]   'arrow'
(11b)   -[h-t'as]   'shoot [O] with bow and arrow'

(12a)   [xał]   'club'
(12b)   -[h-xał]   'handle stick-like [O] (uncontrol)'

(13a)   [tsęł]   'axe'
(13b)   -[tsęł]   'handle [compact O] (uncontrol)'

(14a)   [chįh xeł]   'box'
        stick pack
(14b)   -[chįh]   'handle stick-like [O] (control)'

    Sapir (1921-3) analyzed verb stems in Athabaskan as being underlyingly nominal, with 'third modal' elements (certain verb prefixes) acting as category-changing morphemes. Sapir suggested that this analysis would account for the following pan-Athabaskan facts:

> 1. the ease with which a great many evident nouns are transformed into 'verb stems'...
>
> 2. the frequency with which 'verb stems' with a clearly defined verbal force...take on, when isolated, an abstract or concrete nominal significance...
>
> 3. the fact that a number of verb stems refer not to specific activity but to a class of objects. (Sapir (1921-3:141))

Despite these observations, however, there does not seem to be overwhelming evidence that the stem which underlies pairs such as these is nominal, rather than verbal. I suggest instead that the stem which underlies the pairs in (1)-(14) is simply not assigned to a particular lexical category.

2. Level 1 suffixes

2.1 Possessive suffixes

Possessed nouns are marked by one of three suffixes, -è?, -'?, or -∅. The choice of suffix is lexically determined, but -è? is by far the most common suffix.[2] Some examples of each of these suffixes are given below:

-'? possessive suffix

(15) /sə -xəda -'/
 1sPsr moose psd

 [səghədà?]   'my moose'

(16) /sə -da -'/
 1sPsr eye psd

 [sədà?]   'my eyes'

(17) /sə -se -'/
 1sPsr belt psd

 [səzè?]   'my belt'

(18) /jije chu -'/
 berry water psd

 [jije chù?]   'wine (berry's water)'

-∅ possessive suffix

(19) /?ə -t'oh-∅/
 unspPsr nest psd

 [?at'oh]   'nest'

(20) /sə -kǫh-∅/
 1sPsr house psd

 [səkǫh]   'my house'

(21) /nə -zès -∅/
 2sPsr skin psd

 [nəzès]   'your (sg) skin'

(22) /?ə -za -∅/
 unspPsr sand psd

 [?əza]   'sand'

-e? possessive suffix

(23) /sə -dze -è?/
     1sPsr heart psd

     [sədzeè?]   'my heart'

(24) /?ə -ch'ox -è?/
     unspPsr quills psd

     [?ach'oxe?]   '(its) quills'

(25) /sə -?əsba-è?/
     1sPsr goat psd

     [se?əsbaè?]   'my goat'

In (25), the rule of Preglottal Schwa Fronting (26) accounts for the surface form [se]- of the possessive prefix /sə/-:

(26) Preglottal Schwa Fronting:

     ə --> e / ___[$_N$?

(Schwa Fronting does not apply in verbal forms.) In (27), the vowel of the possessive prefix /sə/- has been deleted by the rule of Prefix Vowel Deletion (Ch. 3, 4.2.1):

(27) /sə -èhtàs -è/
     1sPsr sister psd

     [sèhtàsè?]   'my sister'

The characteristics of inalienably possessed nouns are of some interest. There are a number of bound nominal stems, mainly body parts and kinship terms, which require possessive morphology. Such stems are apparently lexically associated with one of the possessive suffixes and are lexically marked as requiring a prefix or preceding nominal. Inalienably possessed nouns, like other nouns, occur as incorporated stems in position 3 of the verbal prefixes. Interestingly, as incorporated stems, the inalienably possessed nouns apparently abandon their lexical subcategorization frames as they lack possessive morphology in such contexts.

Consider the stem /tsi/ 'head'. As an unincorporated stem (28), this noun requires an overt possessor (in the default case, the prefix /?ə/-, which marks an unspecified possessor, is added):

(28) /?ə   -tsi/
      unspPsr head

       [?ətsi?]   '(someone's) head'

However, as an unincorporated stem in (29), no possessive prefix is required:

(29) /ts'ah t'à   -tsi -sə -s -1 -?atl/
      hat   P:inside head cnj 1sS clf handle compact O
             1   3   10 12 13 stem

       [ts'ah t'àtsisəs?atl]   'I wear a hat on my head'

2.2 -e

Some instances of stem-final -e may be regarded as a suffix. Although -e has no discernible semantic or morphological function, there are phonological reasons for regarding it as a suffix. As will be seen later on in this chapter, Sekani has a rule of Suffix Vowel Deletion:

(30) V --> ∅ /] X ___] V

The final vowel of a suffix is deleted before another vowel-initial suffix. In (31)-(32), final -e is deleted before the diminutive suffix:

(31) /ts'ègh-e -azi/
      woman stm dim

       [ts'èghazi]   'small woman'

(32) /nə -tsèdl -e -azi/
      thm small stm dim

       [nətsèdlazi]   'he, she is small'

But other instances of stem-final -e are not deleted before a vowel-initial suffix:

(33) [dəbe]   'sheep'

       [dəbeazi]   'small sheep'

I suggest that the final -[e] in [dabe] is part of the stem, whereas in [ts'èghe], the final -[e] is a suffix.

Some additional examples of stem-final suffixal -[e] are given below:

noun + -e̱

(34) [ɤughe̱]   'fish'
(35) -[chitl'e̱]   'younger brother'

verb + -e̱

(36) [najùe̱]   'he, she is absent'
(37) [dat'àde̱]   'he, she is thin'
(38) [dak'àse̱]   'he, she is short'
(39) [awàse̱]   'he, she itches'
(40) [?adèhgùge̱]   'he, she squats'

Again, the properties of incorporated stems with respect to this suffix are of interest. The suffix -e̱ is systematically absent from stems which are incorporated into the verbal prefixes.³ Consider the stem /tl'òn/ 'circle, circle of water'. As an unincorporated stem, /tl'òn/ occurs with the suffix -e̱:

(41) [tl'òne]   'bend in river'
      *[tl'ǫ?]

However, when incorporated into the verbal prefixes, the stem lacks this suffix:

(42) /tl'ǫ̀ -də -t'ax/
      circle der fly
       3   9 stem

      [tl'ǫ̀dət'ax]   'he, she flies in a circle'

(43) /tl'ǫ̀ -ghə-lį -ɤ/
      circle Prg flow asp
       3   10 stem

      [tl'ǫ̀ghəlįɤ]   'whirlpool'

(44)   /tl'ǫ -də -sa -ɬeh/
       circle der cnj handle pl O
         3   9 10 stem

       [tl'ǫdèsɬeh]   'he, she puts [pl O] in a circle'

2.3 -hu human plural

-hu is one of two human plural suffixes in Sekani. The other suffix is -ge/ghe, discussed in 3.3. Nouns are lexically marked for which of these suffixes they take.

Some examples of -hu human plural are provided below:

(45a) [ts'ùda]   'child'
(45b) [ts'ùdahu]   'children'

(46a) [?ach'e]   'girl'
(46b) [?ach'ehu]   'girls'

Evidence from affix order (see 3.3) is consistent with a level 1 analysis of -hu.

The initial consonant of -hu is deleted if the stem to which it attaches is consonant-final. This rule is informally stated in (47):

(47)   h Loss:

       h --> ∅ / C___

Its application can be seen in (48) below:

(48a) [dakeɬ]   'Indian person'
(48b) [dakeɬu]   'Indian persons'

The meaningless suffix -e is also absent in forms which contain this plural suffix:

(49a) [ts'èghe]   'woman'
(49b) [ts'èghazi]   'small woman'
(49c) [ts'èghu]   'women'

As indicated by the diminutive form (49b), stem-final -e in this form is analyzable as a suffix because it is deleted before a vowel-initial suffix. The plural form in (49c) suggests that the suffix -e is not present in the plural form underlyingly. In 3.3 I will present evidence that -e and the possessive suffix -e? are not deleted before consonant-initial suffixes. If stem-final -e were part of the stem, the surface form *ts'èghehu would be expected. The underlying representations of the singular and plural forms of these nouns must differ:

(50a) /ts'ègh-e/   'woman'
(50b) /ts'ègh-hu/   'women'

2.4 Instrumental stems

An instrumental suffix -*y* occurs on a few nouns:

/xe/ 'pack'

(51a) [xe*y*]   'pack' [N]

(51b) /k'è-na-nə -d -xe -h/
       per C 2sə clf pack asp
       2   5 12 13 stem

       [k'ènǫgeh]   'you [sg] pack [O] around'

/tl'u, tl'un/ 'tie'

(52a) [tl'u*y*]   'rope'

(52b) /mə -è-tl'u-?ə -nə -tl'ų-h/
       3sO P tie unspO 2sS tie Imp

       [mètl'u?įtl'ųh]   'you [sg] tie up O'

(In (52b), the stem tl'u is also incorporated as a level 5 verb prefix.) This suffix only occurs on these two nouns in my corpus.

2.5 Phonology: Nasalization

The domain of the rule of Nasalization suggests that the possessive suffixes, as well as the meaningless suffix -e, are added on level 1. As discussed in Ch. 1, nearly all nasal vowels in Sekani can be derived from syllable-final /Vn/ sequences. In the following pair, the nasal consonant in (61b) is not syllable-final and thus Nasalization does not apply:

(53a) [tsǫ?]   'shit'

(53b) [sə -tsòn-è?]   'my shit'
    1sPsr shit psd

Now consider the diminutive form of this stem:

(53c) [tsǫ̀-azi]   'small shit'
    shit dim

Nasalization precedes diminutive suffixation but follows possessive suffixation. This suggests that the diminutive suffix is added on a non-initial level of the lexicon, and furthermore, that the possessive suffix is added on the first level. If -è? were suffixed on level 2 or later, Nasalization would presumably have applied to the stem before the possessive suffix could be added, as it has in the diminutive form of this stem. This can be seen in the following derivation:

stem   /tsòn/

level 1
  Nasalization   [tsǫ]

level 2
  possessed noun suffix [tsǫ-è]

                        *-[tsǫ̀è?]

However, if the possessive suffix is added on the first level of the lexicon, the fact that Nasalization does not first apply to nasal-final stems before the addition of the possessive suffix is accounted for.

Similar data involving nasal-final stems suggest that the stem-forming suffix -e should be added on level 1. Consider the aspectually suffixed stem /yha-n/ 'grow' (Pf):

(54a) [tlį yon -e]   'old dog'
    dog grown

206

(54b) [tlį yon -azi]
       dog grown dim

       [tlį yǫazi]   'old, decrepit dog'

Nasalization has applied to the form in (54b), which contains the diminutive suffix, but does not apply to the form in (54a) which contains the suffix -e.

Additional evidence which suggests that -e -è? belong on level 1 is provided by affix order, as will be seen in section 3 below.

2.6 Summary

The possessive suffix -e? possessive and the meaningless suffix -e stem-formative precede the application of Nasalization to stems, suggesting that these suffixes are added on level 1, in contrast to other vowel-initial suffixes. Evidence from affix order to be presented in 3.3 suggests that -hu human plural is also added on level 1.

3. Level 5 Suffixes

3.1 Nominalizing Suffixes

Nouns may be derived from any of the major lexical categories--noun, verb or postposition--through a nominalizing process which I hypothesize to be a level 5 process.

There are three non-zero nominalizing suffixes in Sekani: -i 'human singular', -ne 'human plural', and -i. The non-zero suffixes also attach to verbs in relative clauses.

3.1.1 Examples

In this section I provide examples of each kind of derived nominal:

   -∅ nominalizing suffix

(55) [na -be]
      rev swim
      5   stem   'otter'

(56)   /sə -h -tsʼi/
       cnj clf be sour
       10 13 stem

       [sahtsʼi]   'pepper'

(57)   /ɬè   -s -d -tlʼų/
       in half cnj clf tie
       2   10 13 stem

       [lèstlʼų]   'knot'

(58)   /nà -nə -sə -d -tlʼų/
       cont term cnj clf tie
       2   9   10 13 stem

       [nànèstlʼų]   'fence'

(59)   /dah-də -s-ghǫ/
       up thm ? be hairy
       2   9   stem

       [dahdəsghǫ]   '(tree moss species)'

(60)   /ʔə -də -s-xət/
       unspO thm ? saw O
       7   9   stem

       [ʔədəsxət]   'saw'

(61)   /hà -sa -da -də -sə -ʔǫ/
       up sun thm thm cnj compact O is in position
       2   3   9   9   10 stem

       [hàsadadèzʔǫ]   'sunrise'

(62)   /mə -kʼe -də-sa -h -tsʼi/
       3sO P:on pl cnj clf pl sit
       1   1   9 10 13 stem

       [məkʼedèhtsʼi]   'couch'

(63)   /ʔə -tsʼa -gǫ̀/
       unspO unspS dry O
       7   8   stem

       [ʔatsʼagǫ̀ʔ]   'dried meat'

       -i̧ human singular

(64)   [tse -kʼeh-i̧] 'Sekani person'
       mountain P:on nom:hum sg

(65)   [də -k'al   -į]   'white person'
        thm be white nom:hum sg

(66)   [sə   -k'àh -į]   'my spouse'
        1sPsr marry nom:hum sg

(67)   /sə -ę̇h-ɫàgh-į/
        1sPsr ? one nom:hum sg

        [sę̇hɫàghį]   'my friend, partner'

(68)   /dəne wha-wə -də -h -?įh -į/
        people 1pO thm thm clf teach nom:hum sg

        [dəne whawədah?įhį]   'teacher'

        -ne human plural

(69)   [tse   -lǫh-ne]   'Ft. Ware people'
        mountain end nom:hum pl

(70)   [tsǫ̀? kǫh -ne]   'Ft. St. John people'
        shit house nom:hum pl

(71)   [?įh -k'àh -ne]   'married couple'
        recp marry nom:hum pl

(72)   [keyih nà -jèɫ -ne]   'people who live in town'
        town cont live nom:hum pl

(73)   /ɫàhde   ə -h -ts'į-ne/
        1 place epen clf born nom:hum pl

        [ɫàhde ahts'įne]   'family (of one household)'

(74)   /ɫə -a -d -ghǫ   -ne/
        recp cnj clf kill pl O nom:hum pl

        [ɫagǫne]   'soldiers'

        -i

(75)   /nə -sə -d -dəs   -i/
        term cnj clf twist nom
         9   10 13 stem

        [nèsdəsi]   'twisted tree'

(76)   /tsɨ -gha ə   -s -d -tl'ụ-i /
        head hair epen cnj clf tie nom
                       10 13 stem

        [tsigha əstl'ụi]   'braids'

209

(77) /dah-ʔə   -ts'ə -sə -l -ya   -i/
      up unspO unspS cnj clf pl O be in position nom
      2   7   8   10 13   stem

      [dahʔətsʼahyai]   'glasses'

(78) /ʔə   -i̧là gha-də -i -n -ʔǫ   -i/
      unspPsr hand P   thm asp Pf compact O be in position nom
                      9   9   11   stem

      [ʔi̧là? ghadi̧ʔǫi]   'ring'

(79) /mə -kʼeh tsəz   də -chʼel-i/
      3sO P:on firewood wood split nom
                          9   stem

      [makʼeh tsəz dəchʼeli] 'chopping block'

(80) [u -s-d -lus -i]   'toboggan, sled'
      thm ? clf drag nom
      9   13   stem

(81) /kwàn mə -tʼà   də -sə -kwʼàn-i/
      fire 3sO P:inside fire cnj burn nom
                          9   10 stem

      [kwàn mətʼà? dèzkwʼàni] 'stove'

(82) /hà-nə -h -yheh -i/
      up der clf grow nom
      2 9   13 stem

      [hànahyhehi]   'cultivated plants'

In most of the preceding forms, the base of the derived nominal is a verb. However, the nominalizing suffixes can also be attached to nouns and postpositions, as indicated by (64) and (70).

3.1.2 Level Ordering: Nasalization

The domain of Nasalization suggests that the nominalizing suffixes are added on level 5.

Stem-final nasal vowels, rather than nasal consonants, occur before the vowel-initial nominalizing suffixes. As discussed in 2.5, this suggests that the nominalizing and diminutive suffixes belong to the same level, and that the possessive suffixes are placed on an earlier level. Consider the following nominals suffixed with -i:

(83)   /sa-tsʼa -da -i̧ -ʔo̧   -i/
       ?   unspS thm asp compact O be in position nom

       [satsʼadi̧ʔo̧i]   'pendant'

(84)   /ma -è-da -s-ji̧-i/
       3sO P thm ? ? nom

       [mèdasji̧i]   'binoculars'

(85)   /chu   ma -kʼeh-sa -ko̧   -i/
       water 3sO P:on cnj contained O be in position nom

       [chu makʼehsako̧i]   'washstand'

If the nominalizing suffixes were added on level 1, before Nasalization
applied, these stems should have final nasal consonants rather than nasal
vowels, as do the level 1 suffixes -e and -è:

(86)   *-[ʔoni], *-[jini], *-[koni], etc.[4]

The fact that nasal vowels occur instead of nasal consonants suggests that the
nominalizing suffixes belong to a non-initial level of the lexicon. Level 5
is an arbitrary choice.

It should be noted that many derived nominals are 'phrasal,' in that they
apparently consist of more than one word. Informally, two kinds of 'phrasal'
nominals may be distinguished. Fixed lexical expressions, such as 'teacher'
(86) and 'braids' (94) above, and examples like the following, may contain
more than one word:

(87)   /ma -èh   kʼè-na-d -gùx -i/
       3sO P:by means of per C   clf drive nom
                          2   5   13 stem

       [mèh kʼagùxi]   'car'

(88)   /dàda   kʼè-na-d -ghe -h -i/
       sickness per C clf pack C nom
                2   5 13 stem

       [dàda kʼagehi]   'magpie' (packs sickness around)

(89) /tən nà -gha-tl'ų -i/
      ice down cnj tie   nom
              2   10 stem

      [tən nàghatl'ųi]   'icicle'

It should be noted that the same set of non-zero suffixes (-i, -į, and -ne)
that appear on what are here analyzed as derived nominals mark verbs in
relative clauses:

(90) /łughe nə -chà -i   kayənassən/
      fish   thm big nom I want

      [łughe nəchài kayənassən]

      'I want a big fish'

(91) /i   dəne ə -jən -į   mə -yez natsį/
      dem person epen sing nom:hum sg 3sPsr throat is bad

      [i dəne əjinį məyez natsį?]

      'the person who is singing has a bad voice'

(92) /?àkwène mə-k'à -sə -s -da   -ne   ghįzų/
      3p   3 P:by cnj 1sS sg sit nom:hum pl they are nice

      [?àkwène mək'àsəsdane ghįzų]

      'the people I stay with are nice'

(93) /?eyę ts'ah tà-tsi -sə -l -?atl   -i/
      3s   hat   up head cnj clf compact 0 be nom:hum sg

      [?eyę ts'ah tàtsih?adlį]

      'the one who is wearing a hat'

3.1.3 Possessed Derived Nominals

    Derived nominals may be possessed, just like other nouns:

(94a) /dah-?ə -ts'ə -sə -l -ya   -i/
      up unspO unspS cnj clf pl O be in position nom

      [dah?əts'ahyai]   'glasses'

212

(94b)   /sə -dah?əts'ahyai-è/
        1sPsr glasses   psd

        [sədah?əts'ahyaè?]   'my glasses'

(The rule of Suffix Vowel Deletion has applied in (94b).)

(95a)   /də -tsəs-i/
        der whip nom

        [dətsəsi]   'whip'

(95b)   /sə -dətsəsi -è/
        1sPsr whip   psd

        [sədətsəsè?]   'my whip'

(96a)   /mə-k'eh-s -d -da -i/
        3s P:on cnj clf sg sit nom

        [mək'esdai]   'chair'

(96b)   /sə- mək'esdai-è/
        1sPsr chair   psd

        [səmak'esdaè?]   'my chair'

(97a)   /?ə -bil -i/
        unspO swing nom

        [?əbili]   'swing'

(97b)   /sə- ?əbili-è/
        1sPsr swing psd

        [se?əbilè?]   'my swing'

Phonological evidence from Nasalization indicates that the possessive suffix -è? which occurs in these possessed derived nominals cannot be added to possessed derived nominals on the first pass through level 1. Consider some examples of possessed derived nominals which are derived from nasal-final stems:

(98a)   /sa-ts'ə -də -i -?ǫ   -i/
        ? unspS der asp compact O is in position nom

        [sats'ədi?ǫi]   'pendant'

213

(98b) /sə -sats'ədî?ǫi-è/
       1sPsr pendant   psd

       [səsats'ədî?ǫè?]   'my pendant'

(99a) /mə -è-də -s-jį-i/
       3sO P thm ? ? nom

       [mèdəsjįi]   'binoculars'

(99b) /sə -mèdəsjįi -è/
       1sPsr binoculars psd

       [səmèdəsjįè?]   'my binoculars'

(100a) /chu mə -k'eh-sə -kǫ   -i/
       water 3sO P:on cnj contained O be in position nom

       [chu mək'ehsəkǫi]   'washstand'

(100b) /sə- chu mək'ehsəkǫi-è/
       1sPsr washstand   psd

       [səchu mək'ehsəkǫè?]   'my washstand'

The stems of the forms in (98)-(108) contain nasal vowels, rather than nasal consonants. If the possessive suffix -è? were added on the first pass through level 1, forms with stem-final nasal consonants should result, as in [sətsòne?] 'my shit', [səgòne?] 'my arm'. The possessed derived nominals with stem-final nasal vowels suggest that the possessive suffix -è? is added at a point in the derivation after Nasalization has applied. Plausibly, this point follows the addition of the level 5 nominalizing suffixes:

(101) level 1   Nasalization
       level 5   nominalizing suffix
       level 1   possessive suffix

Affix order also suggests that the possessive suffixes should be added after the nominalizing suffixes are added. In section 4 I will argue that the possessive prefixes are added on level 1. In the following examples, note that a possessive prefix occurs to the left of a level 5 verbal prefix:

(102a) /mə -e-ʔə -da   -i/
       3sO P unspO pl eat nom

       [meʔədai]   'food'

(102b) /mə- meʔədai-è/
       3sPsr food   psd

       [məmeʔədaè?]   'his, her food'

(103a) /mə -èh   k'è-na-d -gùx -i/
       3sO P:by means of per C clf drive nom

       [mèh k'ą̀gùxi]   'car'

(103b) /sə- mèh k'ą̀gùxi -è/
       1sPsr car   psd

       [samèh k'ą̀gùxè?]   'my car'

(104a) /ʔįh -là nà -ghə-n -ʔa   -i/
       recpO P down cnj Pf compact O be in position nom

       [ʔįhlà nàghį̀ʔai]   'coveralls'

(104b) /sə- ʔįh lànàghį̀ʔai-è/
       1sPsr coveralls   psd

       [seʔįhlà nàghį̀ʔaè?]   'my coveralls'

Affix order suggests that the possessive prefixes are added after level 5 verb prefixation in these forms. I posit a loop from level 5 back to level 1 to account for the structure of possessed derived nominals:

(105) ┌─ level 1   possession
       └─ levels 1-5   verb formation

3.1.4 Locative nominals

Before leaving the topic of derived nominals in Sekani, I would like to briefly illustrate the structure of derived locative nominals.

The morphemes d<u>ah</u>/d<u>ih</u> refer to two-dimensional locations; -<u>gàh</u> refers to a one-dimensional location.[5] These suffixes are frequently, but not exclusively, found on place names:

215

(106a) [chu chi dạh]   'Tacheeda L., Tudick L.'
       water big nom:loc

(106b) [chu chi gàh]   'Tacheeda L. creek'

(107a) [?azàze   dịh]   'Azouzetta L.'
       flying squirrel nom:loc

(107b) [?azàze gàh]   'Atunatche Creek' (flows out of Azouzetta L.)

(108a) [chu yaze dịh]   'Chuyazega L.'
       water rough nom:loc

(108b) [chu yaze gàh]   'Chuyazega R.'

Some additional examples of dạh/dịh are given below:

(109) [bàt   -ka   da-   ch'ị dịh]
       stomach P:for for oneself do,be nom:loc

       'kitchen'

(110) /da   -sa -lị   dịh/
       forth cnj flow nom:loc

       [dèzlị dịh]   'lake outlet'

(111) /ła -ts'a -a -d -ghọ   dạh/
       recp unspS cnj clf kill pl O nom:loc

       [łats'agọ dạh]   'War Lake'

(112) /saba   -azi dịh/
       Dolly Varden trout dim nom:loc

       [sabazi dịh]   'Sabai Lake'

(113) /kweh dịh/   'Arctic Lake'
       grave nom:loc

One would expect these morphemes to be added in the lexicon on the same level as the other nominalizing suffixes. However, there is some evidence that dạh/dịh and gàh are not lexical morphemes.

The possessive suffix -è? always occurs inside of dạh/dịh, whereas -è? always occurs to the right of the nominalizing suffix -i in possessed derived nominal forms. Compare the following with the possessed derived nominals given in 3.1.3:

(114a) [ʔədəzla dạh]   'warehouse'

(114b) [seʔədəzlaè̱ʔ dạh]   'my warehouse'

(115a) [hàʔənəyeh dạh]   'garden'

(115b) [səhàʔənəyehè̱ʔ dạh]   'my garden'

Secondly, the diminutive suffix -azi can only occur inside of dạh/dịh, while (as I will show in 3.2) -azi can occur inside or outside of the other nominalizing suffixes:

(116a) [tl'ogh-e   dạh]   'meadow'
       grass stm nom:loc

(116b) [tl'oghazi dạh]   'small meadow'

(116c) *[tl'oghe dạhazi]

(117a) /nàn   hà-wə-h -kǫ   dịh/
       earth up ar clf dig nom:loc

       [nàn hàwahkǫ dịh]   'hole in the ground'

(117b) [nàn hàwahkǫazi dịh]   'small hole in the ground'

(117c) *[nàn hàwahkǫ dịhazi]

3.2 Diminutives and other adjectives

3.2.1 Diminutives

There are two diminutive suffixes in Sekani, -azi 'small' and -azịị̂ʔ 'tiny, baby'. (The latter suffix is glossed 'ddim'.) Some examples of each suffix are given in the forms in (118)-(119) below:

(118a) [bùs]   'cat'

(118b) [bùs-azi]   'small cat, kitten'
       cat dim

(118c) [bùs-azịị̂ʔ]   'tiny newborn kitten'
       cat ddim

(119a) [gusbay]   'sucker' (fish)

(119b) [gusbay-azi]   'small sucker'

(119c) [gusbay-azį?]   'tiny, baby sucker'

Diminutive forms of verbs are also possible. At least -azi may be suffixed to verbs, as can be seen in (120)-(122):

(120a) /ə -s -whàs-e/
       epen 1sS itch stm

       [əswhàse]   'I itch'

(120b) [əswhàsazi]   'I itch a little bit'

The stem-final vowel -e in (120b) has been deleted by the rule of Suffix Vowel Deletion.

The diminutive suffix is lexicalized in some forms (especially those which denote inherently small objects or measurements), both nouns (121)-(129) and verbs (130)-(132).

(121) [?įbazi]   'weasel'

(122) [?įhsyazi]   'spider'

(123) [dlǫazi]   'mouse'

(124) [k'ǫjazi]   'bear cub'

(125) /nǫj   -e -azi/
       big game animal stm dim

       [nǫjazi]   'bird'

(126) /dət'on-e -azi/
       duck   stm dim

       [dət'onazi]   'bird'

(127) [chusk'azi]   'chickadee'

(128) [dachusdəst'azi]   'hummingbird'

(129) [?ùzęhazi]   'owl species'

(130a) [nətsàdl-e],   'he, she is small'

(130b) [nətsàdlazi]   "

(131a) [dək'às-e],   'he, she is short'
(131b) [dək'àsazi]   "

(132a) [dət'àd-e],   'he, she is skinny'
(132b) [dət'àdazi]   "

The verbs in (130)-(132) which contain the diminutive suffix are far more common than the forms which lack the diminutive suffix. In fact, for some speakers, the forms without the diminutive suffix are unacceptable.

A variety of evidence suggests that the diminutives belong to a non-initial level of the lexicon. First, as discussed in 2.5, the fact that Nasalization precedes diminutive suffixation suggests that the diminutive suffixes are not added on level 1, as are the possessive suffixes:[6]

(133a) [tsǫ̀?]   'shit'
(133b) [sətsòne̲?]   'my shit'
(133c) [tsǫazi]   'small shit'

Additional support for a non-initial level ordering assignment of the diminutive suffix is provided by consideration of affix order. (1) The nominalizing and diminutive suffixes are apparently unordered with respect to each other, suggesting that these suffixes belong to the same level. In surface forms, affix order reflects the semantically most plausible constituent structure:

   i-azi

(134a) [sə -k'àh -į]
       1sPsr marry nom   'my spouse'

(134b) /sə -k'àh -į -azi/
       1sPsr marry nom dim

       [sək'àhạzi]   'my dear spouse'

azi-į

(135a) [nətsə̀dlazi]   'he, she is small'

(135b) /nə -tsə̀dl-e -azi-į/
       thm small stm dim nom:hum sg

       [nətsə̀dlazį]   'small person'

ne-azi

(136a) [tse   k'eh-ne]   'Sekani people'
       mountain P:on nom:hum pl

(136b) /tse   k'eh-ne   -azi/
       mountain P:on nom:hum pl dim

       [tse k'ehnazi]   'dear Sekani people'

(2) The suffix -azi occurs to the left of the sentential morphemes a̜ optative and gho̜ positive interrogative:

(137a) /nà -h -chi̜ɬ ghǫ/
       adv clf rain Q

       [nàhchi̜ɬ ghǫ]   'Is it raining?'

(137b) [nà -h -chi̜ɬ-azi ghǫ] 'Is it raining a little bit?'
       adv clf rain dim Q

(138a) /chu   gho-ì -d -dǫ̀   ą/
       water Op 1dS clf drink Op

       [chu ghùdǫ̀ą]   'we [du] have a drink' Op

(138b) [chu ghùdǫ̀-azią]   'we [du] have a little drink' Op
                dim

This is consistent with the level 5 analysis of these suffixes: morphemes added in the lexicon should occur inside of morphemes generated by the syntax.

(3) Finally, note that the diminutive suffix always occurs to the right of the non-zero possessive suffixes -`? and -è?:

(139a) [ts'ùda]   'child'

(139b) /mə   -ts'ùda-`/
       3sPsr child psd

       [məts'ùdà?]   'his, her child'

(139c) /mə -tsʼùda-ʼ -azi/
       3sPsr child psd dim

       [mətsʼùdàzi]   'his, her small child'

(140a) [bes]   'knife'

(140b) [mə -bes -èʔ]   'his, her knife'
       3sPsr knife psd

(140c) /mə-bes-è -azi/   'his, her small knife'
              psd dim

       [məbesàzi]

These data are consistent with an analysis in which the possessive suffix is added before the diminutive suffix.

3.2.2 -zàʔ prototypical

The suffix zàʔ (-zàazi) deserves mention. The noun to which this suffix attaches is translated as 'normal, plain, medium-sized'; i.e., such nouns are prototypes of their class. Some examples of this suffix are given below:

(141a) [dane]   'man, person'

(141b) [dənezàazi]   'Indian person'

(142a) [jèzʔo]   'gun'

(142b) [jèzʔoazi]   'small gun (e.g. .22 caliber)'

(142c) [jèzʔozàazi]   'average gun (e.g. .30-.30)'

(143a) [ɬès]   'flour, bannock'

(143b) [ɬèsazi]   'small bannock'

(143c) [ɬèszàʔ]   'plain, basic bannock'

(144a) [bes]   'knife'

(144b) [besazi]   'small knife'

(144c) [beszàazi]   'plain knife, e.g. table knife'

-zàʔ occurs to the right of the nominalizing suffixes:

(145a) [usdlusi] 'toboggan'

(145b) [usdlusizàazi] 'sled'

(146a) [mèhk'ągùxi] 'car'

(146b) [mèhk'ągùxizàazi] 'truck, car'

Since there is no evidence that -zà? can attach to any lexical items but nouns, I suggest that -zà? is added on level 5, following attachment of the nominal suffixes.

3.3 Human plural -ge/ghe

There are two human plural suffixes in Sekani: -hu, discussed in 2.3, and -ge/ghe, to be discussed in this section.[7] Nouns are lexically marked for which of these suffixes they require.

Some examples of forms containing -ge/ghe are given below:

(147a) [tsaɬtsəl] 'baby'

(147b) [tsaɬtsəl-ge] 'babies'
        hum pl

(148a) /sə -èhtàs -è/
    1sPsr sister psd

    [sèhtàsè?] 'my sister'

(148b) [sèhtàsè-ge] 'my sisters'
        hum pl

(149a) /sə -chatl'e/
    1sPsr younger brother

    [sachatl'e] 'my younger brother'

(149b) [sachatl'ege] 'my younger brothers'

Because -ge/ghe and -hu are both plural suffixes one might be tempted to assign them to the same level. However, the surface order of these suffixes with respect to the diminutive suffix -azi is different.

-hu always occurs to the left of -azi:

(150) /ts'ègh -hu   -azi/
        woman   hum pl dim

       [ts'èghuazi]   'small women'
       *[ts'èghazihu]

(151) /ts'ùda-hu   -azi/
        child   hum pl dim

       [ts'ùdahuazi]   'small children'
       *[ts'ùdazihu]

However, -ge always occurs to the right of -azi:

(152) /sə-   chu   -è -azi-ge/
        1sPsr daughter psd dim hum pl

       [səchuàzige]   'my small daughters'
       *[səchuègazi]

(153) /sə-   chų-è -azi-ge/
        1sPsr son psd dim hum pl

       [səchųàzige]   'my small sons'
       *[səchųègazi]

These data suggest that -ge/ghe human plural belongs to a later level than does -hu human plural. Accordingly, I analyze -ge/ghe as a level 5 suffix, ordered after the diminutive suffixes.[8]

3.4 Level 5 suffixes: Summary

Nasalization and affix order suggest that the diminutive and nominalizing suffixes are added on a non-initial level of the lexicon, which is arbitrarily assumed to be level 5. The human plural suffixes -ge/ghe cannot occur to the left of the diminutive suffixes. Accordingly, I analyze -ge/ghe as level 5 suffixes, ordered after diminutive suffixation.

Possessed derived nominals require a loop from level 5 back to level 1.

4. Compounds and prefixes

In this section I discuss the properties of (1) compounds and (2)

possessive and oblique object prefixes. Evidence for level ordering
assignments is provided by the rules of Continuant Voicing and Nasalization.

In 4.1 I provide a brief description of the inventory of possessive and
oblique object prefixes and in 4.2, of compounding types. In 4.4 I discuss
level ordering assignments, making use of evidence from the domains of
Nasalization and Continuant Voicing (4.3).

4.1 Possessive prefixes and oblique objects

As discussed in 2.1, possessed nouns are marked in two ways. A
possessive suffix (which may be phonologically ∅) is required. In addition, a
non-null possessive prefix or nominal possessor is also required.

In (154) I provide a list of the possessive prefixes in Sekani. With the
exception of the reflexive prefix, these are identical to the oblique object
prefixes and to the verbal direct object prefixes which occur in prefix
position 7:

(154) singular dual   plural   reflexive
1   sə   naxə   whə
2   nə   naxə
3   mə   ghuyə   də
4   yə   ghiyə
unsp   ʔə
area   wə
recp   ɤə/ʔih

The 4th person prefixes are 'disjoint anaphors': they are used when the
subject and object of the sentence are both third person and are obligatorily
disjoint in reference. An example is provided in (155):

(155) /yə -sə -ch'ǫ/
       4sO cnj shoot dead

       [yə̀zch'ǫ]   'he, she$_i$ shot him, her$_j$ dead'

See Saxon (1984 (a,b) to appear) for additional information about cognates to
this prefix or other pronominal prefixes in Dogrib (a closely related

language).

The oblique object prefixes (objects of postpositions) are identical to the possessive prefixes in (154) above with the noted exception of the reflexive prefixes. The reflexive possessive prefix da- requires a third person antecedent. However, the reflexive oblique object and direct object prefix ?ada- does not require a third person antecedent: its antecedent may be first, second or third person. This difference in inflection between postpositions and nominals is important, providing evidence that postpositions and nouns are distinct lexical categories, as first pointed out by Rice (to appear) for Slave. Some examples from Sekani which illustrate the difference between the prefixes da- and ?ada- are given in (156)-(160) below:

    ?ada- reflexive oblique object

third person antecedent:

(156) /?àkwàne ?ada-dagha k'èdǫh-gha-da -da -tsagh/
       3p   refl P:for adv   3p der thm sew
                            2   8 9   9 stem

      [?àkwàne ?adadagha k'èdǫhghadadatsagh]

      'They sew for themselves.'

non-third person antecedent:

(157) /naxane ?ada-dagha k'èdǫh-da -da -ah -tsagh/
       2p   refl P:for adv   der thm 2pS sew
                            2   9   9 12 stem

      [naxane ?adadagha k'èdǫhdadahtsagh]

      'You [pl] sew for yourselves.'

(156) and (157) indicate that the oblique object prefix ?ada- may be used regardless of whether its antecedent is third person or not. Now compare da-, the reflexive possessive prefix:

da- reflexive possessive prefix

third person antecedent:

(158)   /Sam də-   ts'ahgh-è   làdap k'è -wə-?aɣ   ą/
            refl hat   psd table P:on Op handle compact O Op

   [Sam dats'ahghè? làdap k'èwə?aɣ ą]

   'Sam puts his own hat on the table.' Op

(159)   /də -ghə-tsi   ka-na -ghə-də -u -t'às ą/
            refl 3p head P rev 3p der Op cut   Op

   [dəghutsi? kanaghədut'às ą]

   'They cut their own hair.' Op

non-third person antecedent:

(160)   /sə   -įla -'   sə -ı   -t'às/
            1sPsr hand psd cnj 1sPf cut

   [sįlà? sit'às]   'I cut my hand.'
   *[dįlà?]

The reflexive possessive prefix da- cannot be used with a non-third person antecedent, as seen in (160).

4.2 Compounds

Each of the major lexical categories occurs in Sekani nominal compounds: noun + noun, postpositional phrase + noun, noun + verb. Some examples of each type of compound are provided below:

   noun + noun

(161)   [xəda ts'è?]   'cow moose'
            moose female

(162)   [ts'à? k'ède]   'cellar'
            plate place

(163)   [ɣughe mèyikahi]   'fish dipper'
            fish   dipper

(164)   [tl'ogh ts'à?]   'basket'
            grass   plate

(165)   [dəchin yù?]   'bush medicine'
            stick medicine

226

postpositional phrase + noun

(166) /tl'ogh tah wa-dane -`/
grass P:among ar-people-psd

[tl'ogh tah wədənè?]   'Ft. Ware people'

(167) [chin tah tlį]   'coyote'
stick P:among dog

(168) [tsà? ghǫh yhèɤ]   'beaver trap'
beaver P:for trap

(169) [gat tah kǫh]   'Ft. St. John'
spruce P:among house

(170) [?alà? t'ah kǫh]
spruce bark P:under house

'smoke house'

(171) [tsəz gha kǫh]   'woodshed'
firewood P:for house

noun + verb

(172) [tsi? ?atl]   'pillow'
head compact O be in position

(173) /?ə- įla -` ?ǫ/
unspPsr hand psd compact O be in position

[?įlà? ?ǫ]   'ring'

(174) [dəl tsogh]   'bile'
blood yellow

(175) [kw'əs tsədle]   'bead'
cloud small

(176) [?įh -ts'i dəs]   'tornado, twister'
recp wind twist

(177) [dəne ts'at]   'dead person'
person die

(178) [tse gày]   'Clear Mt.'
mountain white, light

(179) [chu yon -e]   'waves'
water grown

(180) [chu zəl]   'soup'
water warm

In the preceding compounds, the verb stem in the second member of the compound lacks the usual verbal morphology. Compare (180) and (181), for example:

(181) [chu sə -zəl -i]   'warm water'
      water cnj warm nom

I now turn to phonological evidence for the level ordering assignments of possessive prefixation, oblique object prefixation, and compounding.

4.3 Continuant Voicing

The phonological rule of Continuant Voicing is of central importance in a level-ordered analysis of these structures.

4.3.1 Basic data

In general, there is no contrast between voiced and voiceless stem-initial fricatives in underlying representations. Surface voicing is predictable. Following Rice (to appear), I assume that stem-initial fricatives are underlyingly voiceless in this position, with a voicing rule providing surface voicing in appropriate environments. This is a controversial position in Athabaskan linguistics (cf. Cook 1984, Kari 1976), but I believe that Rice has provided good arguments for the underlyingly voiceless nature of the continuants. Moreover, these arguments are based on consideration of a wider range of stem-initial data than I have seen in any discussion which claims that stem-initial fricatives are underlyingly voiced.

The initial fricatives of noun and postposition stems are generally voiceless when unprefixed,[9] but voiced when the stems are prefixed or preceded by a nominal possessor or object. These alternations are summarized in (182):

(182)   s ~ z
        ł ~ l
        yh ~ y
        x ~ gh
        wh ~ w

A first approximation to Continuant Voicing is given in (183):

228

(183) [+cont] --> [+voice] / X [___ ...]_{N,P}

The effects of Continuant Voicing can be seen in a wide variety of morphological structures. First consider alternations involving possessed noun stems:

(184a) [xàs]   'planing tool'
(b)   [saghàsè?]   'my planing tool'

(185a) [whəs]   'rose, thorn'
(b)   [sawasè?]   'my rose, thorn'

(186a) [sas]   'bear'
(b)   [səzasè?]   'my bear'

(187a) [se]   'belt'
(b)   [Peter zè?]   'Peter's belt'

(188a) [ɬès]   'flour, bannock'
(b)   [bosdən   lèsè?]   'white person's bannock'
       white person

Continuant Voicing applies regardless of whether the possessor is nominal or pronominal.

Various derivational prefixes are also within the domain of Continuant Voicing:[10]

(189a) [sa]   'sun'
(b)   [iza(nah)]   'month'

(190a) [ɬugh-e]
       fish stm   'fish'

(b)   [ta   -lugh]
       water fish   'salmon'

(191a) [yhin]   'song'

(b)   [sayine?]   'my song'

(192a) [xeɣ]   'pack'

(b)   [?a-   gheɣ-e]   'Carrier Indian'
       work pack stm

The initial continuant of the second member of a compound is voiced:

(193a) [yhis]   'hill'

(b)   [chu   chi yis]   'Tudick Lake hill'
       water big hill

(194a) [yhę̀ɣ]   'trap'

(b)   [tsà? yę̀ɣ]   'beaver trap'
       beaver trap

(195a) [xàz]   'windfall roots'

(b)   [tse   ghàz-e]   'Old Friend Mt.'
       mountain roots

Since postpositions and inalienably possessed nouns are always preceded by an object or possessor, these stems are always voiced, if continuant-initial:

inalienably possessed nouns

(196) [mazi?]   'his, her body'

(197) [?alà?]   'boat'

(198) [saghà?]   'my hair'

(199) [sawaz]   'my leg'

      -gha   postposition

(200) [?ədə -gha ?a -s -ch'į]
       refl0 P   work 1sS be, do

      'I work for myself'

(201) [də   -kʼàhį gha-de -z -ya]
       reflPsr spouse P   der cnj sg go

       'he, she left his, her own spouse'

       -ghǫh   postposition

(202) [ʔadə -ghǫh ah -d -lį]
       reflO P   2pS clf be

       'you [pl] take care of yourselves'

(203) [mama ghǫh nà -s -i -chį]
       mother P   cont cnj 1sPf dream

       'I dreamed about mother'

       -la   postposition

(204) [sə -la-nə -chʼà?]
       1sO P 2sS help

       'you [sg] helped me'

(205) [sə   -kè? la u -s -tõn]
       1sPsr foot P thm 1sS hold

       'I hold it with my foot'

To summarize, Continuant Voicing applies to fricative-initial stems in a variety of morphological contexts: in possessed nouns, nouns which are the second member of compounds, postpositions, nouns which contain derivational prefixes, etc. These structures all have one thing in common: the noun or postposition stem which they contain is not word-initial.

4.3.2 Incorporated stems

Since postposition stems and inalienably possessed nouns do not occur in isolation, it is generally impossible to provide alternations between voiced and voiceless continuant-initial stems for this latter set. There is one environment, however, where inalienably possessed nouns sometimes occur without possessive morphology. This is in the incorporated stem position, verbal prefix position 3. Continuant-initial incorporated stems have uniformly voiceless initials:

(206a) [whazàghè?]   'our language'

(206b) [k'è   -sàgh   -e -də -d   -dah]
       around language vb der clf sg goes

       [k'èsàghedədah]   'he, she walks around talking to him-, herself'

(207a) [xeɬ]   'pack'

(207b) /nà -xeɬ -də -nə -ʔàh/
       down pack der 2sS handle compact O

       [nàxeɬdįʔàh]   'you [sg] put your pack down'

(208a) [sa]   'sun'

(208b) /hà-sa -də -į -n -dlat/
       up sun der asp Pf sun shine

       [hàsadįdlat]   'the sun is shining'

(209a) [yhin]   'song'

(209b) /k'è-yhən-e -də -d -dah/
       per sing vb der clf sg go

       [k'èyhinedədah]   'he, she walks around singing'

(210a) [əzəɬ]   'he, she shouts'

(210b) /k'è-səl -e -də -d -dah/
       per shout vb der clf sg go

       [k'èsəledədah]   'he, she walks around shouting'

Notice that the incorporated stems in the preceding examples occur to the right of additional level 5 prefixes. Thus the incorporated stems meet the structural description of Continuant Voicing, yet they have not undergone the rule. Apparently Continuant Voicing does not apply on level 5, the point at which the stems are incorporated into the verb prefixes. In fact, this conclusion is independently required to account for the phonological properties of certain compounds, as will be seen in 4.4.2.

4.3.3 Continuant Voicing vs. Voicing Assimilation

As discussed in Ch. 3, 2.2.1, continuant-initial verb stems are voiceless when preceded by a voiceless prefix, and otherwise voiced. The rule of Voicing Assimilation accounted for alternations between verb-initial voiced and voiceless fricatives. Since the initial fricatives of nouns and postpositions also exhibit voicing alternations which are superficially similar to those described by the rule of Voicing Assimilation, we might consider collapsing the rules of Continuant Voicing and Voicing Assimilation, as has been the standard analysis of these voicing alternations prior to Rice's research.

Close inspection of the data reveals one important difference between the voicing alternations in verbs and those in nouns and postpositions: whereas a verb stem assimilates in voicing to the voicing of a preceding segment, the voicing of a noun or postposition stem does not depend on whether the noun or prefix which precedes it ends in a voiced or voiceless consonant. Consider the following examples of voiced stem-initial continuants which are preceded by voiceless segments:

(211) /bùs sàs/
       cat skin

       [bùs zàs]   'cat skin'

(212) /ma-   dǫh -xà/
       3sPsr lips hair

       [madǫh ghà?]   'his whiskers'

(213) /?ih -gha -?a -gha-na -d -yhàts/
       recp P   unspO 3pS cnj clf scare O

       [?ihgha?aghidzàts]   'they scared each other'

(214) [làglos gha kǫh]   'belfry'
       bell   P   house

(215) /dzèh ghǫh yhè-da -na -s -?àɫ/
gum P adv thm thm 1sS chew

[dzèh ghǫh yhèdanas?àɫ] 'I chew on gum'

The rules of Continuant Voicing and Voicing Assimilation cannot be collapsed.

4.3.4 Possessed continuant-initial compounds

Additional data involving compounds indicate that the facts of Continuant Voicing are more complicated than just discussed. Consider the following possessed compounds:

(216a) [sa -dze -è?]   'watch'
        sun heart psd

(216b) [sasadzeè?]   'my watch'

(217a) [sa -ba]   'Dolly Varden trout'
        sun father

(217b) [sasabaè?]   'my Dolly Varden trout'

cf.
(218) [iza]   'month'

(219a) [ɣughe-?as -è?]   'fish weir'
        fish weir psd

(219b) [saɣughe ?asè?]   'my fish weir'

cf.
(220) [salughè?]   'my fish'

(221a) [xada -jè?]   'moose horn'
        moose horn

(221b) [saxada jè?]   'my moose horn'

cf.
(222) [saghadà?]   'my moose'

Continuant Voicing has failed to apply to the stem-initial fricatives of these compounds. These stems are clearly within the domain of Continuant Voicing, as indicated by the examples in 4.3.1.

How might Continuant Voicing be revised to account for these data?

Intuitively, the reason why Continuant Voicing fails to apply is that the continuant-initial stem occurs in the left, rather than right, branch of the compound [xədə jè?]. We might think of putting two conditions on the original rule of Continuant Voicing: Continuant Voicing applies (1) only to stems which occur in the right branch of a word stucture tree, and (2) only if the right branch does not branch:

(223) [+cont] --> [+voice] / X [___ ...]$_{N,P}$

condition: [___...] contains no internal brackets

Unfortunately this analysis runs into trouble when the original (unproblematic) data presented in 4.3.1 are reconsidered. Continuant Voicing applies to possessed stems like the following:

(224) [Peter zè?]   'Peter's belt'
(225) [bosdən lèsè?]   'white person's bannock'

The constituent structure of possessed stems like [Peter zè?] 'Peter's belt' is plausibly something like the structure in (226), in which the possessed stem and the possessive suffix form a constituent:

(226)
```
          N
         / \
        N   N
        |  / \
        | N
        | |
      Peter se
```

Given this analysis of possessed nouns, se 'belt' occurs in the branching right constituent of a word structure tree, which under the current hypothesis ought to block Continuant Voicing, yet Continuant Voicing of course applies here, yielding Peter zè?. Perhaps what is needed is a formal way of distinguishing branching structures which contain affixes from branching structures which contain stems.

4.4 Level ordering

We have seen that Continuant Voicing can apply to the right branch of a variety of morphological structures which contain continuant-initial noun and postposition stems. In the absence of counter-evidence, we might assume that all of the morphology that triggers Continuant Voicing belongs to the same level, but it remains to be determined which level this is.

4.4.1 Nasalization

The rule of Nasalization provides evidence that possession is a level 1 process. Consider forms like the following:

(227a) [ʔə-   t'ǫʔ]
       unspPsr leaves   'leaves'

(227b) [sə-   ʔə-   t'ǫ   -èʔ]
       1sPsr unspPsr leaves psd

       [seʔat'ǫ̀èʔ]   'my (its) leaves'

In 2.5 I argued that the possessive suffix should be analyzed as a level 1 suffix because possessive suffixation precedes Nasalization. Yet in (227b), Nasalization has apparently preceded possessive suffixation. In Ch. 7 I will suggest that these and other examples of 'repossessed' nouns contain two layers of possessive morphology:

(228)

[se ʔə t'ǫ èʔ]

In this analysis, the possessive suffix can still be assigned to level 1: in forms like (227b) it is added on the second cycle of level 1. On the first cycle in (227b), the unspecified possessive prefix ʔə- is affixed. Since the prefixation of ʔə- must precede the suffixation of -èʔ, which is a level 1 suffix, ʔə- itself must be a level 1 prefix. Moreover, since the possessive prefix ʔə- triggers Continuant Voicing, this suggests that all of the

morphology which lies within the domain of Continuant Voicing should be
assigned to level 1. Thus I conclude that the oblique objects, nominal
derivational prefixes, and possessive prefixes, are added on level 1. In
addition, Compounding occurs on level 1.

4.4.2 Domain of Continuant Voicing

As noted by Rice (to appear, 1986) Continuant Voicing distinguishes two
kinds of compounds in Slave: there exist compounds whose second member is
voiceless, even if continuant-initial.

Such compounds occur in Sekani also, although they are scarce. Consider
the following examples:

(229) /sə -tl'à   -sə̀s -è/
       1sPsr buttocks skin psd

       [sətl'à sə̀sè?]   'my trousers'

(230) /ɣès -sə̀s/
       flour skin

       [ɣès sə̀s]   'sack of flour'

(231) /mə- xès   sə̀s/
       3sPsr egg   skin

       [maghès sə̀s]   'his scrotum'

(232) /mə- xès -ɣè/
       3sPsr egg ?

       [maghès ɣè?]   'his testicles'

(233) /chįh   xeɣ/
       stick-like O pack

       [chįh xeɣ]   'box'

Clearly there is nothing exceptional about the second member of these
compounds. Compare the following:

(234) [?azə̀s]   'hide, skin'

(235) [səghelè?]   'my pack'

The ('type 2') compounds in (229)-(233) must be formed on a later level of the lexicon, outside the domain of Continuant Voicing, whereas 'type 1' compounds are formed on level 1 along with the other morphology that causes Continuant Voicing.

Since the only other level of the lexicon on which nominal word formation rules are found is (somewhat arbitrarily) level 5, it seems reasonable to assign the type 2 compounds to level 5. This preserves the generalization that nominal word formation occurs on two levels of the lexicon.

4.4.3 The loop

Notice that the initial continuants of type 2 compounds are voiced when these compounds are possessed:

(236) /ma-   xès   sàs/
       3sPsr egg   skin

       [maghès sàs]   'his scrotum'

(237) /ma-   xès -ɣę̀/
       3sPsr egg   ?

       [maghès ɣę̀?]   'his testicles'

The type 2 compounds thus contrast with type 1 compounds in two ways: the initial continuant of the second member of the compound is voiceless; and the initial continuant of the first member of the compound is voiced, if the compound is possessed. Apparently a loop from level 5 back to level 1 is required:

stems   [xès] [sàs]

level 5
  compounding 2   [[xès] [sàs]]

  Bracketing Erasure   [xès sàs]

level 1
  possession   [ma [xès sàs]]

  Continuant Voicing   [ma [ghès sàs]]

4.5 Summary

In this section I have suggested, on the basis of the rules of Continuant Voicing and Nasalization, that the compounding and prefixation word formation rules be assigned to levels 1 and 5 of the Sekani lexicon:

level 1	oblique objects	Continuant Voicing
	possessive prefixes	Nasalization
	Compounding 1	
level 5	Compounding 2	

A loop from level 1 back to level 5 is required to account for the phonological properties of possessed type 2 compounds.

5. Conclusion

Two levels of phonology and morphology can be distinguished within nouns and postpositions. As seen in Ch. 3, restrictions on affix order generally correlate with the domains of phonological rules. However, a loop between levels is required, which suggests that facts about affix order cannot always be taken at face value.

Notes.

1. Anyone who is familiar with Keren Rice's work will recognize how heavily indebted this chapter is to her research.

2. In other Athabaskan languages, the cognates to -è? and -'? are suffixed to different categories of possessed nouns. For example, in Tutchone (Ritter 1983), the cognate of the tonal suffix marks inalienably possessed nouns, while the cognate of -è? marks alienably possessed nouns.

3. This suffix should not be confused with a homophonous suffix -e, which occurs on incorporated verbal stems and denotes an action which is subordinate to that of the main verb. Compare (238) and (239), which differ only in presence or absence of this suffix:

(238) /k'è-chu -e -də -d -dah/
       per water vb der clf sg goes
       2   3   3   9   13   stem

       [k'èchuedədah]   'he, she walks around drinking'

(239) /k'è-chu -də -d -dah/
       per water der clf sg goes
        2   3   9 13 stem

       [k'èchudədah]   'he, she wades around'

Some additional examples of this suffix are given below:

(240) /k'è-ts'agh-e -də -d -dah/
       per yawn   vb der clf sg goes
        2   3   3   9 13 stem

       [k'èts'aghedədah]   'he, she walks around yawning'

(241) /də   -k'àhį̀ èh k'è-səl -e -də -d -dah/
       reflPsr spouse P per shout vb der clf sg goes
                              2   3   3 9 13 stem

       [dək'àhį̀ èh k'èsəledədah]

       'he, she walks around shouting at his, her spouse'

4. Stem-final -[oni] in (242) is a problem for this analysis:

(242) [dèztoni]   'log'

However, the stem /ton/ in 'log' might be a rare exception to Nasalization (see Ch. 1).

5. In the Ft. Ware dialect of Sekani, -[gàh] is a postposition meaning 'by, along'.

6. The cognate suffix in some Athabaskan languages is consonant-initial. Consider the following Navajo forms (Young and Morgan 1980:64):

(243) shash yáázh   'bear cub'
       bear dim

(244) 'ashkii yázhí   'little boy'
       boy   dim

With facts like this in mind, an alternative interpretation of the data in (155) might come to mind. Following Marlett and Stemberber (1984), one might consider positing an empty consonant as the initial segment of the diminutive suffix in Sekani: /Cazi/. The empty consonant would block Nasalization; thus there would be no reason not to assign diminutivization to level 1. However, having posited /Cazi/, one would then predict that the initial consonant would block vowel deletion rules, as well as resyllabification. However, rules like Suffix Vowel Deletion and a Deletion (243)-(244) do apply in diminutive forms, thus indicating that a /Cazi/ representation of this suffix is not only ad hoc, but untenable.

(245) /mə   -įlà -azįį?/
       3sPsr hand ddim

       [mįlàzįį?]   'his, her (baby) hand'

(246) /?èga -azįį?/
       spoon ddim

       [?ègazįį?]   'baby spoon'

Similar arguments from vowel deletion also indicate that the nominalizing suffixes /i/ and /į/ are not consonant-initial.

7. The human plural nominalizing suffix -ne is also used as a human plural suffix.

8. The lexically governed choice of -ge/ghe or -hu is somewhat messier than my discussion in the text might suggest. There is a great deal of idiolectal variation in the choice of these suffixes. Some speakers use -ge/ghe with some nouns while other speakers use -hu. Moreover, for some speakers, -ge/ghe and -hu are free variants for some nouns. The phonological shape of the suffix is also quite variable. The suffixes -gu/ghu/huge are variants of -ge/ghe. The former variants appear to be historically derived from -ge+hu, etc.

9. Some exceptions to the basic generalizations about where voiced and voiceless noun stems occur should be noted.

   Some noun stems must be marked as exceptions to Continuant Voicing:

(247) [sase]   'my mother's brother'

(248) [asatl'e]   'younger brother' voc

(249) [ase]   'father-in-law' voc

(250) [asu]   'mother-in-law' voc

The vocative forms in (248)-(250) might be formed on level 5, after Continuant Voicing shuts off. However, -/se/ 'mother's brother' in (247) must simply be marked as an exception to the rule.

   The following stems, which begin with voiced fricatives even in isolation, pose a more serious problem.

(251) [ya]   'sky'

(252) [yà?]   'louse'

(253) [yù?]   'medicine'

(254) [yas]   'snow'

(255) [ghàje]   'goose'

(256) [yàtòne]   'deer'

The initial fricatives of the stems in (251)-(256) are underlyingly voiced.
In (255)-(256) the voiced fricative may be part of a prefix.

10. ?a- and i- are clearly prefixes. ta 'water' might be a noun or a prefix.
I have no other examples of this morpheme, except perhaps in (257):

(257) [ta   -màh]   'shore'
       water edge

Chapter Five

The Bracketing Erasure Convention

In the Lexical Phonology model, the addition of each new layer of morphology is accompanied by a set of brackets, as shown in (1):

(1)   underlying stem   [B]

       Prefix [A-   [A [B]]

       Suffix -C]   [[A [B]] C]

In many versions of the theory of Lexical Phonology, lexical rules are assumed to apply cyclically. Thus in Lexical Phonology, as in any theory of cyclic phonology, one function of brackets is to delimit cyclic domains, distinguishing old from new morphological information.

In SPE it was proposed that the amount of word-internal bracketing that phonological rules have access to is constrained by means of a universal Bracketing Erasure Convention, according to which internal brackets are erased at the beginning of every cycle. In an SPE derivation of the structure [A [B]] in (1) above, the first rule to apply on the cycle defined by A is the erasure of the brackets surrounding B:

(2)   [A B]

The theory of Lexical Phonology also includes a Bracketing Erasure Convention, although the current version of this convention is considerably weaker than that proposed by SPE.

Certain Sekani rules require a still further weakening of the Bracketing Erasure Convention (BEC). In this chapter, I will argue that stems and classifiers in Sekani are exceptions to the Bracketing Erasure Convention, thus supporting the proposals of Kiparsky (1983) (and Hammond 1984) that marked exceptions to Bracketing Erasure exist.

I begin this chapter with a brief discussion of the need for some sort of

Bracketing Erasure Convention. In section 2 I discuss the motivation for the current version of the BEC, in which brackets are not erased cyclically, but only at the end of a level. In section 3 I turn to the Sekani data which are a problem for this latter version of Bracketing Erasure. The rules of Conjugation a̲ Deletion, Perambulative Reduction, Continuant Voicing, and Suffix Vowel Deletion are rules of the level 3 (or later) phonology, yet they must differentiate stems from affixes. I will propose that stems and classifier prefixes are marked with labelled brackets, and that a revised version of level-final Bracketing Erasure, Exceptionable Bracketing Erasure, does not apply to labelled brackets.

1. Motivation for Bracketing Erasure

In general, rules which apply at the edges of words or non-initial levels or provide evidence for the Bracketing Erasure Convention. Such rules apply in contexts of the sort given in (3):

(3)   ___]   or   [___

Unless internal brackets have been erased at the point in the derivation that the rule applies, such rules will overapply, applying to the edges of all prior cycles.[1] Thus without the Bracketing Erasure Convention, 'word-initial', 'word-final', 'level n-initial', and 'level n-final' will be impossible to formalize in Lexical Phonology.

For example, consider the rule of Final Devoicing in Russian, as formulated by Kiparsky (1985):

(4)   C --> [-voiced] / ___]

This rule applies to forms like the following:

(5a)   sat̲   'garden' (nom. sg.)
(5b)   sad̲a   'garden' (gen. sg.)

If there were no Bracketing Erasure Convention, the obstruent -[d] on the

inner cycle of [[sad]a] would meet the structural description of Final
Devoicing, and Final Devoicing would incorrectly apply to this word:

(5c)   *sata

Word-internal Bracketing Erasure is thus required to prevent rules like
Russian Final Devoicing from overapplying.

The assignment of stress in Malayalam compounds (Mohanan (1982)) also
illustrates the need for Bracketing Erasure. Basically, there are two types
of compounds in Malayalam, cocompounds and subcompounds. According to
Mohanan's analysis, subcompounds are formed on level 2, and cocompounds, on
level 3. The stems of a cocompound are individually stressed, as seen in (7),
but an entire subcompound (6) contains only one primary stress.

(6)   [[máta] [widweeṣam]]
        religion hatred   'hatred of religion'
(7)   [[[ácchan] [ámma]] maarə]
        father   mother pl   'parents'

The subcompound in (6) contains only one primary stress, whereas each stem of
the cocompound in (7) contains a primary stress. Mohanan (1982) analyzes
stress placement as a level 3 rule:[2]

(8)   level 2   Subcompounding

       level 3   Stress
                  Cocompounding

Thus the following derivations are required:

(9)   Subcompound   Cocompound

level 2
  Subcompounding   [[mata][widweeṣam]   ---

  BEC   [mata widweeṣam]   ---

level 3
  Stress   [máta widweeṣam]   [ácchan] [ámma]

  Cocompounding   ---   [[ácchan][ámma]]

level 4
    Inflection   ---   [[[ácchan][ámma]]maarə]

If the domain of stress assignment is defined as the largest string [...] which contains no internal brackets, then Bracketing Erasure must precede level 3 stress assignment so that the internal structure of subcompounds can be ignored by the stress assignment rule.

2. Motivation for non-cyclic, level-final Bracketing Erasure

As observed by Pesetsky (1979), the SPE Bracketing Erasure Convention was inconsistent with the need to distinguish old from new information on any given cycle, as required by, e.g., the Strict Cycle Condition. Pesetsky suggested instead that the Bracketing Erasure Convention be weakened to the version in (10):

(10)   The last rule of any cycle is: erase internal brackets.

Mohanan (1982), on the basis of Malayalam causative data, proposed a weaker version of Bracketing Erasure, which he named the Opacity Principle (11):

(11)   The internal structure at one stratum is invisible to the processes at another.

Additional research by Kiparsky (1982, 1983) on English deverbal nouns and by Rice (1982) on Slave Voicing Assimilation in verbs has confirmed the need for the weaker (Opacity Principle) version of the Bracketing Erasure Convention. In all these cases, rules require access to the structure of the current level.

Consider the argument from Slave. According to the rule of Voicing Assimilation, stem-initial fricatives are voiced when preceded by a voiced segment; otherwise, the fricative remains voiceless. (The Sekani rule discussed in Ch. 3, 2.2.1, is identical.)

(12)   [+cont] --> [+voiced] / [+voiced] [___ ...],
       where [...] contains no inner brackets

Some Slave data which are accounted for by this rule are presented in (13)-(16):

(13a) /ná -h -whe/
　　　 cont 1sS live

　　　 [náhwhe]　　　　　　'I live, stay'

(13b) [náwe]　　　　　　　'he lives, stays'

(14a) /he -h -se/
　　　 epen 1sS shout

　　　 [hehse]　　　　　　'I shout'

(14b) [heze]　　　　　　　'he shouts'

(15a) /he -h -xa/
　　　 epen 1sS lace

　　　 [hehxa]　　　　　　'I lace'

(15b) [heɣa]　　　　　　　'he laces'

(16a) /ná -ʔe -ne -h -ɬu/
　　　 cont? unspO thm? 1sS sew

　　　 [náʔenehɬu]　　　　'I sew'

(16b) [náʔenelu]　　　　　'he sews'

Only stem-initial fricatives undergo Voicing Assimilation. Compare (13)-(16) with forms which contain prefix-initial voiceless fricatives, such as whe-conjugation in (17)-(18):

(17) /ne -'whe-i -h -k'e/
　　　2sO cnj 1sPf clf shoot

　　　[néwhihk'e]　　　　'I shot you [sg]'

(18) /de -whe-íd -die/
　　　incp cnj 1pS pl go

　　　[dewhídie]　　　　　'we [pl] started out'

The conjugation prefix remains voiceless, even though it is preceded by a voiced segment.

In order for this rule to be able to distinguish stems (level 1 domains) from level 2 prefixes while applying on level 2, Bracketing Erasure must not apply cyclically. Consider the incorrect form that would be derived if Bracketing Erasure were to apply cyclically to (18):

```
stem                    [die]

level 2
  subject prefix        [í[die]]
  BEC                   [ídie]

  cnj prefix            [wh[ídie]]
  BEC                   [whídie]

  inceptive prefix      [de[whídie]]
  Voicing Assimilation  [de[wídie]]
  BEC                   [dewídie]

                       *[dewídie]
```

If Bracketing Erasure applies cyclically, stems will be indistinguishable from affixes on level 2. However, if Bracketing Erasure is the last rule of level 2, stems will be identifiable as the information delimited by the innermost set of brackets:

```
level 1
  stem                  [die]

level 2
  subject prefix        [í[die]]
  cnj prefix            [wh[í[die]]]
  inceptive prefix      [de[wh[í[die]]]]
  Voicing Assimilation  ---
  Bracketing Erasure    [dewhídie]

eventually              [dewhídie]
```

Voicing Assimilation will thus be blocked from applying to the prefix <u>whe</u>- if Bracketing Erasure is not cyclic.

3. Violations of the Bracket Erasure Convention in Sekani

Sekani also requires a non-cyclic, level-final version of the Bracketing Erasure Convention, but as will be seen in this section, even the version in (11) is too strong. Several rules which apply on level 3 or later must be able to identify the left or right edges of level 1. If Bracketing Erasure removes all internal brackets on level 1, this information about the extent of level 1 will be lost.

I propose that exceptions to the Bracketing Erasure Convention occur in Sekani. Specifically, I suggest that the brackets associated with stems and classifier prefixes are labelled in Sekani:

(19) $[_1$ $_1]$

Moreover, I suggest that Bracketing Erasure does not apply to labelled brackets:

(20)   Exceptionable Bracketing Erasure Convention

The last rule of level n is: erase unlabelled internal brackets.

I will refer to the stronger form of the BEC as the Exceptionless Bracketing Erasure Convention.

As noted above, exceptions to Bracketing Erasure in English have also been observed by Kiparsky (1983) and by Hammond (1984). In these cases, the exceptionality is associated with a particular affix, such as -ity. The exceptions to Bracketing Erasure in Sekani are similar: only stems and classifier prefixes are exceptional.

In this section I first discuss the rules of Conjugation a Deletion, Perambulative Reduction, and Continuant Voicing, which apply on level 3 or later and distinguish stems from prefixes. In the remaining section I consider the rule of Suffix Vowel Deletion, which distinguishes stems from suffixes.

3.1 Conjugation a Deletion

The rule of Conjugation a Deletion, also extensively discussed in Ch. 3, 4.2.5, poses a problem for level-final Bracketing Erasure. This rule must

refer to the external bracketing of level 1 when it applies on levels 3 and 4.
If Bracketing Erasure applies at the end of level 2 as predicted, this
information about the extent of level 1 will be lost.

3.1.1 Evidence for Bracketing Erasure

First note that despite the problem which this rule poses for Bracketing
Erasur, the rule also supports the existence of some sort of erasure of word-
internal bracketing, as Conjugation a̱ Deletion is sensitive to local
morphological complexity but disregards more distant complexity. As we will
see, the existence of a Bracketing Erasure Convention prevents the under-
application of Conjugation a̱ Deletion in forms which contain classifier
prefixes.

As discussed in Ch. 3, 5.2.5, the rule of Conjugation a̱ Deletion deletes
the vowel of a̱-final conjugation and mode prefixes when no subject (position
12) or mode (position 11) prefixes intervene between the conjugation or mode
prefix and the optional classifier prefix or verb stem:

(21)   a --> ∅ / V $\begin{Bmatrix} s \\ n \\ gh \end{Bmatrix}$ ___ [(clf) stem]
        $\begin{Bmatrix} [+cnj] \\ [+mod] \end{Bmatrix}$

(In 3.2 below, I will present arguments for the formulation of this rule,
including arguments against a phonological restatement of the context [(clf)
stem].) Recall the following examples, which involve the conjugation prefixes
/'sa 'na/. The vowel of the conjugation prefix has been deleted in the (b)
forms:

(22a)   /na -sa -s -d -kwi/
        rev cnj 1sS clf V:vomit
         5   10 12 13 stem

        [nasa̱skwi]   'I vomited'

(22b)   /na -sə -d -kwi/
        rev cnj clf V:vomit
        5   10 13 stem

        [naskwi]   'he, she vomited'

(23a)   /ts'e-ghu-nə -s -h -sit/
        adv 3pO cnj 1sS clf V:wake up
        2   7   10 12 13 stem

        [ts'eghùnassit]   'I wake them up'

(23b)   /ts'e-sə -nə -h -sit/
        adv 1sO cnj clf V:wake up
        2   7   10 13 stem

        [ts'esihsit]   'he, she wakes me up'

In (23b), the conjugation prefix [n] surfaces as nasalization and raising (to

[i]) of the preceding [ə].

(24a)   /kǫh   sə -gha-wə-'nə-n -?ǫ/
        house 1sO P ar cnj Pf V:handle compact O

        [kǫh sawàni?ǫ]   'he, she gave me a house'

(24b)   /kǫh   sə -gha-wə-'nə-?àh/
        house 1sO P ar cnj V:handle compact O
                    1   1   7 10 stem

        [kǫh sawę̀?àh]   'he, she gives me a house'

In (24b), the vowel of the prefix which precedes the conjugation prefix [n]

has become nasalized and undergone n-Conjugation ə Fronting.

(25a)   /?ə -gha-s -d -ts'èt/
        unspO cnj 1sS clf eat
        7   10 12 13 stem

        [?aghasts'èt]   'I ate something'

(25b)   /?ə -gha-d -ts'èt/
        unspO cnj clf eat
        7   10 13 stem

        [?ats'èt]   'he, she ate something'

The segment [gh] that results from the application of Conjugation ə Deletion

to the /ghə/ conjugation and mode prefixes must undergo the additional rule of

Gamma Lowering:

(26)   Gamma Lowering

   gh --> a / ___ [...],   where [...] contains no inner brackets

                    /?ə-ghə-d-ts'èt/

Conjugation a Deletion   ∅
Gamma Lowering   a
Prefix Vowel Deletion   ∅

                    [?ats'èt]

(27a) /sə -ghə-n -ts'èt/
       1sO cnj Pf V:scratch
        7   10 11 stem

       [səghits'èt]   'he, she scratched me'

(27b) /?ədədə-ghə-d-ts'èt/
       refl   cnj clf V:scratch
        7   10 13 stem

       [?ədədats'èt]   'he, she scratched him-, herself'

The fact that Conjugation a Deletion is blocked by the presence of a position 11 or 12 prefix but applies regardless of whether a position 13 prefix is present suggests the following analysis:

(28)   Classifier WFR
       Bracketing Erasure
       Conjugation WFR
       Conjugation a Deletion

Bracketing Erasure must follow the prefixation of the classifiers and precede the rule of Conjugation a Deletion. For this reason, I assign the classifier prefixes to level 1 along with stems.

The following derivations of nasaskwi 'I vomited' and naskwi 'he, she vomited' illustrate this analysis:

level 1
  stem   [kwi]   [kwi]
  classifier prefix   [d[kwi]]   [d[kwi]]
  BEC   [d kwi]   [d kwi]

```
level 2
  1s subject prefix      [s[d kwi]]         ---
  conjugation prefix     [sa[s[d kwi]]]     [sa[d kwi]]
  Conjugation a Del      ---                [s [d kwi]]
  BEC                    [sa s d kwi]       [s d kwi]

level 5
  reversative prefix     [na[sa s d kwi]]   [na [s d kwi]]

eventually               [nasaskwi]         [naskwi]
```

Bracketing Erasure must precede Conjugation a Deletion in order to allow the latter rule to apply in morphologically complex forms which contain a classifier prefix.

3.1.2 The problem for Bracketing Erasure

In Ch. 3, 3.2, I argued that a level ordering distinction, motivated by the rules of s- and n-Conjugation Fronting, exists between the verbal prefixes of positions 8 and 9. The existence of this level ordering distinction, as well as the need for Conjugation a Deletion to apply on level 3 and level 2, creates a problem for Exceptionless Bracketing Erasure.

If level-final Bracketing Erasure removes all internal brackets at the end of level 2, the application of Conjugation a Deletion will be blocked on level 3 because the innermost set of brackets given in the context of the rule will be in the wrong place: the brackets will not occur to the right of the conjugation and mode prefixes, but will include these prefixes. The derivation of [?ats'èt] 'he, she ate something' in (29) illustrates this problem:

```
(29)                     /?a  -gha-d  -ts'èt/
                         unsp0 cnj clf V:eat 0
level 1
  classifier prefix      [d [ts'èt]]
  BEC                    [d ts'èt]

level 2
  conjugation prefix     [gha [d ts'èt]]
  Conjugation a Deletion ---
  BEC                    [gha d ts'èt]
```

```
level 3
  object prefix         [?a[gha d ts'èt]]
  Conjugation a Deletion ---

eventually              *[?aghats'èt]
should be               [?ats'èt]
```

The structural description of Conjugation a Deletion fails to be met in two places in (29). First, on level 2, no vowel precedes the prefix gha and the rule does not apply. Second, on level 3, no brackets are present to delineate the level 1 domain, due to the application of the BEC at the end of level 2.

However, if stems and classifier prefixes are marked as exceptions to the Bracketing Erasure Convention, the correct output will be obtained. Level 2 Bracketing Erasure will not erase the stem and classifier brackets because the brackets which contain the stems and classifier prefixes are labelled $[_1$. The derivation in (30) illustrates this analysis:

```
(30)
level 1
  classifier prefix     [₁d [₁ts'èt₁]₁]

  BEC                   [₁d [₁ts'èt₁]₁]

level 2
  conjugation prefix    [gha [₁d [₁ts'èt₁]₁]]

  Conjugation a Deletion ---

  BEC                   [gha [₁d [₁ts'èt₁]₁]]

level 3
  object prefix         [?a [gha [₁d [₁ts'èt₁]₁]]]

  Conjugation a Deletion [?a [gh [₁d [₁ts'èt₁]₁]]]

  Gamma Lowering            a

  Prefix Vowel Deletion     ∅

eventually              [?ats'èt]
```

Conjugation a Deletion and Gamma Lowering are accordingly revised:

(31) Conjugation a̲ Deletion

$$a \rightarrow \emptyset \; / \; V \begin{Bmatrix} s \\ n \\ gh \\ [+cnj] \\ [+mod] \end{Bmatrix} \; \_\_\_ \; [_1$$

(32) Gamma Lowering

$$gh \rightarrow a \; / \; \_\_\_ \; [_1$$

Labelled brackets replace the context "[...], where [...] contains no inner brackets" with the simpler context $[_1$.

3.1.3 Possible reanalyses of Conjugation a̲ Deletion

Introducing labelled brackets is clearly a step in the wrong direction, as far as a theory of phonology is concerned. Labelled brackets are reminiscent of boundaries, which Lexical Phonology claims to have eliminated through level ordering and allowing 'boundary-sensitive' phonological rules to apply in the lexicon. The introduction of labelled bracketing removes some of the theory-internal motivation for the central claim of the model--allowing phonology to apply in the lexicon--since the postulation of word-internal boundaries would provide a way for boundary-sensitive phonological rules to apply in the syntax, as in the SPE model.

As an example of the less constrained theory that labelled brackets would allow, notice that the rules discussed in Ch. 3, 2.2 (the D-Effect Rule, Palatalization, and Voicing Assimilation) which apply to stem-initial segments could now be analyzed as word level or post-lexical rules. With labelled brackets, only theory-internal considerations, such as whether a rule has lexically marked exceptions, would provide a reason for assigning these rules must apply to level 1.

Thus before concluding that only a new version of the Bracketing Erasure Convention will allow us to analyze Conjugation a̲ Deletion satisfactorily, it is worth considering whether some aspect of this analysis can be changed so that the rule does not crucially refer to labelled brackets.

3.1.3.1 Merging levels 2-4

The most obvious way in which the analysis could be changed would be to remove the distinction between levels 2, 3, and 4. The evidence presented in Ch. 3 indicated that levels 2-4 are a single phonological domain for the purposes of many rules, yet only the rules of s- and n-Conjugation Fronting and Conjugation Tone Mapping provide evidence that they are separate domains.

Consider s- and n-Conjugation a Fronting. These rules apply only on level 2, providing evidence that the level 2 domain includes verb prefixes 9-12 and level 3 consists of most of the positions 7-8 prefixes. If levels 2 and 3 were merged into a single level, labelled brackets would not be required by the rule of Conjugation a Deletion. However, not recognizing the level ordering distinction leads to unnecessary complication in accounting for the rules given above. One would be forced to adopt a diacritic analysis of the prefixes which trigger these rules, in much the same way that Kari (1976:209) was forced to account for similar facts in Navajo:

(33)   si --> 0 / ASP + ___ + i + X + [

Notice that Kari's rule makes use of the prefix position label ASP(ECT) as a diacritic for the rule to refer to.

The diacritic analysis misses the generalization that all prefixes which trigger the Fronting rules occur in the same position.[3] It might be objected that the prefixes which trigger these rules do not actually all occur in the same surface position, as exemplified in Ch. 3, 3.1.4. However, I argued in Hargus (1987) that an analysis of the position of these prefixes which is equivalent to their surface order will make it difficult to account for certain facts concerning the application of s-Conjugation a Fronting in forms which contain level 2 prefixes which occur to the left of the level 4 prefixes ts'ǝ and ghǝ:

(34) [ts'ǝsdli] 'we are cold'

(35) [tlį dahnaghats'èstl'ų] 'we tied up the dog'

If ghǝ occurred to the left of ts'ǝ underlyingly, and were diacritically marked as a trigger for the s- and n- Conjugation rules, the Fronting rule would become considerably more complicated, since it would have to look beyond the immediately preceding prefix to find a trigger for the rule.

Merging levels 2 and 3 seems to be a worse alternative (for Sekani) than labelled brackets.

3.1.3.2 A morphological formulation

Suppose the formulation of Conjugation ǝ Deletion were changed so that the rule does not crucially refer to the leftmost edge of level 1. Certainly some morphological features must be added to the rule to distinguish the position 10 and 11 conjugation and mode prefixes ghǝ from the homophonous position 8 animate plural subject prefix ghǝ. The latter does not alternate with ǝ when preceded by position 7 prefixes:

(36) [tlįge ?ǝ   -ghǝ-tsagh]
      dogs unspO 3pS cry
            7   8   stem

      [tlįge ?ǝghatsagh]   'the dogs are howling'

(37) /wǝ -ghǝ-ts'it/
      thm 3pS tell lie
      7   8   stem

      [waghats'it]   'they tell a lie'

If the rule must be complicated by morphological features anyway, then the possibility of restricting it to forms which do not contain a position 11 or 12 prefix by means of morphological features ought to be considered.

However, a morphological analysis of the rule soon runs into difficulties. Person/number features would have to prevent the rule from applying in first and second person singular, first person dual and second person plural forms while allowing it to apply in first person plural, third person plural and third person singular forms. Moreover, of the latter forms, only those which do not contain the perfective prefix /n/ in position 12 will be allowed to undergo the rule. But adding a feature [-perfective] to the rule would be overly restrictive: forms which contain the /d/ and /l/ classifier prefixes are morphologically perfective even though they lack the perfective prefix,[4] and in such forms, Conjugation <u>a</u> Deletion can apply (see (30), (34), and (35)).

3.1.3.3 A syllable-based rule

Observe that in forms which contain a subject prefix in position 12 or the perfective prefix in position 11, the conjugation and mode prefixes are not syllable-final. This suggests that the relevant context for the rule is not the adjacency of the prefix to the level 1 domain, but perhaps simply a restriction to syllable-final position:

(38) $a \longrightarrow \emptyset \,/\, V \begin{Bmatrix} s \\ n \\ gh \end{Bmatrix} \underline{}]_{syll}$

This formulation would correctly prevent the rule from applying to forms like (25a) and (27a) above. However, it would also incorrectly prevent its application to forms like (39b) which contain the classifier prefix <u>h</u>:

(39a)   /?ə -də -gha-s -h -xǫh/
       unspO Fut Fut 1sS clf V:snore
       7   9   11 12 13 ste

       [?ədaghasxǫh]   'I will snore'

(39b)   /?ə -də -gha-h -xǫh/
       unspO Fut Fut clf V:snore
       7   9   11 13 stem

       [?ədahxǫh]   'he, she will snore'

In (39b), the prefix gha- is not syllable-final, but Conjugation a Deletion has applied. Thus Conjugation a Deletion cannot be reformulated as a syllable-based rule.

3.1.4 Conjugation a Deletion: Summary

The rule of Conjugation a Deletion refers to the leftmost edge of level 1 when it applies on level 3, in violation of the Exceptionless Bracketing Erasure Convention. I have shown how the rule can be accounted for under the Exceptionable version of the BEC: stems and classifier prefixes are marked with labelled brackets, which remain untouched by level-final Bracketing Erasure. I have considered a number of possible reformulations of this rule, including a reanalysis of the Sekani lexicon, before concluding that Bracketing Erasure must be weakened in this way.

In the following sections, I will consider other rules which apply on level 3 or later, referring to portions of level 1. Such cases provide additional support for the Exceptionable version of the Bracketing Erasure Convention.

3.2 Perambulatives

As mentioned in Ch. 3, motion verbs in Sekani may undergo an aspectual derivation which I have labelled 'perambulative', following Kari (1979). This construction is characterized by the prefixes k'è- (position 2), na- customary/habitual (position 5), and the d- classifier (position 13). One of the aspectual suffixes -ts or -h, which characterize the customary aspect, may also be present in surface forms.

The following second person singular forms are illustrative:

(40) /k'è-na-n -d -lit   -ts/
      per C 2sS clf V:float C
       2   5 12 13 stem

      [k'ènǫdlits]   'you [sg] float around'

(41)   /k'è-na-n -d -zùt/
       per C 2sS clf V:skate

       [k'ènǫdzùt]   'you [sg] skate around'

(42)   /k'è-na-n -d -be -h/
       per C 2sS clf V:swim C

       [k'ènǫbeh]   'you [sg] swim around'

As will be seen below, these second person singular forms provide the best evidence for the underlying forms of the morphemes which occur in this construction. Only the rule of a Raising has applied in these forms.

In first and third person singular and second person plural forms in which no prefix occurs between na customary and the subject prefix, the rule of Perambulative Reduction applies:

(43)   k'è-na --> k'an / ___ (C) [(clf) stem

Note that a Raising must precede Perambulative Reduction, which it bleeds, since Perambulative Reduction does not apply to second person singular forms.

The application of Perambulative Reduction can be seen in forms like (44)-(46) (cf. (42) above):

(44)   /k'è-na-d -beh/
       per C clf V:swim

       [k'abeh]   'he, she swims around'

(45)   /k'è-na-s -d -beh/
       per C 1sS clf V:swim

       [k'asbeh]   'I swim around'

(46)   /k'è-na-ah -d -beh/
       per C 2pS clf V:swim

       [k'ahbeh]   'you [pl] swim around'

In deriving (46), I assume that a Deletion (see 3.4 below) precedes Perambulative Reduction:

/k'è-na-ah-d-beh/

a Raising	--
a Deletion	∅
Perambulative Reduction	k'an
Perambulative na Deletion	--

eventually   [k'ąhbeh]

In forms in which a prefix occurs between na customary and the optional position 12 subject prefix, na is deleted:

(47)   Perambulative na Deletion

na --> ∅ / k'è ___

The application of this rule can be seen in the following forms:

(48)   /k'è-na-whè -na -i -s -d -dah/
       per C incp der der 1sS clf V:sg go
       2   5 6   9   9   12 13 stem

       [k'èwhènàsdah]   'I start to walk around'

(49)   /k'è-na-ts'a-d -beh/
       per C 1pS clf V:swim
       2   5 8   13 stem

       [k'èts'abeh]   'we swim around'

(50)   /k'è-na-na -l -?įh/
       per C thm clf V:sneak
       2   5 9   13 stem

       [k'èna?įh]   'he, she sneaks around'

(51)   /k'è-na-wa-d -beh/
       per C Op clf V:swim
       2   5 11 13 stem

       [k'èwabeh]   'he, she swims around' [Op]

In the preceding forms, the perambulative prefix occurs to the left of a prefix of positions 6-11, and the prefix na is absent in the surface forms.[5] Perambulative Reduction thus precedes and bleeds Perambulative na Deletion.

Perambulative Reduction is a problem for an Exceptionless Bracketing Erasure. The structural description of Perambulative Reduction cannot be met until level 5, but the rule refers to the leftmost edge of the level 1 domain.

If Bracketing Erasure applies at the end of level 1, this information about the extent of level 1 will be lost.

It is worth considering whether Perambulative Reduction could be reformulated so that its context did not refer to level 1. One attempt might be as in (52):

(52)   k'èna --> k'an / ___ (C) d C

Since all verb stems are consonant-initial, the consonant cluster /dC/ would uniquely identify the classifier-stem sequence. However, the d classifier is not always present in perambulative forms. As Rice (to appear) has noted for Slave, the prefixes na 'back, again' and na customary require the d classifier, but d only appears in intransitive verbs. Thus in perambulatives (which contain na customary underlyingly), the d classifier only occurs in intransitive perambulative forms. Compare the following transitive forms with the examples given above:

(53)   /k'è-na-n -?ah/
       per C 2sS V:handle compact O

       [k'ęnǫ?ah]   'you [sg] carry [compact O] around'

(54)   /k'è-na-n -leh/
       per C 2sS V:handle pl O

       [k'ęnǫleh]   'you [sg] carry [pl O] around'

(55)   /k'è-na-n -h -tsus/
       per C 2sS clf V:handle cloth-like O

       [k'ęnǫhtsus]   'you [sg] carry [cloth-like O] around'

If the d classifier were present in these verbs, the verb stems in (53) and (54) would surface as [t'ah] and [dleh], respectively. In (55), the h classifier would not be present on the surface if /d/ classifier were also present underlyingly.

A phonological reanalysis of the context in which Perambulative Reduction applies appears to be impossible. Given Exceptionable Bracketing Erasure, however, the rule can be easily reformulated as follows:

(56)   k'è-na --> k'an / ___ (C) [$_1$

Thus Perambulative Reduction provides evidence that stems and classifiers are exceptions to the Bracketing Erasure Convention.

3.3 Continuant Voicing in derived nominals

In Ch. 4, sec. 4 I argued that the structure of possessed derived nominals required an analysis in which the possessive morphology is added on a loop back to level 1 from level 5:

(57)   level 5   verb formation
       ¦
       level 5   nominalizing suffixes
       ¦
       level 1   possession,
                    compounding 1

In possessed derived nominals and derived nominals which occur inside of type 1 compounds, the phonological rule of Continuant Voicing must distinguish stems from prefixes on the loop back to level 1, thus presenting another problem for Exceptionless Bracketing Erasure.

Recall the rule of Continuant Voicing, also discussed in Ch. 4, which accounts for alternations between voiced and voiceless stem-initial fricatives in noun and postposition stems:

(58)   [+cont] --> [+voice] / X [$_{N,P}$ ___...], X ≠ ∅

Stem-initial fricatives are voiced when they are preceded by any level 1 morpheme, which may be a prefix or a stem, and otherwise voiceless:

(59a) [se]   'belt'
(59b) [sazé?]   'my belt'

(60a) [yheɤ]   'trap'
(60b) [tsà? yèɤ]   'beaver trap'

If Continuant Voicing is a level 1 rule, and type 2 compounds are formed on level 5, then the fact that type 2 compounds do not undergo Continuant Voicing is accounted for.

As predicted by this analysis, the stem-initial fricative of a possessed derived nominal or nominal embedded in a compound is voiced, not voiceless, as seen in (61) and (62):

(61) /mə -sùt   -i/
     3sPsr V:skate nom

     [mazùdi]   'his, her tongue'

(62) /chən -ɣa   -i/
     wood pl O are in position nom

     [chin lai]   'lizzard'

Howver, Continuant Voicing does not apply indiscriminately to any noun or postposition stem-initial fricative. In Ch. 4, I pointed out that Continuant Voicing fails to apply to stem-initial fricatives in possessed type 1 compounds, even when these are word-initial:

(63a) [sa -ba]   'Dolly Varden trout'
      sun father

(63b) [səsabaè?]   'my Dolly Varden trout'

Moreover, the stem-initial fricative of a derived nominal remains voiceless if it is not word-initial in the derived nominal:

(64a) /ts'ə -h -xəl   -i/
      unspS clf V:play a musical instrument nom

      [ts'ahxəli]   'guitar'

(64b) [səts'ahxəlè?]   'my guitar'

(65a) /?ə -də -s-xət/
      unspO der ? V:saw O

      [?ədəsxət]   'saw'

(65b) [se?ədəsxədè?]   'my saw'

In order for Continuant Voicing to apply, the fricative must be word-initial as well as stem-initial.

In keeping with this generalization, word-initial, prefix-initial fricatives in derived nominals do not undergo Continuant Voicing:

(66a) /sa -h -kàt   -i/
       cnj clf V:flat nom

       [sahkàdi]   'cloth covering'
(66b) [sasahkàdi]   'my cloth covering'

(67a) /sa -ts'a -da -ì -ya   -i/
        ?   unspS thm asp V:pl O nom

       [sats'adìyai]   'necktie'
(67b) [sasats'adìyaè?]   'my necktie'

The word-initial fricatives in these possessed derived nominals remain voiceless because they belong to prefixes, not stems.

These last forms present a problem for level-final Bracketing Erasure. Possessed derived nominals which contain word-initial stem-initial fricatives undergo Continuant Voicing on the loop back through level 1:

(68)
level 5
  nominalization   [[sùd]$_{Vi}$]$_N$

  Bracketing Erasure   [sùdi]$_N$

level 1
  possessive prefix   [sa[sùdi]$_N$]

  Continuant Voicing   [sa[zùdi]$_N$]

eventually   [sazùdi]

However, if Bracketing Erasure erases all internal bracketing at the end of level 5, then prefix-initial fricatives will be indistinguishable from stem-initial fricatives when the possessive prefixes are added on level 1:

(69)
level 5
  Nominalization WFR   [[sahkàd]$_{Vi}$]$_N$

  Bracketing Erasure   [sahkàdi]$_N$

level 1
  Possessive WFR   [sə[sahkàdi]_N]

  Continuant Voicing   [sə[zahkàdi]_N]

eventually   *səzahkàdi

In order to prevent Continuant Voicing from applying to all word-initial prefixes, stems must be distinguishable from prefixes on the loop back through level 1.

With the Exceptionable Bracketing Erasure Convention, Continuant Voicing is easily revised to account for these data:

(70)   [+cont] --> [+voice] / X [_1 ___] = P, N
                                        X ≠ ∅

Given the persistence of stem bracketing, prefix-initial fricatives will not undergo Continuant Voicing in possessed derived nominals like <u>səsahkàdi</u> 'my cloth covering'.

(71)
level 1
  stem   [_1kàt]

  classifier   [_1h[_1kàt]]

  Bracketing Erasure   --

level 2
  conjugation   [sə [_1h [_1kàt_1]_1]]

  Bracketing Erasure   --

level 5
  Nominalization WFR   [[sə [_1h [_1kàd_1]_1]]i]

  Bracketing Erasure   [sə[_1h [_1kàd_1]_1]i]

level 1
  Possessive WFR   [sə[sə[_1h [_1kàd_1]_1]]i]]

  Continuant Voicing   ---

eventually   səsahkàdi

Continuant Voicing has failed to apply because the fricative is not adjacent to a labelled bracket.

In order to account for the distribution of stem-initial voiced fricatives in possessed derived nominals, the rule of Continuant Voicing must be able to distingush between stems and prefixes on later levels of word formation. Thus derived nominals provide additional evidence that stems are exceptions to Bracketing Erasure in Sekani.

3.4 Suffix Vowel Deletion

So far I have discussed three rules--Conjugation a̱ Deletion, Perambulative Reduction, and Continuant Voicing--which apply on level 3 or later and refer to the leftmost edge of level 1 in the context of the rule. In this section, I will consider a rule that refers to the right edge of stems on level 5 or later.

3.4.1 Basic data

In Ch. 4 I referred to the following rule of Suffix Vowel Deletion, which deletes the final vowel of a suffix before a vowel-initial suffix:

(72)   V --> ∅ /] X ___] V

I will now consider this rule in more detail. Suffix Vowel Deletion is motivated by alternations like the following:

(73a)   /mə -bes -è/
        3sPsr knife psd

        [mabesè?]   'his, her knife'

(73b)   /mə -bes -è -azi/
        3sPsr knife psd dim

        [mabesa̱zi]   'his, her small knife'

(74a)   /ʔə -bil -i/
        unspO V:swing nom

        [ʔabili̱]   'swing'

267

(74b)   /mə -ʔə -bil -i -è/
        3sPsr unspO V:swing nom psd

        [meʔəbilè?]   'his, her swing'

(75a)   /ɣugh-e/
        fish stm

        [ɣughe]   'fish'

(75b)   /ɣugh-e -azi/
        fish stm dim

        [ɣughazi]   'small fish'

(76a)   /də -k'al -i/
        thm V:white nom:hum sg

        [dək'ali]   'white person'

(76b)   /də -k'al -i   -azi/
        thm V:white nom:hum sg dim

        [dək'alazi]   'dear white person'

(77a)   /nə -tsədl-e -azi/
        thm small stm dim

        [nətsədlazi]   'he, she is small'

(77b)   /nə -tsədl-e -azi-i/
        thm small stm dim nom:hum sg

        [nətsədlazi]   'small person'

(78a)   /ʔa -gheɣ -e -ne/
        adv N:pack stm nom:hum pl

        [ʔagheɣene]   'Carrier people'

(78b)   /ʔa -gheɣ -e -ne -azi/
        adv N:pack stm nom:hum pl dim

        [ʔagheɣenazi]   'dear Carrier people'

   The preceding data are summarized in (79):

(79) e+è?   --> è?
      i+è?   --> è?
      i+azi   --> azi
      è+azi   --> àzi
      e+azi   --> azi
      į+azi   --> ązi
      azi+į   --> azį
      ne+azi --> nazi

These rules can be collapsed into a rule of Suffix Vowel Deletion (80):

(80)   V --> ∅ /] X ___] V

According to this rule, a vowel-final suffix is deleted before a vowel-initial suffix. As will be seen below, the inclusion of the first bracket, which indicates that the vowel belongs to a suffix and not a stem, poses a problem for level-final Bracketing Erasure.

3.4.2 Stem vs. suffix vowels

Suffix Vowel Deletion distinguishes suffix vowels from stem vowels. The latter are generally not deleted before suffix vowels, as the following examples indicate:

(81a) [dəgi]   'swan'

(81b) /sə -dəgi-è/
      1sPsr swan psd

      [sədəgiè?]   'my swan'

(81c) /dəgi-azi/
      swan dim

      [dəgiazi]   'small swan'

(82a) [tsà?]   'beaver'

(82b) /sə -tsà -è?/
      1sPsr beaver psd

      [sətsàè?]   'my beaver'

(83a)   [ʔə   -ch'į̀]   'job'
        unspPsr job

(83b)   /sə -ʔə   -ch'į̀-èʔ/
        1sPsr unspPsr job psd

        [seʔach'i̱è̱ʔ]   'my job'

(83c)   /ʔə   -ch'į̀-azi/
        unspPsr job dim

        [ʔach'i̱a̱zi]   'small job'

(84)   /də -k'ǫ̀   -azi/
        thm V:midget dim

        [dək'ǫ̱azi]   'he, she is midget-sized'

(85a)   [dəje]   'groundhog'

(85b)   /sə -dəje   -èʔ/
        1sPsr groundhog psd

        [sədəje̱è̱ʔ]   'my groundhog'

(85c)   /dəje   -azi/
        groundhog dim

        [dəje̱a̱zi]   'small groundhog'

(86)   /mə -ʔə -da   -i/
        3sPsr unspO V:pl eat nom
                  7   stem

        [meʔəda̱i̱]   'food'

(87)   /keyih nà -jè   -į̀/
        town cont V:live nom:hum sg
                   2   stem

        [keyih nàjè̱į̀]   'town dweller'

(88)   /whə-ghǫh-ə   -lį̀ -į̀/
        1pO P   epen V:be nom:hum sg
         1   i   stem

        [whǫhəlį̱į̱]   'nurse' (takes care of us)

(89)   /i   tlį dəne   sə -gha-ya-nə -n -h -chį   -i/
        dem dog person 1sO P 3sO cnj Pf clf handle animate O nom

        [i tlį dəne sayànįhchįi]

        'the dog someone gave me'

a-final stems provide the only exceptions to the generalization that stem vowels do not delete before suffix vowels. Stem-final a is deleted before an a-initial suffix:

(90a)   [tsà?]   'beaver'

(90b)   /tsà   -azi/
        beaver dim

        [tsàzi]   'small beaver'

(90b) is accounted for by the rule of a Deletion (see Ch. 3, 4.2.1):

(91)   a --> ∅ % a [___

Now consider (90c):

(90c)   /sə   -tsà   -è -azi/
        1sPsr beaver psd dim

        [sətsàazi]   'my small beaver'

In (90c), stem-final a does not delete because it is not immediately followed by the diminutive suffix -azi in its underlying representation:

(92)   /sə-tsà-è-azi/

a Deletion   --
Suffix V Deletion   ∅

                [sətsàazi][6]

a Deletion must precede Suffix Vowel Deletion.

    To summarize, Suffix Vowel Deletion deletes the first vowel of a sequence of two suffix vowels. This rule generally applies only to suffix vowels, not to sequences which contain a vowel-final stem.

3.4.3 Problems for Exceptionless Bracketing Erasure
3.4.3.1 Possessed derived nominals

In Ch. 4 I argued that the possessive suffix, like the possessive prefixes, is added to derived nominals on the loop from level 5 back to level 1. This raises a problem for the Exceptionless Bracketing Erasure Convention.

As just exemplified, the nominalizing suffix i is deleted in forms which also contain the possessive suffix è?. An example of this was given above in (74b); additional examples are provided below:

(93a) /ts'ə -h -xəl   -i/
       unspS clf V:play musical instrument nom

       [ts'ahxəli]   'guitar'

(93b) [səts'ahxəlè?]   'my guitar'

(94a) /də -tsəs -i/
       der V:whip nom

       [dətsəsi]   'whip'

(94b) [sədətsəsè?]   'my whip'[7]

As exemplified in (81b) above and in (95) and (96) below, stem-final i is not deleted when the possessive suffix is added:

(95a) [k'i]   'birch'

(95b) [sək'iè?]   'my birch'

(96a) /mə -k'e-də-sə -h -ts'i/
       3sO P pl cnj clf pl sit
       1 1 9 10 13 stem

       [mak'edèhts'i]   'couch'

(96b) [səmak'edèhts'iè?]   'my couch'

Stem-final i thus contrasts with the nominalizing suffix i with respect to Suffix Vowel Deletion. If Bracketing Erasure removes all internal brackets at the end of level 5, it will not be possible to distinguish stem vowels from suffix vowels on the loop back through level 1. Consider the contrast between dagi 'swan' and datsasi 'whip'. The diminutive forms of these nouns provide additional evidence that the final i is part of the stem in 'swan' but is a suffix in 'whip':

(97)   [datsasazi]   'small whip'

(98)   [dagiazi]   'small swan'

If all internal brackets were erased at the end of level 5 in 'whip', Suffix Vowel Deletion would fail to apply to this form because no internal structure would be available to indicate that it was a derived nominal:

(99)   [dagi]   [datsasi]

       -[dagiè?]   *-[datsasiè?]

However, if stem-final bracketing is still available at the end of level 5 to indicate that the final -i in 'whip' is not part of a stem, then Suffix Vowel Deletion can apply in this form as required:

output of level 5   [da [₁tsas₁] i]

level 1
  possessive suffix   [[da [₁tsas₁] i] è]

  Suffix Vowel Deletion   ∅

Given the Exceptionable Bracketing Erasure Convention, Suffix Vowel Deletion can be revised:

(100) V --> ∅ / ₁] X ___] V

Only vowels which are not adjacent to ₁] will be deleted by this rule. Suffix Vowel Deletion will be blocked by a labelled bracket.

3.4.3.2 Stem-final vs. suffixal -[e] and -[è?]

Another set of data involving Suffix Vowel Deletion which were a problem for the stronger version of the Bracketing Erasure Convention are easily accounted for if stems are identifiable with labelled brackets.

Consider level 1 suffixes of the shape [e è?]. These suffixes are deleted before another suffix vowel:

(101a) [ts'èghe]   'woman'

(101b) [ts'èghazi]   'small woman'

(102a) /sə -chu   -è/
       1sPsr daughter psd

       [səchuè?]   'my daughter'

(102b) /sə -chu   -è -azi/
       1sPsr daughter psd dim

       [səchuàzi]   'my dear daughter'

As exemplified above, stem-final [e] is not deleted before a suffix vowel:

(103a) [ghàje]   'goose'

(103b) [ghàje-azi]   'small goose'
       goose dim

(104a) /sə dəne-`/
       1sPsr man psd

       [sədənè?]   'my man'

(104b) /sə -dəne-` -azi/
       1sPsr man psd dim

       [sədənèazi]   'my dear man'

In Ch. 4 I argued that -[e] and -[è?] are level 1 suffixes, based on phonological evidence from nasal-final roots. If Bracketing Erasure takes place at the end of level 1 the distinction between structures containing stem-final -[e] -[è] and suffixal -[e] -[è] will be merged:

	stem-final [e]	suffixal [e]
level 1		
stem	[ts'ègh]	[ghàje]
suffixation	[[ts'ègh]e]	--
BEC	[ts'èghe]	--

274

```
level 4
  diminutivi-    [[ts'èghe]azi]           [[ghàje]azi]
  zation

  Suffix Vowel        --                       --
  Deletion

eventually      *ts'ègheazi               ghàjeazi
```

Thus on level 5, Suffix Vowel Deletion will be unable to distinguish stem-final [e è] from suffixal [e è] because the internal structure of level 1 has been deleted.

Of course, if labelled brackets are allowed, then suffixal -e and stem-final -e are easily distinguished:

```
                stem-final [e]          suffixal [e]
level 1
  stem          [₁ts'ègh₁]              [₁ghàje₁]

  suffixation   [[₁ts'ègh₁]e]              --

  BEC              --                      --

level 5
  diminutivi-   [[[₁ts'ègh₁]e]azi]      [[₁ghàje₁]azi]
  zation

  Suffix Vowel        ∅                      --
  Deletion

eventually      ts'èghazi               ghàjeazi
```

The alternative to allowing stems to be marked as exceptions to Bracketing Erasure would be a diacritic analysis of the stem-final [e] in words like ts'èghe. Although some of the deleting stem-final e's have an apparent stem-forming function, most of the deleting, stem-final -e's have no clear function, as discussed in Ch. 4, 2.2. In any analysis, they must be considered part of the basic lexical entry of the roots to which they will be suffixed. However, despite the fact that many instances of suffixal -e must be considered lexically specified, this does not mean that they are not suffixes. In the Athabaskan languages, it is not uncommon for lexical entries to consist of several (nonadjacent) morphemes, as discussed in Ch. 2, 3.4.2.

As further examples, note that verbs like 'tell lie' and 'handle cloth-like O' consist of discontinuous morphemes:

(105)   /gho-ts'it/   'tell lie'
         7   stem

(106)   /h -tsus,tsùz/   'handle cloth-like O' (Imp, Pf)
         13 stem

Discontinuous strings of prefixes can also be associated with a single meaning:

(107)   /ts'e də/   'into fire'
         2   9

(108)   /ta də/   'misplaced, lost'
         2 9

Given the need for these kinds of lexical representations, there is no reason why 'woman' could not have the representation in (109), in which -e is part of the lexical entry, but still a suffix:

(109)   /ts'ègh e/   'woman'
         stem   sfx

(109) would still differ minimally from (110) and (111), which do not undergo Suffix Vowel Deletion:

(110)   /dəne/   'man'
         stem

(111)   /ghàje/   'goose'
         stem

To summarize, there appear to be no compelling reasons to adopt a diacritic analysis over a suffixal analysis of the stem-final e's.

4. Conclusion

In this chapter I have presented evidence that exceptions to the Bracketing Erasure Convention must be allowed. I have discussed four Sekani rules which crucially refer to stems or classifier prefixes (level 1 morphology) on level 3 or later. As a means of encoding this exceptionality into the grammar of Sekani, I have proposed that exceptions to the Bracketing Erasure Convention are marked with labelled brackets. I have also proposed a slight reformulation of the BEC as the Exceptionable Bracketing Erasure Convention, which erases only unlabelled brackets.

The analysis adopted here supports the proposal of Kiparsky (1983) that violations of the Bracketing Erasure Convention are linked to certain kinds of morphology within a language. It is significant that the violations of the BEC in Sekani all involve a certain morphological domain. I know of no level 5 rules which crucially refer to the prefixes of position 9, for example.

In the next chapter I return to the Exceptionable Bracketing Erasure in my analysis of the phonological rule of Epenthesis in Sekani.

Notes.

1. In theory, the Strict Cycle Condition would prevent most cyclic rules from applying entirely within inner cycles. However, if word level rules are exceptions to the Strict Cycle Condition (Kiparsky 1985), or if lexical rules are not necessarily cyclic (Mohanan 1986), then these sorts of rules still provide an argument for the Bracketing Erasure Convention.

2. In Mohanan (1986), it is assumed that all levels are noncyclic and that stress is assigned on level 2.

3. As noted in Ch. 3, the level 2 prefix da in 'kindle fire' exceptionally fails to undergo Conjugation a Fronting:

(112) [kwàn nadàsihk'ǫ]   'I kindled a fire'
      *[kwàn nadèehk'ǫ]

Thus the prefix da must be marked as an exception to s-Conjugation a Fronting. I also noted in Ch. 3 that the level 3 prefixes wa and ya unpredictably undergo n-Conjugation a Fronting.

The existence of prefixes which must be marked for whether or not they undergo these a Fronting rules of course weakens the argument against a diacritic analysis, but does not in itself seem to be a strong reason for abandoning the level ordering distinction between levels 2 and 3. As discussed in Ch. 3, 4.2.6, the na prefixes of position 5 must be exceptionally marked as triggers for the rule of na Absorption, but this is not a compelling reason for abandoning the level ordering distinction which falls between prefixes 6 and 7.

4. This is clear from stem variation, for example:

(113) /yidà -n -d -xe -n/
    inside cnj clf pack Pf

    [yidǫgį]   'he, she packed [O] inside'

5. Reversative na may be present in surface forms of perambulative aspect verbs:

(114a) /k'è-na-tsį -da-tsįh/
    per C sniff der V:sniff

    [k'ètsįdatsįh]   'he, she sniffs around'

(114b) /k'ènatsįdatsįh/   'he, she sniffs around again'

As far as I know, these are the only forms in which both na's occur underlyingly. Since na customary is deleted, it is impossible to determine what the underlying order of the na prefixes is.

6. Notice that this form does not surface as *[satsàazi], with two adjacent low tone [a]'s. The tone of the possessive suffix is exceptionally mapped to the stem vowel a when it is set afloat by Suffix Vowel Deletion:

(115)   L
         ∕
         á   a

Compare the following a-final stem:

(116) [chəba]   'poplar'

    [sə -chəba -è?]   'my poplar'
     1sPsr poplar psd

    /sə -chəba -è -azi/
     1sPsr poplar psd dim

    [səchəbàazi]   'my small poplar'
    *[səchəbaàzi]

7. Compare the following verb:

(117) /u -da -gha-s -h -tsas -e/
    rep Fut Fut 1sS clf V:whip Fut

    [udaghastsase]   'I will whip it'

Chapter Six

Epenthesis

Sekani, like many other Athabaskan languages, contains a phonological rule of Epenthesis.[1] The level on which this rule applies is of some analytical and theoretical interest. I consider a number of possible level ordering assignments before concluding that it is a level 5 rule. However, as a level 5 rule, it must refer to stem bracketing, and thus can be added to the list of Sekani rules which pose a problem for exceptionless versions of the Bracketing Erasure Convention.

I have organized this chapter as follows. In section 1 I justify the rule of Epenthesis. In sections 2 and 3 I provide a preliminary analysis of the domain and formulation of the rule, and in section 4 I consider rule ordering in more detail. In section 5, I summarize the likely historical origin of Epenthesis, and propose, following Rice (1983), that Epenthesis is a level 5 rule. The interaction of Epenthesis with an additional rule, Stray n Deletion, discussed in section 6, provides further evidence that Epenthesis is a level 5 rule.

1. Introduction

The forms in (1) and (2) indicate that the underlying shape of the first person singular subject prefix is /s/, and that the category of the third person singular subject is not morphologically marked:

(1a) /na -s -h -xęh/
       rev 1sS clf thaw O
       5   12 13 stem

      [nasxęh]   'I thaw out [O]'

(1b) /na -h -xęh/
       rev clf thaw O

      [nahxęh]   'he, she thaws out [O]'

(2a) /nà -nə -s -l -ʔį̇/
      adv der 1sS clf hide
       2   9 12 13 stem

      [nànəsʔį̇ʔ]   'I hide'

(2b) /nà -nə -l -ʔį̇/
      adv der clf hide

      [nànaʔį̇ʔ]   'he, she hides'

This is the analysis of the subject prefixes that has been assumed in previous chapters.

The forms in (1) and (2) contain syllabic prefixes that have been added by the morphology. Now consider the following forms, in which no syllabic prefix is morphologically specified:

(3a) /s -d -yhən/
      1sS clf sing
      12 13 stem

      [əsjin]   'I sing'

(3b) /d -yhən/
      clf sing

      [ajin]   'he, she sings'

(4a) /tl'ogh s -dòt/
      grass 1sS smoke O
            12   stem

      [tl'ogh əsdòt]   'I smoke grass'

(4b) /tl'ogh dòt/
      grass smoke O

      [tl'ogh adòt]   'he, she smokes grass'

(5a) /s -h -ch'ès/
      1sS clf roast O
      12 13 stem

      [əsch'ès]   'I roast [O]'

(5b)   /h -chʼès/
       clf roast O

       [ahchʼès]   'he, she roasts [O]'

(Note that the rule of Schwa Lowering has applied in (5b).) In each of these forms, a syllabic element ([a] or [ə]) appears. This vowel is the output of the rule of Epenthesis.

Before proceeding with the details of Epenthesis, I would first like to point out another possible interpretation of the data in (1)(5). All of the forms in (3)-(5) are in the imperfective mode. In early studies of the phonology of Athabaskan languages (e.g., Sapir and Hoijer 1967), the cognate of the epenthetic syllabic element was sometimes analyzed as a marker of one of the conjugation classes of the imperfective mode, the y-imperfective. However, Krauss (1970:226) observed that the y-imperfective is in complementary distribution with the ∅-imperfective (another conjugation class of the imperfective) in this analysis, amounting to loss of generalization. Moreover, as noted by Kari (1975, 1976), in a morphological analysis of the syllabic segment in (3)-(5), it is necessary to assume that this syllabic element is deleted in all but the first and third person singular forms; i.e., in those forms that lack a syllabic subject prefix.

As a final strike against analyzing the epenthetic vowels in (3)-(5) as an imperfective morpheme, notice that these vowels are not limited to the imperfective mode. Consider the following perfective forms:

(6)   /sə -d -yhi/
       cnj clf breathe
       1O 13 stem

       [əsji]   'he, she breathed'

(7)   /sə -d -yhǫ/
       cnj clf grow
       1O 13

       [əsjǫ]   'he, she is old'

Although such data were observed and puzzled over in the early analyses, the presence of the epenthetic vowel in these perfective forms was not related to the presence of the epenthetic vowel in the imperfective forms.

Rice (1983) has insightfully described the conditions under which the epenthetic vowel occurs, and I will summarize her description: every verb in the Athabaskan languages consists of a stem preceded by at least one syllabic prefix. If no syllabic prefix is added by the morphology, then a vowel is added by Epenthesis to ensure that the verb contains a syllabic element to the left of the verb stem in its surface form.

In a phonological analysis, then, the presence of the epenthetic vowel in non-imperfective forms like (7) is easy to explain. Epenthesis will simply apply to the output of Conjugation ə Deletion in a form like (7). Conjugation ə Deletion is stated informally in (8):

(8) $\quad$ ə --> ∅ / $\left\{\begin{matrix} s \\ n \\ gh \end{matrix}\right\}$ ___ [(clf) verb stem]
$\qquad\qquad\qquad \left\{\begin{matrix} [+cnj] \\ [+mode] \end{matrix}\right\}$

The output of Conjugation ə Deletion, as applied to the prefixes /'sə/ and /'nə/, will be a form which lacks a syllabic prefix in third person singular forms. Epenthesis can then apply to create the appropriate surface form:

$\qquad\qquad\qquad$ /sə-d-yhǫ/

Cnj ə Del $\qquad\qquad\qquad$ ∅
Epenthesis $\qquad\qquad\qquad$ ə

$\qquad\qquad\qquad$ [asjǫ]

Thus a phonological rule of Epenthesis accounts for the presence of the epenthetic vowel in imperfective as well as non-imperfective forms.

2. The domain of Epenthesis--a first approximation

In the preceding section we saw that an epenthetic vowel appears in the following places:

--to the left of prefixes in positions 12, 13

--to the left of the conjugation prefix (position 10)

In the forms of the preceding section, the epenthetic vowel was word-initial, which might suggest that Epenthesis is a postlexical rule.

Now consider some additional data. In the following forms, the epenthetic vowel is not word-initial, but occurs within a word. Notice that the epenthetic vowel occurs to the right of the level 5 prefixes in all cases where it is word-internal:

(9) /ghǫzų sa -ghǫh lį/
    well 1sO P be
         1 1 stem

[ghǫzų sǫh<u>a</u>lį]   'he, she takes good care of me'

(10) /dah-sa -h -tsus/
     up cnj clf handle cloth-like O
     2 10 13 stem

[dah<u>a</u>htsus]   'he, she hangs up [cloth-like O]'

(11) /ya -ghǫh-na -yah/
     4sO P cnj sg goes
     1 1   10 stem

[yǫh<u>i</u>yah]   'he, she gets to [O], walking'

These data suggest that the epenthetic vowel is inserted after the level 2 prefixes have been added, but before the level 5 prefixes.

An additional complication must be mentioned. In examples (9)-(11), the level 5 prefix is consonant-final. However, forms which contain vowel-final level 5 prefixes lack an epenthetic vowel in their surface forms:

(12) /ɬè   -s -tl'ųh/
     in half 1sS tie
     2   12 stem

[ɬèstl'ųh]   'I tie a knot'

(13)   /nà -wàt/
        cont walk fast
        2   stem

        [nàwàt]   'he, she walks fast'

(14)   /?adalè e -h -kwi/
        blood P clf vomit O
               1 13 stem

        [?adalè? ehkwi]   'he, she vomits blood'

In keeping with the hypothesis that Epenthesis applies before the level 5 prefixes are added, information about whether or not a prefix will be added on level 5, and thus whether it is vowel- or consonant-final, is presumably unavailable at the point in the derivation that Epenthesis applies. Suppose that a formulation of Epenthesis is posited which looks only rightward to see if no syllabic prefixes have been added:

(15)   Epenthesis:

        $\emptyset \rightarrow \vartheta \;/\; \underline{\quad} \; C_0 \; [_V$

Then all that is required is an additional rule which deletes the epenthetic vowel if a vowel-final level 5 prefix is added. Recall from Ch. 3, 4.2.1, that Sekani has a rule of Prefix Vowel Deletion, given in (16):

(16a) $\vartheta \rightarrow \emptyset \;\%\; \underline{\quad} \; V$

(16b) $i \rightarrow \emptyset \;\%\; \underline{\quad} \; V$

(Prefix Vowel Deletion is actually two rules, with (16a) ordered before (16b).) In Ch. 3 I proposed that one difference between levels 2-4 and level 5 was that Prefix Vowel Deletion ceases to apply after level 4. However, suppose that only rule (16b) shuts off after level 4. Then (16a), Schwa Deletion, will be available to remove the epenthetic vowel if a vowel-final level 5 prefix is present. This analysis is illustrated in the derivation of (14) -ehkwi:

                        /h-kwi/

Epenthesis   ə

```
level 5
  morphology        e-ə
  Schwa Deletion    e-
```

eventually   [ehkwi]

Thus in verbal forms which lack syllabic levels 2-4 prefixes, the epenthetic vowel surfaces in only two cases: when no level 5 prefix is present, or when a level 5 prefix which ends in a consonant is added.

3. Formulation of Epenthesis

In the formulation of Epenthesis given in (15), I included the level 1 (verb stem) bracket [$_V$, without any real justification for including it in the rule:

(15) $\emptyset \rightarrow \partial\ /\ \_\_\_\ C_0\ [_V$

In this section I will show that it is indeed necessary to include stem bracketing in the rule. I will consider two alternative formulations of this rule. One of these does not rely crucially on stem bracketing, and is not observationally adequate. The other formulation I will consider is that proposed by Rice (1983), in which stem bracketing is available on a later level through an ingenious use of syllable structure.

3.1 The importance of stem bracketing

One possible interpretation of Epenthesis is that it is simply the manifestation of a surface constraint on well-formed verbs:

(17)   [σ   σ $_V$]

Verbs must fit a syllabic template consisting of at least two syllables. Of course, verbs would be allowed to exceed this template, as they often do, but the template might be regarded as a lower bound on the phonetic length of verbs.

However, note that Epenthesis applies even to verb stems which are disyllabic:

(18) /s -whàse/
      1sS itch
      l2 stem

      [aswhàse]   'I itch'

(19) /h -whàse/
      clf tickle O
      l3 stem

      [ahwhàse]   'he, she tickles [O]'

(20) /ʔəlà h -t'oghəs/
      boat clf paddle O
            l3 stem

      [ʔəlàʔ aht'oghəs]   'he, she paddles the boat'

If Epenthesis simply counted the number of syllables in a word, then it presumably would not need to apply in forms like (18)-(20). However, if Epenthesis is sensitive to stem bracketing, then the epenthetic vowel will correctly be inserted in these forms.

3.2 A syllable-based rule of Epenthesis?

So far we have seen that an epenthetic vowel is present in surface forms under the following conditions:

(21) C-final level 5 prefix   ___   no syllabic levels
      no level 5 prefix   2-4 prefixes

The syllabic element added by Epenthesis is present only when no syllabic levels 2-4 prefixes are added. To capture this generalization, Rice (1983) has proposed a syllable-based version of this rule to account for data in Slave which are analogous to these Sekani facts.

In recognition of the need for Epenthesis to refer to stem bracketing, Rice proposes that the following word formation rule applies to verb stems on level 1:

(22)   6
      [[v] v]

286

As a level 1 rule, the word formation rule in (22) ensures that every verb stem is preceded by at least one syllabic prefix in its surface form. The syllable added by the level 1 word formation rule can be filled by a syllabic prefix which is added on levels 2-4 by the morphology. However, if no syllabic prefix is added, then a vowel fills the empty syllable position, by the rule of Epenthesis:

(23) $\emptyset \longrightarrow e\ /\ \underset{---}{\overset{\sigma}{\triangle}}$

(The epenthetic vowel in Slave is e [ ].) Rice argues that Epenthesis applies on Slave level 4 (= Sekani level 5) to fill any empty syllable positions that have not been filled by the levels 2-3 word formation rules. She also argues that Epenthesis must precede the level 4 word formation rules.

This analysis has several nice consequences. First, a word level analysis of Epenthesis does not overgenerate: the epenthetic vowel is inserted only when no syllabic levels 2 or 3 prefixes are present. Second, the empty syllable provides a way of identifying the stem or level 1 domain on a later level which is not adjacent to level 1.

Theoretically, the analysis is also quite appealing. Since word level Epenthesis, a phonological rule, precedes the word level word formation rules, it indicates that levels 3 and 4 are linked through the phonology (as observed by Rice 1983), providing strong support for the Lexical Phonology model. Moreover, if one takes the position that syllable structure is an autonomous, rather than derived, property of phonological structure (Anderson 1982b), Lowenstamm and Kaye (1985)), the analysis is very much in keeping with the research strategy suggested by Anderson (1982b:18):

> ...there is reason to believe that segmental rules of epenthesis can be completely prohibited.

However, there is really no evidence that Epenthesis in the Athabaskan languages is a syllable-based rule. In fact, 'epenthesis' is something of a misnomer. This rule inserts a prothetic vowel in certain environments, much like the rule of Prothesis in Mohawk described by Michelson (1981). Thus the epenthetic vowel does not break up consonant clusters, or perform similar functions, as do syllable-based rules of epenthesis in other languages.

In what follows I will assume a linear version of Epenthesis.[2] Given the conclusion in Ch. 5 that stems are marked with labelled brackets, a syllable-based version of this rule is not required to circumvent the Bracketing Erasure Convention.

4. Rule ordering

To summarize, Epenthesis applies in verbal forms which lack syllabic level 2-4 prefixes. The epenthetic vowel surfaces only when no level 5 prefix is present, or when a consonant-final level 5 prefix is present. These facts suggest that Epenthesis applies on levels 2, 3, 4 or 5.

Since Epenthesis must refer to stem bracketing, the first hypothesis which comes to mind might be that Epenthesis is an early rule of the phonology. The data presented in Ch. 3 indicated that most of the rules of levels 2-4 are identical; thus Epenthesis might be a (cyclic) rule of levels 2, 3 and 4. In this section I consider the necessary orderings of a level 2 rule of Epenthesis with other level 2 phonological and morphological rules, and conclude that Epenthesis must be assigned to a later level.

4.1 Conjugation rules

In section 1 it was seen that Epenthesis must apply to the output of Conjugation a Deletion in certain forms (Ch. 3, 4.2.2). An epenthetic vowel appears in verb forms which contain th d classifier and the /`sə/ or /`nə/ conjugation prefixes, and in which the conjugation prefix is word-initial or preceded by a consonant-final level 5 prefix. An example is given in (24):

(24)   /`sa-d -yhǫ/
       cnj clf grow

       [asjǫ]   'he, she is old'

                                 /`sa-d-yhǫ/
Conjugation a Deletion   ∅
Epenthesis   a

                                 [asjǫ]

Epenthesis must follow Conjugation a Deletion.

Epenthesis must also follow Conjugation Tone Mapping (see Ch. 3, 4.2.2). Recall that Conjugation Tone Mapping applies on levels 2-4 of the verbal prefixes. The low tone of the conjugation prefixes /`sa/ and /`na/ is mapped to a preceding levels 2 and 3 vowel:

(25)   L   L
         ╱   ╱
       V́   sa   V́   na

Consider the forms asjǫ (24) and yǫhiyah (26). Since the vowel inserted by Epenthesis is not linked to a low tone in these forms, this suggests that level 2 Epenthesis follows Conjugation Tone Mapping, as the following derivation indicates:

(26)   /ya -ghǫh-`na-yah/
       4sO P   cnj sg go
       1   1   10 stem

       [yǫhiyah]   'he, she gets to him, her, walking'

                                 /`n-yah/
Conjugation Tone Mapping   --
Epenthesis   a n -yah
Nasalization   ą -yah
a Raising   į -yah

eventually   [yǫhiyah]

Epenthesis must also follow two additional level 2 rules that involve the conjugation prefixes. These are the rules of s- and n-Conjugation a Fronting (Ch. 3, 3.2). Recall that position 9 (level 2) prefixes of the shape /Ca/

become [Ce] in certain forms when followed by the conjugation prefixes /ˈsə/ or /ˈnə/. In n̲-Conjugation forms, only those forms in which the [n] of the conjugation prefix is syllable-final (third person singular, and first and third person plural) undergo the rule of n̲-Conjugation ə Fronting:

(27) n̲-Conjugation ə Fronting:

   ə --> e / ___ n]$_{syll}$

An example of the application of this rule can be seen with the position 9 prefix /də/ 'wooden O':

(28) /yidà -də -nə -leh/
      inside wood cnj handle pl O
       2   9   10   stem

      [yidàd<u>e</u>leh]   'he, she carries [pl O] inside'

cf.
(29) [d<u>e</u>chin]   'wooden'

In s̲-Conjugation forms, only forms which contain a low tone (this excludes 1d forms) undergo the rule of s̲-Conjugation ə Fronting:

(30) s̲-Conjugation ə Fronting:

               L
               |
       ə --> e / ___ s

Alternations involving the position 9 prefix /nə/ 'face' illustrate this rule:

(31a) /nə -sə -kàt/
      face cnj slap
       9   10 stem

      [nèzkàt]   'he, she slapped [O] on the face'
cf.
(31b) [nə -kàt]   'he, she slaps [O] on the face'
      face slap
       9   stem

The /ˈsə/ conjugation prefix is not present in the imperfective form in (31b).

In a form like [əsjq], it is clear that the vowel inserted by Epenthesis has not undergone s̲-Conjugation ə Fronting:

```
                       /s-d-yhǫ/
Cnj a Fronting          --
Epenthesis              a-s-d-yhǫ
```

And in a form like [yǫhiyah], n-conjugation a Fronting has not applied to the output of Epenthesis. Thus a level 2 rule of Epenthesis would have to follow the a Fronting rules.

4.2 Position 12 subject prefixes

The rule of L Deletion discussed in Ch. 3, 4.2.3, indicated that the position 12 subject prefixes are added on level 2. Level 2 Epenthesis also must follow the addition of these prefixes. Since the first person singular subject prefix /s/ contains no syllabic element, Epenthesis will apply in this form. The effect of Epenthesis is apparent in the surface forms of verbs which contain this prefix and no syllabic prefixes:

(32) /s -h -ch'ès/
      1sS clf roast O
      12 13 stem

      [asch'ès]   'I roast [O]'

(33) /s -d -yhan/
      1sS clf sing

      [asjin]   'I sing'

(34) /s -tsagh/
      1sS cry

      [astsagh]   'I cry'

Level 2 Epenthesis cannot apply until after /s/ has been added by the morphology:

```
stem                        /tsagh/

level 2
  subject prefix            s-tsagh
  Epenthesis                as-tsagh
```

The reverse ordering will incorrectly result in *[satsagh].

4.3 Summary

If Epenthesis is a levels 2-4 rule, it must follow several level 2 rules, given in (35):

(35)   Conjugation a̱ Deletion
       s̱- and ṉ-Conjugation a̱ Fronting
       Conjugation Tone Mapping
       affixation of position 12 subject prefixes

Epenthesis must be extrinsically ordered after many level 2 rules, but not before a single level 2 rule.

This ordering seems quite suspicious. It suggests that a generalization is being missed about where Epenthesis applies in the Sekani lexicon. If Epenthesis were instead assigned to a level later than level 2, say, level 3 or 5, the level ordering assignment would accomplish what would otherwise have to be stated separately in several rules.

Suppose Epenthesis were assigned to level 3. One descriptive generalization that emerged from Ch. 3 was that in Sekani, if a phonological rule applies on level 3 or 4, it also applies on level 2 (but not vice versa). However, a level 3 analysis of Epenthesis would run counter to this generalization. Moreover, if Epenthesis were a level 3 rule, it would still be necessary to order it after Conjugation Tone Mapping.

In fact, it is not necessary to violate the "if level 3 or 4, then level 2" generalization. As I will suggest in the following section, a level 5 analysis of Epenthesis is possible.

5. Level 5 Epenthesis

Rice (1983) suggests that Epenthesis was originally a post-lexical phonological rule. As discussed in Ch. 3, sec. 5., the level 5 or "disjunct" verbal prefixes are historically the most recently incorporated of the Athabaskan verbal prefixes. Rice (1983:10) provides a historical summary of Epenthesis and its relation to the level 5 prefixes in the Athabaskan languages:

> While these prefixes must be considered part of the verb word phonologically, they are clearly less bound to the verb than are the [levels 2-4] prefixes. Epenthesis...was very likely originally a post-lexical rule. It filled a syllable position before a verb stem if there was no prefix; the disjunct prefixes were not part of the verb word.

Given the probable post-lexical origin of Epenthesis, we might suppose it is still a comparatively late rule of the phonology, applying on level 5.

Indeed, a level 5 analysis of Epenthesis is possible and has no apparent negative consequences. First note that if Epenthesis applies on level 5, its formulation must be more complicated than that proposed in (15). As shown in 3.1, Epenthesis must refer to stem bracketing, like other rules discussed in Ch. 5, sec. 3. Since stems are exceptions to Bracketing Erasure in Sekani, Epenthesis may be formulated as in (36):

(36) $\emptyset \longrightarrow \mathrm{\partial} \: / \: \underline{\quad} \: [\: C_0 \: [_1, \: V$

If Bracketing Erasure Convention removes unlabelled brackets at the end of levels 2 and 3, then the context "$[\: C_0$" will be interpreted as the maximal string that can intervene between level 5 Epenthesis and the stem. Consider a form like (37):

(37)   /də -s -kwəs/
        thm 1sS cough
        9   12   stem

        [dəskwəs]   'I cough'

After levels 2-4 Bracketing Erasure has applied to this form, it will be bracketed as in (38):

(38)   [dəs[$_1$kwəs]]

Level 5 Epenthesis will be blocked from applying to (38) because a syllabic prefix is present. Now consider a form like (39):

(39)   /s -tsagh/
       1sS cry
       12 stem

       [astsagh]   'I cry'

This form will be bracketed as in (40) on level 5, and Epenthesis can thus apply to this form, as required.

(40)   [s[ɨtsagh]]

A level 5 analysis of Epenthesis solves the ordering problem discussed in sec. 4. The formulation of this rule given in (36) provides additional support for the version of the Bracketing Erasure Convention discussed in Ch. 5: in Sekani, stems are exceptions to the Bracketing Erasure Convention.

The data that I will discuss in the next section provide additional evidence that Epenthesis is a level 5 rule.

6. Epenthesis and Stray n Deletion

6.1 Stray n Deletion

Consider the following forms. Observe that the postposition in (41) and (42) alternates in shape between [ka] and [ɨka]:

(41a) /làdi nka-yə -nə -s -sən/
       tea P   thm thm 1sS want
            1   7   9   12 stem

       [làdi kayənassən]   'I want tea'

(41b) /sə -nka-yə -nə -n -zən/
       1sO P   thm thm Pf want
       1   1   7   9   11 stem

       [sɨkayənɨzən]   'he, she wants me'

(42a) /ghàje nka ts'ə-ch'ɨ/
       goose P   1pS be, do

       [ghàje ka ts'ach'ɨ]   'we are hunting a goose'

(42b)   /?ə   -nka ts'ə-ch'į/
        unspO P   1pS be, do

        [?įka ts'ach'į]   'we are hunting something'

As discussed in Chs. 3 and 4, Sekani independently requires the rules of
Nasalization and ə Raising:

(43)   Nasalization:

        Vn --> Ṽ / ___]$_{syll}$

(44)   ə Raising:

        ə --> i / ___ n]$_{syll}$

Thus if /nka/ is the underlying representation of this postposition, its
surface form in the (b) forms will be automatically accounted for by these
rules:[3]

                /sə-nka-yə-nə-n-zən/

Nasalization   ə̃   ə̃
ə Raising   į   į

                [sįkayanįzən]   'he, she wants me'

To account for (41a) and (42a), however, an additional rule will be necessary.
First recall that, as discussed in Ch. 1, Sekani has no syllable onsets of the
shape [nC]. In fact, aside from a few loan words, Sekani onsets may not
contain consonant clusters. Thus, in (41a) and (42a) above, no word-initial
[n] appears in the surface forms [ghàje _ka ts'əch'į] and [làdi _kayənəssən]
because the [n] cannot be syllabified into the onset of the syllable [ka].

To account for the failure of [n] to appear in these forms, we might
simply assume, following Lapointe and Feinstein (1982), that stray segments
are not phonetically realized, rather than deleted by language-specific rules.
However, when additional data are considered below, it will be seen that the
following rule which actually deletes the initial [n] of the postposition is
required:

(45)   Stray n̲ Deletion

$$n \rightarrow \emptyset\ /\ \underline{\quad}\ \begin{array}{c}* \\ \text{syll}\end{array}$$

Any unsyllabified [n]s will be deleted by this rule. As for the domain of this rule, the postposition forms above indicate that it cannot apply until after the level 1 oblique object prefixes have been added. In fact, as we will now see, Stray n̲ Deletion cannot apply until all word formation is complete.

The verbal prefix /n/ 'perfective mode' occurs in prefix position 11. Some forms which contain this prefix are given in (46)-(52):

(46)   /baɬ -də -ghə-n -h -ts'əgh/
       sleep thm cnj Pf clf yawn
       3   9   10 11 13 stem

       [baɬdəghi̱hts'əgh]   'he, she yawned'

(47)   /i -n -h -chùt/
       asp Pf clf take O carefully
       9   11 13 stem

       [i̱hchùt]   'he, she took [O] carefully'

(48)   /əsji ts'ə-n -li̱/
       smart 1pS Pf be
             8   11 stem

       [əsji ts'i̱li̱]   'we are smart'

(49)   /ùya ghə -n -li̱/
       shy 3pS Pf be
           8   11 stem

       [ùya ghi̱li̱]   'they are shy'

(50)   /na-ʔə -n -ni̱h/
       C unspO Pf make O well
       5   7   11 stem

       [naʔi̱ni̱h]   'he, she makes O well customarily'

(51)   /sa -n -h -gàs/
       sun Pf clf black
       3   11 13 stem

       [so̱hgàs]   'pitch black'

(52)   /ʔa -n -là/
       work Pf make O
       2   11 stem

       [ʔǫ̀là?]   'he, she made [O]'

In (51) and (52), the rules of a̱ Raising and Nasalization have applied to derive [ǫ], and in (46) and (48)-(50), a̱ Raising and Nasalization have created surface [i̱].

In the preceding forms the perfective prefix /n/ is preceded by prefixes of various positions: 2, 3, 7, 8, 9, 10. Now consider forms in which the perfective prefix is word-initial. Such forms would be expected to contain an epenthetic vowel, since the verb stem is not preceded by a syllabic prefix, but only by the consonantal perfective prefix /n/. Thus [i̱] would be expected in such forms. These forms do indeed contain an epenthetic vowel, but surprisingly, the perfective prefix is absent:

(53)   /əsji n -li̱/
       smart Pf be
            11 stem

       [əsji a̱li̱]   'he, she is smart'

(54)   /ùya n -li̱/
       shy Pf be
            11 stem

       [ùya a̱li̱]   'he, she is shy'

(The forms in (53) and (54) should be compared with (48) and (49) above for evidence that the perfective prefix is present underlyingly.) Apparently Stray ṉ Deletion has applied in these forms.

6.2 Rule ordering

The forms in (53) and (54), together with those in (46)-(52), indicate that Stray ṉ Deletion follows level 5 prefixation. Thus, if level 5 is a cyclic domain, then Stray ṉ Deletion must be a post-lexical rule. Notice, however, that if Epenthesis precedes Stray ṉ Deletion, Stray ṉ Deletion would have to precede the post-lexical syllabification rules. If post-lexical syllabification precedes Stray n̲ Deletion, then presumably the perfective prefix could not remain stray. Consider the following derivation of [alį] (54):

output of level 1   ∧
                                -[lį]

level 2
  Perfective prefix   ∧
                          [n -lį]

  Syllabification   --

level 5
  Syllabification   --

  Epenthesis   ∧
                          [ə n-lį]

post-lexical
  Stray n̲ Deletion   ∅

  Syllabification
                          | ∧
                         [ə -lį]

It is odd for syllabification rules to be extrinsically ordered after segmental rules. In fact, Harris (1983:77) has suggested that:

> ..prosodic rules precede segmental rules of the same (lexical or postlexical) type, at least in the unmarked case.

If this hypothesis is true, then Stray n̲ Deletion should precede Epenthesis.[4]

Given the formulation of Epenthesis in (36), Epenthesis cannot be a post-lexical rule. It must precede level 5 Bracketing Erasure in order to apply in forms like [daha̲htsus]. Fortunately, there is some evidence (discussed in Ch. 7), that level 5 is not a cyclic domain in Sekani.[5] Thus the following rule ordering is possible:

(55)   level 4 word formation rules
        Stray n̲ Deletion
        Epenthesis
        Bracketing Erasure

Now consider the derivation of [əlį], under this analysis:

```
                                    ∧
output of level 1          -[lį]

level 2                       ∧
  perfective prefix        [n -lį]

level 5
  Stray n Deletion         ∅
  Epenthesis                   ∧
                             ə-lį

post-lexical
  Syllabification          |   ∧
                           ə  -lį
```

If Epenthesis were a level 3 or earlier rule, it would not be possible to order Epenthesis after Stray n Deletion, and forms like (61) əlį would be difficult to account for.

7. Conclusion

There is good evidence for analyzing Epenthesis as a level 5 rule. This analysis eliminates the need for ordering Epenthesis after many level 2 rules. Moreover, if Epenthesis is a level 5 rule, it can follow Stray n Deletion, which clearly follows all prefixation.

Epenthesis provides evidence that stems are exceptions to Bracketing Erasure in Sekani, and thus that the weaker version of the Bracketing Erasure Convention proposed in Ch. 5 is required. Since Epenthesis refers to stem bracketing, it could only apply on level 5 if stem bracketing is still available on level 5.

Notes.

1. The vowel inserted by Epenthesis is sometimes referred to in the Athabaskan literature as the 'peg element' or the 'pepet vowel'.

2. I believe that syllable structure should be regarded as a derived, rather than autonomous, property of phonological representations.

3. Underlying representations like /nka/ are a marked shape for stems. /n/ in these forms might be a prefix. There is some evidence that the initial į-

of stems like (56)-(59) is a prefix:

(56) -[į-la]- 'hand'
     hand

(57) [į-za(-nah)] 'month'
     sun

(58) -[į-lin -é?] 'thigh'
     thigh psd

(59) -[į-ghǫ?] 'nose'
     nose

There are no stems in which į- is followed by a voiceless fricative. If į- is analyzed as a prefix, this fact will be accounted for by Continuant Voicing (Ch. 4, sec. 4), as pointed out to me by Keren Rice. There are many more stems which contain the prefix į- than those which contain the prefix n-. It is necessary to posit both /n/ and /in/ as prefixes.

4. Not everyone agrees that analyses in which prosodic rules follow segmental rules must be ruled out. Kiparsky (1985) has proposed an analysis of Spanish Depalatalization in which this rule applies at the word level, 'ordered before syllabification.' Kiparsky (1985) has also proposed that Icelandic Syllabification precedes u-Epenthesis but follows j-Deletion.

5. Harris (1983) concludes that the word level in Spanish must be a non-cyclic domain in order to avoid ordering certain segmental rules before post-lexical (Re)syllabification rules (but cf. note 6.) See also Kiparsky (1985) for further discussion of the word level.

Chapter Seven

The Cycle

In a non-cyclic derivation, rules are given exactly one chance to apply to a phonological string:

(1)   /A+B+C/

Rule R   a
Rule Q   c

                   [aBc]

However, in a cyclic derivation, each rule in an extrinsically ordered list of rules is given more than one chance: rules apply in cycles to successively larger constituents which are defined by morphological or syntactic structure:

(2)   [A + [B + [C]]]

Rule R
Rule Q   c

Rule R   a
Rule Q

                       [aBc]

Cyclic rule application is thus compositional in nature: the whole is hypothesized to be equal to the sum of its parts.

In the Lexical Phonology model, the two generative components of the lexicon--phonology and morphology--are hypothesized to interact with each other in a way that amounts to cyclic rule application. As proposed by Pesetsky (1979) and by Booij (1981), the phonological rules apply to the output of each cycle of morphology:

(3)   stem
       ↓
      Morph   --> P rule

      Morph   --> P rule
      etc.

For example, the stress contour of [industrialization] (where '1' = primary stress, '2' = secondary stress, etc., as in SPE) is derived in the following way, according to the Lexical Phonology model:

(4)   P rules: stress

    stem   industry   1
                                          industry

    -al   1   2 1
           industry-al   industry-al

    -ize   2 1   3 1   2
           industry-al-ize   industry-al-ize

    -ation 3 1   2   4 2   3 1
           industry-al-ize-ation industry-al-ize-ation

The stress rules are given a chance to apply after each suffix is added. Thus the apparent need for cyclic rule application, which had been unexplained prior to research in the LP framework, is a natural consequence of the way the lexicon is organized.

There has been some controversy over the need for cyclic rule application (i.e., over whether the preceding model is necessary) both in recent and not so recent work in phonological theory. In this chapter I will present evidence from certain segmental rules of the phonology of Sekani for both cyclic and non-cyclic rule application.

I begin this chapter with a brief discussion of the controversy surrounding cyclic analyses and the various attempts to predict the class of cyclic rules. In section 3 I present two pairs of Sekani rules which must apply cyclically, and in section 4, two rules which are post-cyclic. The distribution of cyclic and non-cyclic domains in Sekani is as predicted by Kiparsky (1985) and Harris (1983): the non-cyclic rules in Sekani are all late rules of the lexical phonology.

1. Do cyclic rules exist?

As mentioned above, cyclic rule application has been a controversial topic in phonological theory. Proposed cyclic analyses have rarely stood the test of time.

The theory of rule ordering known as the 'transformational cycle hypothesis' first appeared in SPE, in which Chomsky and Halle argued that cyclic rule application was needed to account for the stress patterns of morphologically complex words. The famous pair in (5) and (6) are nearly identical in terms of their segmental composition, yet the second syllables of the pair contain different degrees of stress:

(5)   3 0 1
           compensation

(6)   3 4 1
           condensation   'act of condensing'

Chomsky and Halle observed that these words are themselves derived from the words in (7) and (8), respectively, whose stress patterns are predictably different:

(7)   1 0 3
           compensate

(8)   3 1
           condense

The underlying stress on the second syllable of condense persists throughout the derivation of condensation. However, since the second syllable of compensate is not stressed at any point in its derivation, the second vowel of compensation surfaces with a completely reduced vowel. In SPE it was shown that a cyclic analysis of the stress rules of English could account for these and other facts in a way that a non-cyclic analysis could not, and was thus empirically required.

Reaction to the proposal that the cycle be incorporated into phonological theory was mixed. The cyclic aspect of the SPE analysis of stress has been criticized by Schane (1975), for example, although more recent metrical treatments of English stress have upheld the cyclic treatment (Kiparsky 1979,

Hayes 1984).

Many cyclic analyses of languages other than English have been proposed following the publication of SPE, and many of these have been criticized as not crucially requiring the cycle.[1] However, I believe that well-motivated cyclic analyses do exist, such as Yer Lowering in Russian (Pesetsky 1979, 1985), or the interaction of Syncope and Umlaut in Icelandic (Kiparsky 1984; also cf. Anderson 1974), or the analysis of Glide Formation, Vowel Reduction and Destressing (or Stress assignment; cf. Hayes (1984)) in Catalán (Mascaró 1976). The Sekani cases discussed in sec. 3 may be added to this collection of evidence for the cycle.

2. Which rules are cyclic?

Just as it would be useful to be able to predict which phonological rules are restricted to derived contexts (see Ch. 2, 5.2), there are certain advantages to being able to predict which rules are cyclic. For one thing, not all rules are cyclic. In Russian, for example, Yer Deletion is demonstrably post-cyclic, just as Yer Lowering is demonstrably cyclic (see Pesetsky 1979, 1985). The usual assumption of cyclic phonology (see Rubach 1984b) is that cyclic and postcyclic derivations form two separate blocks, with cyclic rules preceding the application of postcyclic rules.

Various answers to the question of which rules are cyclic have been proposed. In SPE, it was hypothesized that rules which apply below the level of the word (word-internally) are cyclic, whereas rules which apply at the word level or to constituents larger than a word are non-cyclic. (There is no discussion in SPE of why this division into cyclic and post-cyclic rules should exist, or where it might come from.)

Another hypothesis that has had some currency was the proposal that only stress rules or rules which referred to stress required the cycle (Brame 1972,

Thomas 1975, Anderson 1982a); i.e., no cyclic derivations involving segmental rules should be necessary. Again, it is not clear why this should be true, but there is no need to wonder too deeply about it, because this hypothesis is not true. Many cyclic analyses do indeed involve stress rules (the English and Catalán cases mentioned above do, for example), but many do not (e.g., the Russian and Icelandic cases also referred to as well as the Sekani case discussed below).

In early versions (e.g. Pesetsky 1979) of the Lexical Phonology model, it was thought that there was a correlation between cyclic application and lexical vs. postlexical status: all lexical rules apply cyclically, whereas all post-lexical rules are non-cyclic. However, both aspects of this hypothesis have been recently challenged.

There is some evidence that post-lexical rules may apply cyclically in some languages. See Dresher (1983) for Tiberian Hebrew, McHugh (1984) for Chaga, Shih (1984) for Mandarin, and Kaisse and Shaw (1985) for a list of other cases. If cyclic and postcyclic rule applications form two separate blocks, with cyclic derivations preceding postcyclic ones, then these cases might be handled under the hypothesis that languages may vary at the point in the lexicon that rules cease to apply cyclically. That is, the division between cyclic and non-cyclic derivations might be level 1 in some languages, and it might not exist at all in others.

The hypothesis that all lexical rules are cyclic has also been questioned. For example, Rubach (1984a) has suggested that each level contains a last-cyclic rule component, as well as a fully cyclic component. There is some theory-internal motivation for this hypothesis. As discussed in Ch. 5, level-final Bracketing Erasure must be a last-cyclic rule. Also, Kiparsky (1985) and Harris (1983) have proposed that word level and later rules apply non-cyclically (contra the reported analyses of postlexical cyclic rule application), whereas rules which apply on noninitial levels of the lexicon are cyclic.

A drastic revision of the hypothesis that there is a correlation between cyclic rule application and lexical status has been proposed by Mohanan and Mohanan (1984), Halle and Mohanan (1985), and Mohanan (1986), who maintain that cyclicity is a stipulated property of any levels. According to this view, any level of the lexicon of any language may be cyclic or not.

I believe that well-motivated analyses of lexical rules which must apply noncyclically do exist, such as Dahl's Law in Kikuyu (Myers 1973, cited in Pulleyblank 1986) (although some aspects of this analysis are problematic). However, many of the reported noncyclic analyses (e.g., in Malayalam (Mohanan and Mohanan 1984) or English (Halle and Mohanan 1985) are problematic, relying crucially on whether a rule violates the Strict Cycle Condition or not. However, since the exact formulation of the SCC (or the question of which rules obey it) is currently unresolved (see Ch. 2, sec. 5.2), it seems premature to conclude that a given rule must apply noncyclically because it violates the SCC.

3. Cyclic rule application in Sekani

In this section I discuss two pairs of segmental rules which I will argue apply cyclically.

3.1 Diphthongization and w Vocalization

The levels 2-4 rules of Diphthongization and w Vocalization are unordered with respect to each other, and they must apply cyclically. This is an interesting example of the need for cyclic rule application: cyclic derivations are often posited to resolve ordering paradoxes, yet in this case, the rules are crucially unordered.

3.1.1 Diphthongization

The rule of Diphthongization is informally stated in (9):

(9)   o --> wə / velar___

As discussed in Ch. 1, positing a rule of Diphthongization accounts both for the marked distribution of labio-velars (most labio-velars occur before the vowel ə), as well as a gap in the distribution of velars before surface (non-nasal) [o]. In rare cases, underlying /o/ is preserved after velars, creating alternations between [o] and [wə] after velars. Surface velar + [o] sequences are found before syllable-final ɣ, as can be seen in (10) and (11), or when [o] is nasal, as seen in (12)-(13):

(10)   -[goɣ]   'crawl to O' Fut

(11)   -[gwəts]   'crawl to O' C

(12)   /gho-tsəgh/
        Op cry
        11 stem

        [wətsəgh]   'he, she cries' Op

(13)   /gho-n -tsəgh/
        Op 2sS cry
        11 12 stem

        [ghǫtsəgh]   'you [sg] cry' Op

(Recall that w is phonologically a labio-velar ([ghw]), as is wh ([xw]).) These conditions on Diphthongization may be incorporated into the rule as follows:

(14)   o --> wə / velar___ (C)]_{syll}, C ≠ ɣ
        [-nas]

3.1.2 w Vocalization

The rule of w Vocalization in (15) was discussed in Ch. 3, 4.2.4.

(15)   wə --> u / V ___   domain: levels 2-4

(Recall that the only forms which meet the structural description of this rule are optative forms.) As seen in (12), the optative prefix /gho/ is [wə] in the third person singular form, but not in the second singular form in (13), in which the nasal [ǫ] blocks Diphthongization. Now consider an optative paradigm in which the optative prefix occurs to the right of the level 2 prefix nə:

(16) /nə -gho-s -d -dayh/
      thm Op 1sS clf dance
       9   11 12   13 stem

      [nusdayh]   'I dance' Op

(17) /nə -gho-d -dayh/
      thm Op clf dance

      [nudayh]   'he, she dances' Op

Vocalization has applied to the output of Diphthongization in the forms above:

(18)   /nə-gho-d-dayh/

Diphthongization   wə
Vocalization   u
Prefix Vowel Deletion   ∅

                          [nudayh]

It is worth considering a possible reanalysis of this rule. Suppose that Vocalization were instead formulated as in (19):

(19)   gho --> u / V ___

In this analysis, Vocalization would not interact with Diphthongization at all:

(20)   /nə-gho-d-dayh/

Vocalization   u
Prefix Vowel Deletion   ∅

                          [nudayh]

Instead of applying to the intermediate representation created by Diphthongization, Vocalization would apply to the underlying form of the prefix /gho/. My objection to this analysis is that it amounts to loss of generalization: Vocalization, like Diphthongization, would be blocked when [ǫ] is nasal. Compare the form in (21) with the paradigmatically related forms in (16)-(17) above:

(21) /nə -gho-n -d -dayh/
      thm Op 2sS clf dance
      9   11 12 13 stem

      [naghǫdayh]   'you [sg] dance' Op

A gho --> u analysis of Vocalization would miss the generalization that only forms in which Diphthongization has applied (namely, first and third person singular forms) also undergo w Vocalization. For this reason, I propose that Vocalization applies to the intermediate representation [wə].

Aside from the fact that the domain of this rule is restricted to the levels 2-4 prefixes, as discussed in Ch. 3, an additional restriction must be placed on Vocalization. Vocalization does not apply to forms in which the optative prefix is preceded by the level 2 prefix /u/:

(22) /u -gho-tòn/
      thm Op hold O
      9   11 stem

      [uwatòn]   'he, she holds [O]' Op

(23) /u -gho-h -ch'uh/
      thm Op clf shoot O

      [uwahch'uh]   'he, she shoots [O] repeatedly' Op

This fact is of considerable importance, as will soon be apparent. w Vocalization is accordingly revised:

(24) wə --> u / V ___ ,   V ≠ u

3.1.3 Rule ordering: the gho-gho forms

So far we have seen that Vocalization applies to the output of Diphthongization: Diphthonigzation feeds Vocalization. Now consider forms in which two /o/-final prefixes occur, which I will refer to as 'gho-gho' forms[2]. When the vowel which precedes [w] is underlyingly /o/, Vocalization appears to apply optionally. The (a) and (b)' variants in (25)-(26) are equally acceptable.

(25)   /gho-gho-h -tləgh/
       ar Op clf rub O
       7   11 13 stem

(a)   [wəwahtləgh]   'he, she rubs [area] with medicine' Op
(b)   [wuhtləgh]

(26)   /xo -gho-h -whəse/
       1pO Op clf itch, tickle
       7   11 13 stem

(a)   [whəwahwhəse]   'he, she tickles us' Op
(b)   [whuhwhəse]

How are we to make sense of these data? One possible analysis would be to formulate the following two rules of w Vocalization:

(27a) Vocalization I³

       wə --> u / C   V ___   optional
                [+round]

(28)   Vocalization I

       wə --> u / V ___,   V ≠ u   obligatory

By applying the first of these rules to the forms in (25) and (26), the two surface forms will be generated in accordance with whether or not Vocalization has applied:

(29)   /xo -gho-h-whəse/

Diphthongization   whə wə
Vocalization I   u
(chooses to apply)
Prefix Vowel Deletion   ∅

                             [whuhwhəse]

(30)   /xo -gho-h-whàse/

Diphthongization   whǝ wǝ
Vocalization I   --
(chooses not to apply)
Schwa Lowering   a

                            [whǝwahwhàse]

However, a considerably less complicated analysis of these forms is also available. Recall that Vocalization is blocked when the preceding vowel is [u], a round vowel. Since the output of Diphthongization is an unrounded vowel [ǝ], whereas the input to Diphthongization is a round vowel, [o], the two possible surface variants in the gho-gho forms can be accounted for if w Vocalization and Diphthongization are unordered with respect to each other. A single rule of w Vocalization can be posited:

(31)   wǝ --> u / V ___
                   [-rnd]

When Diphthongization precedes (and feeds) Vocalization, the forms with [u] will be derived, as in (25b) and (26b) above:

(32)   /xo -gho-h-whàse/

Diphthongization   whǝ-wǝ
Vocalization   whǝ-u
Prefix Vowel Deletion   wh-u

                            [whuhwhàse]

When Vocalization precedes (and counter-feeds) Diphthongization, Vocalization will be blocked because the rule does not apply to [gho], only to [ghwǝ]:

(33)   /xo -gho-h-whàse/

Vocalization   --
Diphthongization   whǝ wǝ
Schwa Lowering   a

                            [whǝwahwhàse]

Moreover, the vowel which precedes the optative prefix is round.

311

3.1.4 Diphthongization and Vocalization are cyclic

In the preceding section we have seen that Diphthongization and Vocalization must be unordered with respect to each other in order to account for both surface variants of the gho-gho forms. These forms are compatible with either a cyclic or a non-cyclic analysis of the rules. We have seen how a non-cyclic derivation correctly generates the two forms. Now consider a cyclic derivation of (26), which works equally well. (I have suppressed certain earlier cycles of morphology and phonology.)

(34)   /xo -ghohwhàse/

gho cycle
Diphthongization   wə
Vocalization   --
Prefix Vowel Deletion   --

xo cycle
Diphthongization   whə
Vocalization   u
Prefix Vowel Deletion   wh -u

                    [whuhwhàse]

As seen above, when Diphthongization feeds Vocalization, the form in (34) is generated. When the Vocalization counter-feeds Diphthongization, the form in (35) is generated:

(35)   /xo -ghohwhàse/

gho cycle
Vocalization   --
Diphthongization   wə
Prefix Vowel Deletoin   --

xo cycle
Vocalization   --
Diphthongization   whə
Prefix Vowel Deletion   --

                    [whəwahwhàse]

As in (34), Vocalization is blocked on the xo cycle in (35) by the roundness of the preceding vowel.

So far the cyclic and non-cyclic analyses appear to work equally well.

However, when the original data (presented in 3.1.2) are reconsidered, it will be seen that only a cyclic analysis can generate all and only the correct forms, whereas a non-cyclic analysis of the CV-<u>gho</u> forms, in which Diphthongization and <u>w</u> Vocalization are unordered with respect to each other, will predict incorrect forms.

First consider a cyclic analysis of <u>nudayh</u> 'he, she dances'. If Diphthongization precedes Vocalization in this derivation, only <u>nudayh</u> will be derived, as is correct:

(36) /nə -gho-d -dayh/
      thm Op clf dance
       9   12 13 stem

/nə-gho-d-dayh/

<u>gho</u> cycle
Diphthongization   wə
Vocalization   --
Prefix Vowel Deletion

<u>nə</u> cycle
Diphthongization   --
Vocalization   u
Prefix Vowel Deletion   n - u

[nudayh]

Even if Vocalization precedes Diphthongization, only <u>nudayh</u> is derived (again, as desired):

(37)   /nə-gho-d-dayh/

<u>gho</u> cycle
Vocalization   --
Diphthongization   wə
Prefix Vowel Deletion

<u>nə</u> cycle
Vocalization   u
Diphthongization   --
Prefix Vowel Deletion   n - u

[nudayh]

Regardless of how Diphthongization and Vocalization are ordered with respect to each other on any given cycle, the apparent feeding order of the rules (Diphthongization preceding Vocalization) which is required to derive only [nudayh] is obtained in a cyclic analysis: only the structural description of Diphthongization is met on the gho cycle, and only the structural description of w Vocalization is met on the na cycle.

This is not the case in a non-cyclic analysis. As seen in the derivation in (37), a non-cyclic analysis will correctly derive only the form [nudayh] only when Diphthongization precedes (feeds) Vocalization. When Vocalization precedes (counter-feeds) Diphthongization, *[nawədayh] will be produced:

(38)   /nə-gho-d-dayh/

Vocalization   --
Diphthongization   wə

                              *[nawədayh]

Thus the non-cyclic derivation is unable to accounting for the CV-gho forms if the rules are unordered, as is required for the gho-gho forms.

In a non-cyclic analysis, the only way to predict all and only the correct forms would be to retreat to the bifurcated version of Vocalization given above:

(39a) Vocalization I

       wə --> u / C   V ___   optional
               [+round]

(39b) Vocalization II

       wə --> u / V ___   V ≠ u   obligatory

Another alternative, in the non-cyclic analysis, would be to posit a gho --> u formulation of Vocalization, in which Diphthongization and Vocalization do not interact. But, as discussed above in 3.1.2, this analysis leads to loss of generalization.

A non-cyclic analysis of these rules would be more complicated or redundant than the simple cyclic analysis.[4]

3.2 Possessive suffixation and Nasalization

In this section I will argue that possessive suffixation and Nasalization must apply cyclically. The special interest of this analysis lies in the fact that a phonological rule (Nasalization) apparently must precede a morphological process, possessive suffixation. Moreover, the analysis illustrates the apparently correct prediction of the Lexical Phonology concerning the source of cyclic rule application: the cycle is the result of the interaction of phonology and morphology.

3.2.1 Nasalization

As discussed in Ch. 1, nearly all nasal vowels in Sekani can be derived from syllable-final [Vn] sequences by the rule of Nasalization:

(40) Vn --> Ṽ / ___ (C)]$_{syll}$

The derived nature of nasal vowels is suggested by alternations like the following:

(41a) [sə -tsòn-è?]   'my shit'
      1sPsr shit psd

(41b) [tsǫ̀?]   'shit'

(42a) [sə -gòn-è?]   'my arm'
      1sPsr arm psd

(42b) [sagǫ̀ts'è-lè?]   'my elbow'
            bone

(43a) /yhèɬ nè   -nə -s -ɬeh/
      trap to ground cnj 1sS handle pl O

      [yhèlnènasɬeh]   'I set traps'

(43b) /yhèɬ nè   -n -leh/
      to ground cnj handle pl O

      [yhèɬ nę̀leh]   'he, she sets traps'

The alternation between [Vn] and [Ṽ] in (43a) and (b) is the result of the application of Conjugation a Deletion in the third person singular form:

(44) /nè-na-leh/

Conjugation a Deletion   ∅
Nasalization   ę̀

[nę̀leh]

In addition to accounting for alternations between [Vn] and [Ṽ], this analysis also accounts for the fact that [Vn] and [Ṽ] sequences are largely in complementary distribution. Thus, the rule of Nasalization, which applies to non-derived as well as to derived forms, can considerably simplify the inventory of underlying vowel segments: with the exception of the nasal vowels in the stems -[chų̀ę?] 'son' and -[sk'ų̀ę?], all nasal vowels, even non-alternating ones, can be derived from syllable-final /Vn/ sequences.[5]

In Ch. 4, I argued that Nasalization was a lexical rule, because its application must precede diminutive suffixation:

(45) /tsòn-azi/
     shit dim

     [tsǫ̀azi]   'small shit'

Moreover, as predicted of a lexical rule, there are lexically marked exceptions to Nasalization, as also discussed in Ch. 1.

(46) [?ətsibalyàn]   'bald eagle'

(47) -[tòn]   'hold O; be broken'

(48) [jon]   'here'

The form in (46) is a loan word from Carrier (cf. Carrier Linguistic Committee (1974)).

3.2.2 Repossessed nouns

As discussed in Ch. 4, Sekani, like other Athabaskan languages, morphologically distinguishes alienably from inalienably possessed nouns. The latter always require a possessive prefix or nominal possessor.[6] If no overt possessor is specified, the prefix [ʔə]- 'unspecified possessor' occurs on inalienably possessed nouns. For example, the inalienably possessed noun [dzəghè?] 'outer ear' occurs with the unspecified possessive prefix [ʔə]- in the derived nominal in (49) because no other possessor is specified:

(49) /ʔə -dzəghè gha-də -i -n -ya -i/
  unspPsr outer ear P der der Pf pl O are in position nom

  [ʔədzəghè? ghadįyai]   'earrings'

However, in the compound in (50), the stem [chaba] is the possessor, and the prefix [ʔə]- is unnecessary:

(50) [chəba dzagh -è?] '(a poplar fungus)'
  poplar outer ear psd

The list of inalienably possessed nouns includes body parts and kinship terms, as well as some nouns that might otherwise be thought of as alienably possessed, on semantic grounds:

(51) [ʔət'ǫ?]   'leaves'
(52) [ʔət'oh]   'nest'
(53) [ʔəza]   'sand'
(54) [ʔach'elè?]   'rag'
(55) [ʔəlà?]   'dugout canoe'
(56) [ʔach'į]   'job'

Recall from Ch. 4 that nouns lexically specify that one of three possessive suffixes is required: -[è?], -['?] or -∅.

When inalienably possessed nouns are possessed by other than their natural owner, the 'repossessed' construction, in which there are two layers of possessive morphology, is required. Consider the following:

(57a) /sə -įla - /
  1sPsr hand psd

  [sįlà?]   'my (own) hand'

(57b) [tsà ila-`?]   'beaver's paw'
      beaver hand psd

(57c) /sə -?ə -ila-`/
      1sPsr unspPsr hand psd

      [se?ilà?]   'my (its) hand'

(In (57c), the rule of Preglottal Schwa Fronting has applied:

(58) a --> e / ___ [$_N$?)

Another example of a repossessed inalienably possessed noun is given below:

(59a) [sə -t'oh]   'my nest'
      1sPsr nest

(59b) [dat'one t'oh]   'duck's nest'
      duck   nest

(59c) /sə -?ə -t'oh-è/
      1sPsr unspPsr nest psd

      [se?at'ohè?]   'my (its) nest'

Notice that the possessive suffix -[è?] occurs in the repossessed form of 'nest', even though this stem lexically specifies that no possessive suffix is required. This is apparently characteristic of the repossessed construction: nouns which normally lexically specify -∅ possessive suffix require -è in the repossessed construction.[7]

To summarize, two layers of possessive morphology occur in repossessed forms. The first layer of morphology, the prefix [?ə]-, marks the unspecified original owner and the second layer marks the new owner.

3.2.3 An ordering paradox

As discussed in Ch. 4, the following forms suggest that possessive suffixation precedes Nasalization:

(60) [sagònè?]   'my arm'

(61) [satsònè?]   'my shit'

Suffixation of -[e?] causes the stem-final nasal to be resyllabified with the possessive suffix, blocking Nasalization:

(62)   /tsòn/

possessive suffixation   tsòn-è
Nasalization   --

                               -[tsònę̃]

Now consider the following repossessed nouns:

(63a)   [?at'ǫ?]   '(its) leaves'

(63b)   [se?at'ǫ̀è?]   'my (its) leaves'

(64a)   [?ach'į]   '(its) job'

(64b)   [se?ach'įè?]   'my (its) job'

These forms suggest that Nasalization must precede possessive suffixation:

(65)   [t'òn]

Nasalization   [t'ǫ̀]
Possessive suffixation   [[t'ǫ̀]è]

eventually   [se?at'ǫ̀è?]

An ordering paradox has arisen. In an analysis in which non-alternating nasal vowels are derived from syllable-final /Vn/ sequences, one would expect *[se?at'ònè?] for 'my (its) leaves' if possessive suffixation precedes Nasalization:

(66)   /sa-?a-t'òn-è/

Nasalization   --
ə Fronting   e

                               *[se?at'ònè?]

3.2.4 Nasalization is cyclic

A cyclic analysis provides a way to account for the contrast between (60) and (61), on the one hand, and (63b) and (64b), on the other, without having to posit underlying nasal vowels in the case of all repossessed nouns.

It is clear that repossessed nouns contain two layers of possessive morphology. If Nasalization is a cyclic rule, then its application on the first cycle will both precede and follow possessive suffixation. On the first cycle, suffixation of -/è/ will bleed Nasalization, but suffixation of -∅ will not.

The repossessed nouns may be derived as follows:

(67)   [t'òn]

original possessor cycle
prefix ?ə-   [?ə [t'òn]]
Nasalization   ǫ̀

new possessor cycle
affix sə- and -e   [sə [?ə [t'ǫ̀]] è]
Nasalization
ə Fronting   e

                               [se?at'ǫ̀è?]

However, in [satsònè?], no nasal vowels are derived because this form contains only one layer of possessive morphology:

(68)   [tsòn]

possessive suffixation   [sə [tsòn] è]
Nasalization   --

                               [satsònè?]

Nasalization is blocked in this form because the nasal is not syllable-final.

In this case, the cycle provides a systematic account of the contrast between -[Ṽè?] and [Vnè?]. In a non-cyclic analysis, it would be necessary to posit underlying nasals in all cases where nasal vowels do not alternate with nasal consonants. However, as discussed above, such an analysis of nasal vowels would lead to loss of generalization about the distribution of [Vn] sequences with respect to [Ṽ].

4. Non-cyclic rule application in Sekani

The evidence of the preceding section suggests that levels 1 (as indicated by 3.2) and 2 (as indicated by 3.1) are cyclic domains in Sekani. Now I would like to turn to evidence that level 5 and the post-lexical level are not cyclic domains. Given the current controversy in Lexical Phonology over which rules are cyclic, it is of equal interest to note that some rules in Sekani are clearly non-cyclic.

4.1 Schwa Lowering

In Ch. 3, I referred briefly to the rule of Schwa Lowering, which is stated informally below:

(69)   ə --> a / ___ h]$_{syll}$

Recall the alternations which motivate this rule:

(70a)   /zə -s -h -xeh/
        der 1sS clf kill sg O
        9   12 13 stem

        [zəsxeh]   'I kill [sg O]'

(70b)   /zə -h -xeh/
        der clf kill sg O

        [zahxeh]   'he, she kills [sg O]'

(71a)   /?ə -s -h -xǫh/
        unspO 1sS clf snore
        7   12 13 stem

        [?əsxǫh]   'I snore'

(71b)   /?ə -h -xǫh/
        unspO clf snore

        [?ahxǫh]   'he, she snores'

Schwa Lowering has applied to the prefixes /zə/- and /?ə/- in the third person singular forms, where they are followed by the classifier /h/-.

The interaction of Schwa Lowering with w Vocalization suggests that Schwa Lowering is not a cyclic rule. To see why this is so, first reconsider some of the forms in which w Vocalization does not apply.

4.1.1 w Vocalization and second person plural forms

Forms which contain the second person plural subject prefix /ah/ are among those in which Vocalization (discussed in 3.1 above and repeated below in (72)) does not apply:

(72)   Vocalization

       wə --> u / V ___
              [-rnd]

(73)   /na -gho-ah -?įh/
        asp Op 2pS steal O
        9   11 12   stem

       [nawah?įh]   'you [pl] steal [O]' Op

(74)   /na -gho-ah -d -dayh/
        thm Op 2pS clf dance
        9   11 12 13 stem

       [nawahdayh]   'you [pl] dance'

Apparently, Vocalization does not apply when the vowel which follows [w] ([ghw]) is not [a]. The forms in (73)-(74) suggest that Prefix Vowel Deletion precedes (bleeds) the application of w Vocalization on the next cycle:

(75)   /na-gho-ah-?įh/

gho cycle
Diphthongization   wə
Prefix Vowel Deletion   w -ah

na cycle
Vocalization   --

                              [nawah?įh]

w Vocalization cannot apply because Prefix Vowel Deletion has removed the schwa of the optative prefix.

4.1.2 Schwa Lowering is not cyclic

     Now consider the following forms:

(76)   /ts'ə-gho-h -yhòʔ/
        1pS Op clf blow
        8   11 13 stem

       [ts'uhyhòʔ]   'we blow on [O]' Op

(77)   /ʔə -gho-h -xǫh/
       unspO Op clf snore
       7   11   13   stem

           [ʔuhxǫh]   'he, she snores' Op

If Schwa Lowering were a lexical rule of levels 2-4, it would have to apply cyclically, since Diphthongization and w Vocalization are cyclic rules. However, the wrong forms will be produced if Schwa Lowering applies cyclically, as the following derivation indicates:

(78)   /tsʼə-gho-hyhòɫ/

gho cycle
Diphthongization   wə
ə Lowering   a

tsʼə cycle
Vocalization   --

                        *[tsʼawahyhòɫ]

The cyclic application of Schwa Lowering would bleed w Vocalization, because the output of Schwa Lowering would create a form which is identical to one which contains the second person plural subject prefix /ah/, in which Vocalization does not apply. Of course, the right form will be produced if Schwa Lowering does not apply cyclically:

(79)   /tsʼə-gho-hyhòɫ/

gho cycle
Diphthongization   wə

tsʼə cycle
Vocalization   u
Prefix Vowel Deletion   ø

post-cyclic:
Schwa Lowering   --

                        [tsʼuhyhòɫ]

Clearly, Schwa Lowering must be prevented from applying on level 2 on the cycle in which its structural description is met, in order to derive [tsʼuhyhòɫ], as required. Therefore, Schwa Lowering must not be a cyclic rule.[8]

4.1.3 Is Schwa Lowering a post-lexical rule?

We have seen that Schwa Lowering cannot apply cyclically. The next question to ask is whether it is word level rule or a post-lexical rule.

If Schwa Lowering is a word level rule, it must follow Epenthesis (Ch. 6), since it applies to the output of this rule:

(80) /ə -h -ch'ès/
      epen clf roast 0
           13 stem

      [ah̲ch'ès]   'he, she roasts [0]'

(81) /ə -h -ts'ex/
      epen clf lick
           13 stem

      [ah̲ts'ex]   'he, she licks [0]'

As far as I know, the structural description of Schwa Lowering would not be met between words; i.e. Lowering could not be a sandhi rule. The following combination of words would be required:

(82) [...ə hC...]

But there are no word-initial consonant clusters in Sekani, and there are also no [ə]-final words.

It is perhaps worth noting that Schwa Lowering has many of the hypothesized characteristics of post-lexical rules. It is surface true, has no lexical exceptions, and is not sensitive to word-internal structure. There are no lexical rules which must follow it. This evidence is consistent with the assumption that Schwa Lowering is post-lexical rule.

4.2 a Deletion

The lexical rule of a Deletion was discussed in Chs. 3, 4, and 5:

(83) a --> ∅ / ___ a

Recall that this rule applies to a-a sequences that arise from the suffixation of a-final stems with an a-initial suffix, and the prefixation of an a-final

level 5 prefix to a verb which contains the 2p subject prefix /ah/:

forms containing stem-final /a/

(84a)   /yà   -azi/
        louse dim

        [yàzi]   'small louse'
cf.
(84b)   [yà?]   'louse'

(85a)   /chəba -azi/
        poplar dim

        [chəbazi]   'small poplar'
cf.
(85b)   [chəba]   'poplar'

(86a)   /xəda -azi/
        moose dim

        [xədazi]   'small moose'
cf.
(86b)   [xəda]   'moose'

forms which contain /ah/ (second person plural subject prefix)

(87a)   /nà -ah -d -ts'it/
        down 2pS clf sg/du fall

        [nàhts'it]   'you [du] fall down'
cf.
(87b)   /nà -na -d -ts'it/
        down 2sS clf sg/du fall

        [nànats'it]   'you [sg] fall down'

(88a)   /chu -na -ah -k'əs/
        water rev 2pS clean

        [chunahk'əs]   'you [pl] wash [O]'
cf.
(88b)   [chunak'əs]   'he, she washes [O]'

(89a)   /ʔa -ah -ɬeh/
        adv 2pS handle pl O

        [ʔahɬeh]   'you [pl] make [O]'
cf.
(89b)   [ʔaleh]   'he, she makes [O]'

The rule of a̱ Deletion is somewhat unusual in Sekani. Normally, stem vowels are not deleted before suffix vowels, nor are level 5 prefixes normally deleted.

4.2.1 a̱ Deletion is not cyclic

    In Ch. 3, I noted that forms like the following indicate that Nasalization is a lexical rule:

(90)   /hà-na-ah-ɬeh/
        out rev 2pS handle pl O
         2   5 12   stem

        [hǫ̀ahɬeh]   'you [pl] take [pl O] back out'

(91)   /dà -na -ah -kwi/
        dstr rev 2pS vomit
         4   5   12 stem

        [nadǫ̀ahkwi]   'you [pl] habitually vomit separately'

These forms also indicate that a̱ Deletion cannot be a cyclic rule. To see why this is so, consider the following cyclic derivation of (90):

(92)   /hà-na-ahɬeh/

na̱ cycle
a̱ Deletion   ∅

hà cycle
ṉ Insertion   n
a̱ Raising   o
Nasalization   ǫ
na̱ Deletion   ∅

                        *[hǫ̀hɬeh]

Like Schwa Lowering, a̱ Deletion cannot apply as soon as its structural description is met. a̱ Deletion must wait until na̱ Deletion has had a chance to apply. a̱ Deletion can be ordered after na̱ Deletion, but if level 5 is a cyclic domain, this will not have the desired effect: the structural description of na Deletion will not be met until the next cycle in the preceding form.

However, if a Deletion is a post-cyclic rule, it can follow na Deletion:

(93) /hà-na-ahɫeh/

n Insertion   n
a Raising   o
Nasalization   ǫ
na Deletion   ∅
a Deletion   --

            [hǫ̀ahɫeh]

This derivation suggests that a Deletion is not a cyclic rule.

4.2.2 a Deletion is not post-lexical

Having established that a Deletion is not cyclic, we might next try to determine whether it is a level 5 or a post-lexical rule. There is some evidence that it is a level 5 rule, rather than a rule of the syntax. Sequences of [a a] which belong to different words do not undergo a Deletion:

(94) [ùya ahɫį]   'you [pl] are shy'
     shy 2pS be

(95) [ʔįka ahch'į]   'you [pl] are trapping'
     unspO P   2pS be, do

(96) [ya àhxal]   'you [pl] threw [stick-like O] in the air'
     sky 2pS handle stick-like O carelessly

The existence of these [aa] sequences suggests that a Deletion does not apply in the syntax.

4.2.3 a Deletion is a level 5 rule

If a Deletion is not post-lexical, and it is not a cyclic rule of level 5, then it can only be a non-cyclic rule of level 5.

However, if a Deletion is a non-cyclic rule of level 5, then a slight problem arises: why do word-internal [aa] sequences exist? If a Deletion is not a cyclic rule, it should not be constrained by the Strict Cycle Condition, and should thus be free to apply in non-derived environments. But in certain second person plural s-conjugation forms, the sequence [aa] arises:

(97) /u -zə -sə -ah -h -ts'ǫ/
      thm thm cnj 2pS clf listen

      [uzàahts'ǫ]   'you [pl] listened to [O]'

(The vowel sequence is derived by level 2 rules which were discussed in Ch. 3, 3.2.1.) One possible solution would be to reformulate the rule in (83) so that it includes a bracket:

(98) a --> ∅ % ___ [a

Then, given the fact that level 2 Bracketing Erasure necessarily precedes level 5 a Deletion, forms like (97) will not undergo a Deletion because they do not meet the structural description of the rule.[9]

The fact that a Deletion is a non-cyclic level 5 rule is compatible with either of two theories of non-cyclic rule application in Lexical Phonology. The rule could be taken as support for the hypothesis of Kiparsky (1985) that the last lexical level is a non-cyclic word level. However, the rule is equally compatible with the hypothesis of Rubach (1984a) that every level contains a post-cyclic rule component.

I have not been able to find evidence that any of the level 5 rules must apply cyclically in Sekani, and for this reason, I adopt Kiparsky's more restrictive model of the cycle. Thus the following picture of cyclic domains in Sekani emerges:

(99)   levels 1-2   cyclic rules

        level 5   post-cyclic rules
        post-lexical

The fact that level 5 is non-cyclic has one nice analytical consequence. As discussed in Ch. 6, Stray n Deletion must follow the level 5 morphological rules. However, if Stray n Deletion is a post-lexical rule, it must crucially

precede the post-lexical syllabification rules, and this is apparently a
marked ordering of prosodic and segmental rules (cf. Harris (1983)). On the
other hand, if level 5 is non-cyclic, Stray n̲ Deletion may be analyzed as a
level 5 rule, ordered after the level 5 word formation rules, and this may
turn out to be the unmarked ordering of phonological and morphological rules
on a noncyclic level (cf. Mohanan (1986), Mohanan and Mohanan (1984):

> ..in a noncyclic lexical stratum phonological rules apply only at the
> end of all the morphological operations at that stratum. (Mohanan and
> Mohanan (1984:594))[10]

4.3 Non-cyclic rules: summary

Two Sekani rules, a̲ Deletion and Schwa Lowering, are demonstrably non-
cyclic. This implies that cyclicity 'turns off' at some point in Sekani.
When this conclusion is compared with the fact that some post-lexical rules in
other languages are cyclic, it suggests that the boundary between cyclic and
non-cyclic domains vary from language to language.

5. Conclusion

Good evidence for the cyclic or non-cyclic application of rules is hard
to find. In this chapter, I have presented all of the evidence that I am
aware of in Sekani for cyclic or non-cyclic rule applications. Given the rich
morphological structure of Sekani, it might be expected that better evidence
for the cycle might be found in Sekani than in languages with relatively
impoverished morphology like English.

The evidence presented in this chapter is relatively independent of
theoretical considerations. I have simply shown that in some cases, cyclic
derivations yield the right results, while in other cases, non-cyclic
derivations derive the correct phonetic forms. The arguments presented in
Rubach (1984b), Halle and Mohanan (1985), and Mohanan and Mohanan (1984) for

cyclic/non-cyclic rule application seem to me considerably weaker than those presented here, in that the arguments are based on whether the rules precede or follow other cyclic rules, or whether their formulations violate current versions of the Strict Cycle Condition.

Not surprisingly, of the three models of cyclic vs. non-cyclic rule application in Lexical Phonology discussed in sec. 2, very little evidence which clearly favors any one of them has appeared, either in this chapter or elsewhere in the literature. The Kiparsky/Harris 'word level' model of the cycle, however, appears to be the most restrictive, in that it makes the strongest predictions about cyclic and non-cyclic rule application. Since the Sekani facts do not require the less restrictive models of Halle and Mohanan (1985) and Rubach (1984a), the analysis discussed here can be construed as evidence in favor of the Kiparsky/Harris model of the cycle in Lexical Phonology.

Notes.
1. For example, Brame (1974) proposed a cyclic analysis of Spanish stress, which was criticized by Suñer (1975), but later upheld by Harris (1983).

   Kuroda (1967) proposed a cyclic analysis of certain segmental rules in Yawelmani, which was criticized by Rice (1969). Kisseberth (1973) proposed a cyclic analysis of vowel deletion and epenthesis rules in Klamath, which was widely criticized (cf. White (1973), Thomas (1974), and Feinstein and Vago (1981), for example). However, the need for the cycle in the analysis of Klamath has been reaffirmed in some of the most recent work on Klamath (Clements and Keyser 1983).

   These are but a few examples; a complete list of proposed cyclic analyses and their counter-analyses would be quite long.

2. Bruce Hayes receives the credit for coining this name.

3. Vocalization I could be simplified to (109) if it does not apply to the output of Diphthongization:

(100)   gho --> u / o ___   optional

4. Notice that the analysis in this section has only provided evidence that level 2 is cyclic. It has not shown that level 3 is also cyclic. The required evidence would be a sequence of prefixes in which CV and gho are

wholely contained within level 3. CV-gho sequences in which the first prefix is a level 3 morpheme are easy to find. An example is given in (110):

(101) /ghə-gho-tsagh/
       3pS Op cry
       8   11 stem

       [ghutsagh]   'they cry'

ghə- is a level 3 prefix and gho-, a level 2 prefix. Thus this form can only be derived in a cyclic manner: but the 'cycle' in this case is imposed by level ordering.

5. This is true except in the case of stems which appear in the incorporated stem position. See Ch. 4.

6. Pam Munro suggested this hypothesis to me. Other examples are provided by 'my (its) skin' below and by 'my (its) leaves' in 3.2.3.

(102a) [ʔə   -zàs]   'hide, skin'
       unspPsr skin

(102b) /sə   -ʔə   -zàs -è/
       1sPsr unspPsr skin psd

       [seʔazèsè?]   'my (its) skin'

7. [jeyǫè?] 'bull moose', with a prevocalic nonalternating nasal vowel, is also problematic. However, its structure might be as in (104):

(103) [[je] [yon] è]
        horn   grown psd

    The form -[sk'ǫè?] 'roe' might contain two layers of morphology, in which ʔə- is an instance of ʔə- 'unspecified possessor', added on the second cycle. If the s is a prefix in this form, it has no meaning which I am aware of. But there are many other mysterious word-internal s's in Sekani, some of which are listed in (105)-(111). The structure of these forms also appears to be prefix-s-stem:

(104) [ʔə-s-ke]   'boy'

(105) [ʔə-s-ba]   'goat'

(106) [ʔə-s-xu]   'mountain potato'
             tooth

(107) [ʔə-s-t'as]   'story'

(108) [dah-də -s-ghǫ]   'tree moss'
        up thm ? be hairy

(109) [ʔə -də -s-tl'às]   'paper'
        unsp thm ? paint

331

(110)   [dàghe -s tsʼi̧le]   '(berry species)'
        ground ? bare, smooth

8. One might consider ordering Schwa Lowering before Diphthongization, thus allowing Schwa Lowering to apply in the lexicon:

(111)   /tsʼə-gho-hyhòɬ/

gho cycle
ə Lowering   --
Diphthongization   wə

tsʼə cycle
Vocalization   u
Prefix Vowel Deletion   ∅

                            [tsʼuhyhòɬ]

However, I assume the formalization of Schwa Lowering given in (112):

(112)   V   C
          ⁎ |
        [+cont] syll
          |
        [+low]

As formulated in (112), Schwa Lowering is not a structure-changing rule, and is thus free to apply on the tsʼə- cycle before Vocalization. (Recall that Diphthongization and Vocalization are unordered with respect to each other.)

9. Of course, with this move, there is also an explanation for why the post-lexical [əə] sequences fail to undergo ə Deletion. These will be bracketed as in (113):

(113)   ..ə] [ə..

This does not mean, however, that ə Deletion could be a post-lexical rule. Presumably, level 5 Bracketing Erasure removes the internal brackets of level 5 before the post-lexical rules apply. If ə Deletion were a post-lexical rule, it could not distinguish [əə] sequences which arise on level 5 from those of the level 2 second person plural s-conjugation forms.

10. Unfortunately, however, there is other evidence that not all of the phonological rules of level 5 follow all of the morphological rules of this level. The level 5 rule of na Metathesis (Ch. 3, 5.2) is arguably morphological. It applies only to the prefixes na customary and na reversative, and not to nearly homophonous prefixes like ná continuative or nà down. na metathesis must follow ə Raising.

Appendix

Sekani Rules

In this appendix I provide an alphabetical list of the Sekani rules which appear in this dissertation. I include an informal formulation of each rule and a reference to some portion of the text where the rule is discussed.

a Deletion

a --> ∅ % a [___   Ch. 3, 4.2.1
                           Ch. 5, 3.4.2
                           Ch. 7, 4.2

a-Low Tone Mapping

          Ch. 5, Notes

a Raising

a --> o / ___ n]syll   Ch. 3, 5.2

Aspiration

s --> h / ___ {h? } [stem   Ch. 3, 2.1.2.4
[+cnj]   {1 }

Assimilation to a

e --> a / ___ a   Ch. 3, 3.2.1.1

Assimilation to e

V --> e / e ___   Ch. 3, 3.2.1.1

Cluster Simplification

C --> ∅ C ___]syll   Ch. 3, 2.1.2.1

Conjugation s Deletion

s --> ∅ / e ___ V   Ch. 3, 3.2.1.1

Conjugation ə Deletion

$$\text{ə} \longrightarrow \emptyset \; / \; V \begin{Bmatrix} s \\ n \\ gh \end{Bmatrix} \underline{\quad} \; [_1$$

$$\begin{Bmatrix} [+cnj] \\ [+mod] \end{Bmatrix}$$

Ch. 3, 4.2.5
Ch. 5, 3.1

Conjugation Tone Mapping

$$\overset{L}{V} \; \text{sə} \qquad \overset{L}{V} \; \text{nə}$$

Ch. 3, 4.2.2

Continuant Voicing

$$[+cont] \longrightarrow [+voice] \; / \; X \; [_1 \underline{\quad} \qquad 1 = N, P$$

Ch. 4, 4.3
Ch. 5, 3.3

D-Effect Rule

```
d-z  --> dz
d-l  --> dl
d-y  --> j
d-gh --> g
d-?  --> t'
```

Ch. 3, 2.2.2

Devocalization

$$u, o \longrightarrow w \; / \; \underline{\quad} \; V$$

Ch. 3, 6.1

Diphthongization

$$o \longrightarrow wə \; / \; velar \; \underline{\quad} \; (C), \; C \neq Y$$
[-nas]

Ch. 1, 5.2
Ch. 7, 3.1

Distributive-na Metathesis

$$\frac{\text{dà}}{4} \; \frac{\text{na}}{5} \longrightarrow 5 \; 4$$

Ch. 3, 5.2.3

Epenthesis

$$\emptyset \longrightarrow ə \; / \; \underline{\quad} \; C_0 \; [_1 \qquad 1 = V$$

Ch. 6

Gamma Loss

    gh --> ∅ / V [p ___ V   Ch. 3, 2.1.2.2

Gamma Lowering

    gh --> a / ___ [1   Ch. 3, 4.2.5
                                              Ch. 5, 3.1

Glottal Stop Insertion

    ∅ --> ʔ / L   Ch. 3, 6.2
                |
              V ___]

h Loss

    h --> ∅ / C ___   Ch. 4, 2.3

h Voicing

      d+h --> C   Ch. 3, 2.1.2.3
   [+clf] |
            [+voiced]

i Lowering

    i --> ə / ___ { s / gh }   Ch. 3, 3.1.4

i Metathesis

    i gho --> 11 9 / ___ i   Ch. 3, 3.1.4.2
    9 11   12

L Deletion

    L --> ∅ / ___ L [stem   Ch. 3, 4.2.3

n Insertion

    ∅ --> n / a ___ na   Ch. 3, 5.2

n Conjugation a Fronting

$$a \rightarrow e \; / \; \begin{matrix} L \\ | \\ \underline{\quad} \; n]_{syll} \end{matrix}$$

Ch. 3, 3.2.2

Nasalization

$Vn \rightarrow \tilde{V} \; / \; \underline{\quad} \; (C) \;]\underline{syll}$

Ch. 1, 5.3
Ch. 4, 2.5
Ch. 7, 3.2

na Deletion

$na \rightarrow \emptyset \; / \; q \; \underline{\quad}$ optional

Ch. 3, 5.2

na Absorption

$a \rightarrow \emptyset \; / \; V \; n \; \underline{\quad}$

Ch. 3, 4.2.6

o Raising

$o \rightarrow u \; / \; \underline{\quad} \; i$

Ch. 3, 3.1.2

Palatalization

$$\begin{matrix} d \\ t \\ t' \end{matrix} \rightarrow \begin{matrix} j \\ ch \\ ch' \end{matrix} \; / \; \underline{\quad} \; i,e,u$$

Ch. 3, 2.2.3

Perambulative na Deletion

$na \rightarrow \emptyset \; / \; k'è \; \underline{\quad}$

Ch. 5, 3.2

Perambulative Reduction

$k'è$-$na \rightarrow k'an \; / \; \underline{\quad} \; (C) \; [_1$

Ch. 3, 5.2
Ch. 5, 3.2

Prefix Vowel Deletion

Schwa Deletion

$ə \rightarrow \emptyset \; \% \; \underline{\quad} \; V$

$i \rightarrow \emptyset \; \% \; \underline{\quad} \; V$

Ch. 3, 4.2.1

Preglottal ə Fronting

  ə --> e / ___ [_N ?   Ch. 4, 2.1

s Conjugation ə Fronting

      L
  ə --> e / | Ch. 3, 3.2.1
     ___ s

s Voicing

  s --> z / ___ [stem   Ch. 3, 2.1.2.4

Schwa Deletion

  See Prefix Vowel Deletion

Schwa Fronting rules

  See Preglottal ə Fronting
    n Conjugation ə Fronting
    s Conjugation ə Fronting

Schwa Lowering

  ə --> a / ___ h]$_{syll}$ Ch. 7, 3.1
           Ch. 7, Notes

Schwa Raising

  ə --> i   Ch. 1, 3.1.2
           Ch. 6, 6.1

Stray n Deletion

  n --> ∅ / ___   Ch. 6, 6.1
      *
     syll

Suffix Vowel Deletion

  V --> ∅ /]$_1$ (X) ___] V Ch. 5, 3.4

Syllabification

Onset rule (universal):   Ch. 1, 5.1

(C) V --> (C) V

Rhyme rule (Sekani):

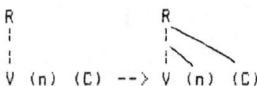

V (n) (C) --> V (n) (C)

Unlinked L Deletion

$$L \longrightarrow \emptyset \,/\, \underset{V}{\underset{\ast}{\_\_\_}}$$ Ch. 3, 4.2.1

Velar Loss

$$\begin{bmatrix} +\text{cont} \\ +\text{round} \end{bmatrix} \longrightarrow \begin{bmatrix} -\text{high} \\ -\text{back} \\ -\text{round} \\ +\text{ant} \end{bmatrix}$$ Ch. 1, 6

Voicing Assimilation

$$\underset{[+\text{voice}]}{L} \text{---} \left[\begin{matrix} -\overset{C}{\underset{|}{}} \\ +\text{cont} \quad \ldots \\ -\text{son} \end{matrix} \right]_{\text{stem}}$$ Ch. 3, 2.2.1
                                                                                  Ch. 5, 2.

w Vocalization

wa --> u / $\underset{[-\text{round}]}{V}$ ___   Ch. 3, 4.2.4
                                                        Ch. 7, 3.1

REFERENCES

Allen, Margaret R. (1978) Morphological Investigations Ph.D Dissertation, Univ. of Connecticut.

Anderson, Stephen R. (1974) The Organization of Phonology. New York: Academic Press.

Anderson, Stephen R. (1975) On the interaction of phonological rules of various types. Journal of Linguistics 11:39-62.

Anderson, Stephen R. (1982a) Differences in Rule Type and their Structural Basis. The Structure of Phonological Representations Part II, ed. by Harry van der Hulst and Norval Smith, 1-25. Dordrecht: Foris.

Anderson, Stephen R. (1982b) The analysis of French Schwa, or, how to get something for nothing. Language 58:534-573.

Anderson (1988) Morphological Theory. Linguistics: The Cambridge Survey II, ed. by F. Newmeyer, 146-191.

Archangeli, Diana (1983) The Root CV-Template as a Property of the Affix. Natural Language and Linguistic Theory 1:347-384.

Archangeli, Diana (1984) An Overview of the Theory of Lexical Phonology and Morphology. MIT Working Papers in Linguistics 7, ed. by M. Speas and R. Sproat, 1-14.

Archangeli, Diana (1985) Yokuts Harmony: Evidence for Coplanar Representation in Nonlinear Phonology. Linguistic Inquiry 16:335-372.

Aronoff, Mark (1976) Word Formation in Generative Grammar. (Linguistic Inquiry Monograph, 1.) Cambridge: MIT Press.

Aronoff, Mark and S.N. Sridhar (1983) Morphological Levels in English and Kannada, or Atarizing Reagan. Parasession on the Linguistic Levels. Chicago: Chicago Linguistic Society. 3-16.

Basbøll, Hans (1985) Stød in Modern Danish. Folia Linguistica 19:1-50.

Booij, Geert E. (1981) Rule Ordering, Rule Application and the Organization of Grammars. Phonologica 1980, ed. by Wolfgang U. Dressler et al., 45-56. (Innsbrucker Beitrge zur Sprachwissenschaft, 36.)

Brame, Michael K. (1972) The Segmental Cycle. Contributions to Generative Phonology, ed. by Michael K. Brame, 62-72. Austin: University of Texas.

Brame, Michael K. (1974) The Cycle in Phonology: Stress in Palestinian, Maltese and Spanish. Linguistic Inquiry 5:39-60.

Carrier, Jill (1979) The Interaction of Morphological and Phonological Rules in Tagalog: A Study in the Relationship between Rule Components in Grammar. Ph.D. dissertation, MIT.

Carrier Linguistic Committee (1974) *Central Carrier Bilingual Dictionary*. Ft. St. James, B.C.

Carrier-Duncan, Jill (1984) Some Problems with Prosodic Accounts of Reduplication. *Language Sound Structure*, ed. by M. Aronoff and R. Oehrle. Cambridge: MIT Press.

Chomsky, Noam (1970) Remarks on Nominalizations. R. Jacobs and P. Rosenbaum, eds., *Readings in English Transformational Grammar*. Waltham, MA: Ginn and Co.

Chomsky, Noam and Morris Halle (1968) *The Sound Pattern of English*. New York: Harper and Row.

Clements, G.N. (1980) *Vowel Harmony in Nonlinear Generative Phonology: An Autosegmental Model (1976 version)*. Bloomington, IL: IULC.

Clements, G.N. (1985) The Problem of Transfer in Nonlinear Morphology. MS.

Clements, G.N. and Kevin Ford (1979) Kikuyu Tone Shift and its Synchronic Consequences. *Linguistic Inquiry* 10: 179-210.

Clements, George N. and Samuel J. Keyser (1983) *CV Phonology: A Generative Theory of the Syllable*. (Linguistic Inquiry Monograph, 9.) Cambridge: MIT press.

Cook, Eung-Do (1984) *Sarcee Grammar*. Vancouver: University of British Columbia Press.

Denniston, Glenda (1981) Sekani. *Subarctic*, ed. by J. Helm. (Handbook of North American Indians, 6.) Washington, D.C.: Smithsonian Institution.

Di Sciullo, Anna-Maria and Edwin Williams (1988) *On the Definition of Word*. (Linguistic Inquiry Monograph, 14.) Cambridge: MIT Press.

Dresher, Bezalel Elan (1983) Post-lexical Phonology in Tiberian Hebrew. *Proceedings of the West Coast Conference on Formal Linguistics* Vol. 2, ed. by M. Barlow, D. Flickinger, and M. Wescoat, 67-78. Stanford: Stanford Linguistics Association.

Dudas, Karen (1974) A Case of Functional Phonological Opacity: Javanese Elative Formation. *Studies in the Linguistic Sciences* 4:91-111.

Feinstein, Mark and Robert Vago (1981) Non-evidence for the Segmental Cycle in Klamath. *Phonology in the 1980's*, ed. by D.L. Goyvaerts, 119-145. Story-Scientia: Ghent.

Greenberg, Joseph (1987) *Language in the Americas*. Stanford: Stanford University Press.

Hall, Tracy (1987) Lexical Phonology and the Distribution of [ç] and [x] in German. MS.

Halle, Morris (1973) Prolegomena to a Theory of Word-Formation. *Linguistic Inquiry* 4:3-16.

Halle, Morris and K.P. Mohanan (1985) Segmental Phonology of Modern English. *Linguistic Inquiry* 16:57-116.

Hammond, Michael (1984) Level Ordering, Inflection and the Righthand Head Rule. *MIT Working Papers in Linguistics* 7. 33-52.

Hardy, Frank (1979) *Navajo Aspectual Verb Stem Variation*. Ph.D dissertation, Univ. of New Mexico.

Hargus, Sharon (1985) Surface Phonology of Ft. Ware Sekani. MS.

Hargus, Sharon (1987) Infixation and Bracketing Erasure in Sekani. *Working Papers in Linguistics* 9, ed. by L. Kenton and S. Weinberger. 83-117.

Hargus, Sharon (1988) A Lexical Analysis of Luiseño Spirantization. Presented at Northwest Linguistics Club meeting, Vancouver, B.C.

Hargus, Sharon (to appear (a)) Underspecification and Derived-only Rules in Sekani Phonology. *Canadian Native Languages in Theoretical Perspective*, ed. by D. Gerdts and K. Michelson. Albany: SUNY Press.

Hargus, Sharon (to appear (b)) Sekani Phonology. *Contributions to Canadian Linguistics*. (National Museum of Man, Mercury Series.) Ottawa: National Museum of Man.

Hargus, Sharon (to appear (c)) Sekani *Gha*: Conjugation or Mode Prefix? *Athapaskan Linguistics*, ed. by K. Rice and E.-D. Cook. Berlin: Mouton.

Harmon, Daniel (1957) *Sixteen Years in the Indian Country: The Journal of Daniel Williams Harmon, 1800-1816*, ed. by W.K. Lamb. Toronto: MacMillan.

Harris, James W. (1983) *Syllable Structure and Stress in Spanish: A Nonlinear Analysis*. (Linguistic Inquiry Monograph, 8.) Cambridge, MA: MIT Press.

Hayes, Bruce (1984) *A Metrical Theory of Stress Rules*. New York: Garland.

Helm, June and Royce Kurtz (1984) *Subarctic Athapaskan Bibliography-1984*. Iowa City: University of Iowa.

Hoijer, Harry (1971) Athapaskan Morphology. *Studies in American Indian Languages*. (University of California Publications in Linguistics, 65.) 113-147.

Honigman, J.J. (1954) *The Kaska Indians: An Ethnographic Reconstruction*. (Yale University Publications in Anthropology, 51.) New Haven: Yale.

Howren, Robert (1971) A Formalization of the Athabaskan 'D-Effect'. *International Journal of American Linguistics* 37:96-113.

Jackendoff, Ray (1975) Morphological and Semantic Regularities in the Lexicon. *Language* 51:639-671.

Jenness, Diamond (1937) *The Sekani Indians of British Columbia*. (Canada Department of Mines and Resources Bulletin No. 84.) Ottawa: National Museum of Canada.

Kahn, Daniel (1979) *Syllable-Based Generalization in English Phonology*. New York: Garland.

Kaisse, Ellen M. and Patricia A. Shaw (1985) On the Theory of Lexical Phonology. *Phonology Yearbook* 2:1-30.

Kari, James (1975) The Disjunct Boundary in the Navajo and Tanaina Verb Prefix Complexes. *International Journal of American Linguistics* 41:330-345.

Kari, James (1976) *Navajo Verb Prefix Phonology*. New York: Garland.

Kari, James (1979) *Athabaskan Verb Theme Categories: Ahtna*. (Alaska Native Language Center Research Papers, 2.) Fairbanks: ANLC.

Kari, James (1988) Affix Positions and Zones in the Athabaskan Verb Complex: Ahtna and Navajo. MS.

Kiparsky, Paul (1974) Phonological Representations *Three Dimensions of Linguistic Theory*, ed. by Osamu Fujimura, 1-136. Tokyo: Institute for Advanced Studies of Language.

Kiparsky, Paul (1979) Metrical Structure Assignment is Cyclic. *Linguistic Inquiry* 10:521-41.

Kiparsky, Paul (1982) Lexical Morphology and Phonology in I.-S. Yange, ed., 3-91. *Linguistics in the Morning Calm*. Seoul: Hanshin Publishing Co.

Kiparsky, Paul (1983) Word Formation and the Lexicon, *Proceedings of the 1982 Mid-America Linguistics Conference*, ed. by F. Ingemann, 3-29. Lawrence: Univ. of Kansas.

Kiparsky, Paul (1984) On the Lexical Phonology of Icelandic. *Nordic Prosody III: Papers from a Symposium*, ed. by C.C. Elert et al. University of Umea. 135-164.

Kiparsky, Paul (1985) Some Consequences of Lexical Phonology. *Phonology Yearbook* 2:85-138.

Kisseberth, Charles (1973) The 'Strict Cyclicity' Principle: The Klamath Evidence. *Studies in Generative Phonology*, ed. by Charles Kisseberth. (Papers in Linguistics Monograph Series No. 3, Linguistic Research Inc., Edmonton, Alberta.)

Krauss, Michael E. (1964) Proto-Athabaskan-Eyak and the Problem of Na-Dene: The Phonology. *International Journal of American Linguistics* 30:118-131.

Krauss, Michael E. (1965) Eyak: A Preliminary Report. *Canadian Journal of Linguistics* 10:167-187.

Krauss, Michael E. (1969) On the classification in the Athabaskan, Eyak and Tlingit languages. *Indiana University Publications in Anthropology and Linguistics Memoir* 24:49-83.

Krauss, Michael E. (1970) Review of *The Phonology and Morphology of the Navajo*

Language, by Edward Sapir and Harry Hoijer. *International Journal of American Linguistics* 36:220-228.

Krauss, Michael E. (1978) Athabaskan Tone. MS.

Krauss, Michael E. and Victor K. Golla (1981) Northern Athabaskan Languages. *Subarctic*, ed. by June Helm (Handbook of North American Indians, 6.), 67-85. Washington, D.C.: Smithsonian Institution.

Krauss, Michael E. and Jeff Leer (1981) *Na-Dene Sonorants*. (Alaska Native Language Center Research Papers, 5.) Fairbanks: ANLC.

Kuroda, S.-Y. (1967) *Yawelmani Phonology*. (MIT Research Monograph No. 43.) Cambridge: MIT Press.

Lanoue, Guy (1983) *Continuity and Change: The Development of Political Self-Definition among the Sekani of Northern British Columbia*. Ph.D dissertation, University of Toronto.

Lapointe, Steven G. and Mark H. Feinstein (1982) The Role of Vowel Deletion and Epenthesis in the Assignment of Syllable Structure. *The Structure of Phonological Representations* Part II, ed. by Harry van der Hulst and Norval Smith, 69-120. Dordrecht: Foris.

Leer, Jeff (1979) *Proto-Athabaskan Verb Stem Variation. I: Phonology*. (Alaska Native Language Center Research Papers, 1.) Fairbanks: ANLC.

Levine, Robert (1979) Haida and Na-Dene: A new look at the evidence. *International Journal of American Linguistics* 45:157-170.

Li, Fang-Kuei (1933) Chipewyan Consonants. *Bulletin of the Institute of History and Philology of the Academica Sinica, Supplementary Volume I: Ts'ai Yuan'Pe'i Anniversary Volume*, 429-467. Peiping.

Li, Fang-Kuei (1946) Chipewyan *Linguistic Structures of Native America*, ed. by C. Osgood, 398-423. (Viking Fund Publications in Anthropology, 6.)

Lieber, Rochelle (1980) The Organization of the Lexicon. Ph.D. dissertation, MIT.

Lowenstamm, Jean and Jonathan Kaye (1985) Compensatory Lengthening in Tiberian Hebrew.

Marantz, Alec (1982) Re Reduplication. *Linguistic Inquiry* 13:435-482.

Marchand, Hans (1966) *The Categories and Types of Present-Day English Word-Formation: A Synchronic-Diachronic Approach*. (Alabama Linguistic and Philological Series, 13.) University of Alabama Press.

Marlett, Stephen A. and Joseph Paul Stemberger (1983) Empty Consonants in Seri. *Linguistic Inquiry* 14:617-640.

Mascaró Joan (1976) *Catalán Phonology and the Phonological Cycle*. Ph.D Dissertation, MIT.

Michelson, Karin (1981) Stress, Epenthesis and Syllable Structure in Mohawk. *Harvard Studies in Phonology* 2, ed. by G.N. Clements, 311-353. Bloomington: Indiana University Linguistics Club.

Mills, Elaine, ed. (1981) *The Papers of John P. Harrington...A Guide to the Field Notes, Vol. I: Alaska/Northwest Coast.* Krauss International Publications.

Mohanan, K.P. (1982) *Lexical Phonology*. Ph.D Dissertation, MIT.

Mohanan, K.P. (1986) *The Theory of Lexical Phonology*. Dordrecht: Reidel.

Mohanan, K.P. and Tara Mohanan (1984) Lexical Phonology of the Consonant System in Malayalam *Linguistic Inquiry* 15:575-602.

Munro, Pamela and John P. Benson (1973) Reduplication and Rule Ordering in Luiseño. *International Journal of American Linguistics* 39:15-21.

Myers, A. (1974) Phonology of Kikuyu. MS.

McHugh, Brian (1984) *Phrasal Tone Rules in Kirua (Vunjo) Chaga*. M.A. thesis, UCLA.

Parr, R.T. (1974) *A Bibliography of the Athapaskan Languages*. (National Museum of Man, Mercury Series, Ethnology Division Paper, 14.) Ottawa: National Museum of Man.

Pesetsky, David (1979) Russian Morphology and Lexical Theory. MS.

Prince, Alan (1987) Planes and Copying. *Linguistic Inquiry* 18:491-509

Pulleyblank, Douglas G. (1986) *Tone in Lexical Phonology*. Dordrecht: Reidel.

Randoja, Tiina (to appear) *Beaver Phonology and Morphology*. Ph.D. dissertation, University of Toronto.

Rice, Keren (1976) *Hare Phonology*. Ph.D Dissertation, University of Toronto.

Rice, Keren (1982) On Stems and Lexical Phonology: An Athapaskan Example. MS.

Rice, Keren (1983) Epenthesis in the Athapaskan Languages and the Linking of Levels. Presented at annual meeting of Canadian Linguistics Association.

Rice, Keren (1985) The Optative and *s and *n Conjugation Marking in Slave. *International Journal of American Linguistics* 51:282-301.

Rice, Keren (1986) The Structure of Slave Compounds. Presented at annual meeting of Canadian Linguistics Association.

Rice, Keren (to appear) *lave Grammar*. Berlin: Mouton.

Rice, Lester A. (1969) Review of *Yawelmani Phonology* by S.-Y. Kuroda. *International Journal of American Linguistics* 35:275.

Ritter, John (1983) Glottalization, Aspiration, and Tone in Tutchone.

Presented at Athabaskan Languages Conference, Fairbanks, AK.

Rotenberg, Joel (1978) The Syntax of Phonology. Ph.D Dissertation, MIT.

Ross, John R. (1972) A Reanalysis of English Word Stress (Part I). Contributions to Generative Phonology, ed. by Michael K. Brame, 229-324. Austin: Univ. of Texas Press.

Rubach, Jerzy (1984a) Cyclic and Lexical Phonology: The Structure of Polish. Dordrecht: Foris.

Rubach, Jerzy (1984b) Segmental Rules of English and Cyclic Phonology. Language 60:21-54.

Sapir, Edward (1921-3) A Type of Athabaskan Relative. International Journal of American Linguistics 2:136-142.

Sapir, Edward and Harry Hoijer (1967) The Phonology and Morphology of the Navaho Language. (University of California Publications in Linguistics, 50.) Berkeley and Los Angeles: U.C. Press.

Saxon, Leslie (1984a) Disjoint Anaphora and the Binding Theory. Proceedings of the West Coast Conference on Formal Linguistics, vol. 3, ed. by M. Cobler et al.

Saxon, Leslie (1984b) Dogrib Pronouns. National Museum of Man, Mercury Series.

Saxon, Leslie (to appear) The Syntax of Pronouns in Dogrib (Athapaskan): Some Theoretical Consequences. Dordrecht: Reidel.

Schane, Sanford (1975) Noncyclic English Word Stress. Essays on the Sound Pattern of English, ed. by D. Goyvaerts and G. Pullum. Ghent: Story-Scientia.

Shih, Chilin (1984) Foot Formation in Mandarin Chinese. [Paper presented at LSA meeting, Baltimore, MD.]

Siegel, Dorothy (1974) Topics in English Morphology Ph.D Dissertation, MIT.

Sproat, Richard (1986) Malayalam Compounding: A Non-Stratum Ordered Account. Proceedings of the West Coast Conference on Formal Linguistics 5, ed. by M. Dalrymple, et al., 268-288. Stanford: Stanford Linguistics Association.

Stanley, Richard (1967) Redundancy Rules in Phonology. Language 43:393-436.

Stanley, Richard (1969) The Phonology of the Navajo Verb. Ph.D Dissertation, MIT.

Stanley, Richard (1973) Boundaries in Phonology. A Festschrift for Morris Halle, ed. by Stephen R. Anderson and Paul Kiparsky, 185-206. New York: Holt, Rinehart and Winston, Inc.

Steriade, Donca (1982) Greek Prosodies and the Nature of Syllabification. Ph.D Dissertation, MIT.

Steriade (1986) Yokuts and the Vowel Plane. Linguistic Inquiry 17:129-146.

Stong-Jensen, Margaret (1987) Lexical Overgeneration in Icelandic. *Nordic Journal of Linguistics* 10:181-205.

Story, Gillian (1979) Problems of Interpretation in Beaver Phonemics. MS.

Story, Gillian (1980) The Athapaskan First Duo-Plural Subject Prefix. MS.

Strauss, Stephen L. (1982) *Lexicalist Phonology of English and German*. (Publications in Language Sciences, 9.) Dordrecht: Foris.

Suñer, Margaret (1975) Spanish Adverbs: Support for the Phonological Cycle? *Linguistic Inquiry* 6:602-605.

Tenenbaum, Joan (1978) *Morphology and Semantics of the Tanaina Verb*. Ph.D dissertation, University of Columbia.

Thomas, Linda (1974) *Klamath Vowel Alternations and the Segmental Cycle*. Ph.D Dissertation, Univ. of Massachusetts.

Thomas, Linda K. (1975) Toward a Cyclic Constraint Hypothesis. *Proceedings of the Chicago Linguistics Society* 11, ed. by Robin E. Grossman, et al., 583-588.

Thompson, Chad (1978) Athabaskan Relativizing Suffixes. MS.

White, Robin (1972) *Klamath Phonology*. Ph.D Dissertation, University of Washington.

Wilbur, R. (1973) The Phonology of Reduplication. Bloomington: Indiana University Linguistics Club.

Wilkinson, David and Kay Wilkinson (1965) [Phonemic analysis of Sekani, McLeod Lake dialect.] MS.

Wilkinson, David and Kay Wilkinson (1969a) *Sekani Reading Book*. Ft. St. James, B.C.: Wilkinson and Wilkinson.

Wilkinson, David and Kay Wilkinson (1969b) *Sekani Bible Story Book*. Ft. St. James, B.C.: Wilkinson and Wilkinson.

Young, Robert (1939) Siccanee Field Notes. MS.

Young, Robert and William Morgan (1980) *The Navajo Language: A Grammar and Colloquial Dictionary*. Albuquerque: University of New Mexico.

For Product Safety Concerns and Information please contact our EU
representative GPSR@taylorandfrancis.com
Taylor & Francis Verlag GmbH, Kaufingerstraße 24, 80331 München, Germany

www.ingramcontent.com/pod-product-compliance
Lightning Source LLC
Chambersburg PA
CBHW072132220426
43664CB00013B/2222